# Reading: The Patterning of Complex Behaviour

# READING

## The Patterning
## of Complex
## Behaviour

## Marie M. Clay

**Heinemann**

**Heinemann Publishers**
Cnr College Road and Kilham Avenue, Auckland 9, New Zealand.
Associated companies, branches and representatives throughout the world.

SBN 435 80234 8
ISBN 0 86863 251 1

© 1979 Marie M. Clay
First published 1972
Reprinted 1973, 1975, 1976, 1977, 1978
Second edition 1979
Reprinted 1982, 1984, 1985, 1987

**Typeset by Jacobson Typesetters Ltd, Auckland**

The pronouns she and he have often been used in this text to refer to the teacher and the child respectively. Despite a possible charge of sexist bias it makes for clearer, easier reading if such references are consistent.

# Contents

## Part 3 First Reading Books

## Part 4   The Reading Process

# Introduction

Reading people have many different theories, many preferred programmes and as many incompatible rationales for doing what they do. If such differences were critical we would be producing mostly problem readers and a few successful readers. That does not happen. Eighty to ninety percent of children learn to read in very diverse programmes. However, reading people often reason in circles about the things that matter to them (after the manner which R.D. Laing captured in his poems 'Knots'). So,

This child cannot read.
Because he cannot read
  we must help him.
He is little, so,
  we break the job into little steps.
Because we break it into little steps
  he can only learn in little steps.
I can only teach one-thing-at-a-time, so
  he can only learn one-thing-at-a-time.
If he can only learn one-thing-at-a-time
  then we should only teach one-thing-at-a-time.
That is why I teach him this before that.
You must not teach him that before this
  because that would upset my programme.

This is a facetious and perhaps unfair exaggeration but it can be backed by serious quotations which are found in recent analyses of the reading process in statements like —

We recommend to teachers an approach which *singles out* reading skills for testing and training *and then* attempts to sequence these in appropriate ways.

In the last 15 years there has been an intensive search for better theories about the reading process. Theories should explain what happens when we read. They should predict what will happen if we change our way of teaching. But our present theories compete for support rather than lead us to clear explanations and predictions. On the one hand the traditional, older view sees reading as an exact process with an emphasis on letters and words, while on the other hand, a more recent set of theories sees reading as an inexact process, a search for meaning during which we sample only enough visual information to be satisfied that we have received the message of the text.

These two major, but different, explanations of the reading process can be contrasted (McConkie and Rayner, 1976). One describes reading as a direct perception process and the other describes it as an hypothesis-and-confirmation process. Critics of the hypothesis-and-confirmation theory say, 'If a person reads a passage up to a point and then attempts to guess the next word, he will be wrong far more often than he is correct.' So hypothesis-and-confirmation is a weak theory they say. Yet this is a strategy that is basic in human perception (Bruner, 1957), and in the way we coordinate movement (Bruner, 1974). It is difficult to imagine how one could avoid hypothesis and confirmation in a perceptual cognitive activity like reading. This is central to Smith's theory of reading (1978)

The direct perception position assumes that the reader uses the visual details of print to get access to his memory. He attends to a word, links what he sees with similar detail remembered from past experiences and in some kind of cognitive operation gets meaning from the text. I think I do this sometimes when I read but I am rather sure that many times I read without paying much visual attention. Could it be that I find it easier to predict and check, and that I use as little direct visual perception as I can get away with?

Descriptive studies of young New Zealand children, learning in a typical beginning reading programme, suggest that they get to direct perception via hypothesis-testing strategies. Perhaps it could be the other way around in other programmes. It may be very important that the child moves flexibly from one type of processing to the other as he reads.

We know how teachers can make the hypothesis-and-confirmation process easier for the child. Choosing a text with a limited range of vocabulary, or with only a few types of sentence structure makes the reading more predictable. Discussing the story with the child, its language, concepts and sequences of events brings the beginner to the point where he can use an hypothesis-and-confirmation process on that text. So for the present let us not take these theories as opposing points of view. We can regard both seriously without adopting either exclusively.

The great debate in reading may be one of the sequence or the order of instruction (Carroll, 1976). Reading is made up of various component behaviours and there are various ways to master these components. The guidelines for a particular training programme are provided by the order in which the skills are emphasized. Starting points vary from one approach to another. Flexible children may be able to approach the task by any of these routes. One may not be better than another for many children.

## Are all children infinitely flexible?

We preselect what children have an opportunity to learn. Their learning is constrained by our schemes and our scheming, by our allegiances and our theories. We construct the learning situation for the child. Do we ever distort it? If we do just a little, how twisted is the growth, how misshapen the tree, by *our* decisions or those of some publisher of reading texts?

I am not convinced that children are infinitely flexible and my training in psychology tells me that the more formalized the teaching sequence, and the more committed the teachers are to it, the larger could be the group of children who cannot keep up with the programme.

We must believe that sequences of instruction make a difference otherwise why would we continually look for better methods and better materials. When one school selects a diagnostic-prescriptive instruction programme, knowing that a neighbouring school has adopted individualized reading in an open-plan classroom, each must believe that one approach is better than another. It is easy to conclude that our usual sequences are necessary sequences, but are they? If children succeed in a programme that is a demonstration of a satisfactory sequence but not of a necessary one.

I had many questions about how certain sequences of instruction affect children's learning when I began to record in detail what children did as they read books.

The observations reported in this book have led me to a new understanding of what happens as we read, and as children learn to read. Those are two different sets of activities. An overview of these insights will be found in the final chapter of this book which could be read before the evidence presented in the rest of the text. The observations were made in a programme of research studies which included two longitudinal studies. During the first, a record was taken *every week* of what children were saying and doing in reading from the time they entered school at 5:0 (i.e. 5 years) through until their sixth birthdays (Clay, 1967). In this study of the first year of instruction I tried to record, by objective procedures and in minute detail, the observable reading 'behaviour'. Behaviour is the key word. The records described what the children did and what they said, with *no prior assumptions* as to how or why they did these things. Following this intensive documentation of reading behaviour during the first year of schooling, tests were administered at 6:0 and again at 7:0 and 8:0.

The second research study began by using groups of children who were 5:0, 5:6, 6:0 and 6:6, and their progress was followed for 6 months. The children were selected to reflect four very different backgrounds of language experience. One group was bilingual in Samoan and English. Another was a group of Maoris who were monolingual in English. A third was an average group of children whose parents spoke English as their mother-tongue. The fourth group came from homes where one parent had professional training and there, it was presumed, the English language would be modelled for the child in all its range of usage (Clay, 1970).

From these studies and several others many insights into the process of learning to read in New Zealand were gained, and these have been set in the perspective of reports from other countries, and of major shifts in theory that have occurred in the last twenty years. The starting point of the research was the prevention of reading failure and because of this the reader will find three emphases in the text.

First, there is more emphasis on how to avoid or detect reading failure and less on how to stimulate successful readers. Secondly, there is more comment on behaviour which is readily observed and less on aspects of reading which concern comprehension and interpretation. This is because the research focussed on objective evidence and did not rely on subjective assessments which are always involved in judgments of how much interpretation or understanding the child engaged in. Thirdly, the children entered school and a teaching programme at 5:0. The behaviour described may require different emphases when beginning readers are older children.

These are field studies which described reading progress under classroom conditions. One question they sought to answer was whether the process of learning to read could be going wrong within a few months of school entry. If this were so it would be folly to wait several years before providing remedial programmes. Published reports suggest that it is unusual for remedial reading instruction to begin before 8:0 in Great Britain or New Zealand, where children do enter school at 5:0. If efforts to prevent reading failure were intensified and began earlier this might reduce the magnitude of the reading problem in the upper school. Why have we waited so long?

# References and Further Reading

Bruner, J.S., 'On perceptual readiness', *Psychological Review*, 64, 1957, 123-152.

Bruner, J.S., Organization of early skilled action. In Richards, M.P.M. *The Integration of a Child Into A Social World*, Cambridge University Press, London, 1974.

Carroll, J., The nature of the reading process. In H. Singer and R.B. Ruddell, (Eds.) *Theoretical Models and Processes of Reading*. IRA, Newark, Delaware, 1976, 8-19.

Clay, Marie M., 'The reading behaviour of five year old children: a research report', *N.Z.J. Educ. Studies*, 2, (1), 1967, pp. 11-31.

Clay, Marie M., 'Language Skills: A Comparison of Maori, Samoan and Pakeha Children Aged 5 to 7 years', *N.Z.J. Educ. Studies*, 1970, 153-162.

Clay, Marie M., *What Did I Write?* Heinemann Educational Books, Auckland, 1975.

Laing, R.D., *Knots*. Pantheon Books, New York, 1970.

McConkie, G.W., and Rayner, K., Identifying the span of the effective stimulus in reading: Literature review and theories of reading. In H. Singer and R.B. Ruddell (Eds.), *Theoretical Models and Processes of Reading*. IRA, Newark, Delaware, 1976, 137-162.

Singer, H., and Ruddell, R.B. (Eds.), *Theoretical Models and Processes of Reading*. IRA, Newark, Delaware, 1976, 8-19.

Smith, F., *Understanding Reading*. 2nd Ed. Holt, Rinehart and Winston, New York, 1978.

# Part 1

# Orientation to Reading

# 1   What is Reading?

Any statement that we like to make about reading is likely to be wrong in some respect. It is so obvious to each of us what we do when we read. If we were to try to teach a deaf child to pronounce the sounds of our language in a clearly understandable way we would realize immediately how complex speaking is. Reading, like speaking, is a very complex process. The 'best' readers have a rich repertoire of responses for solving the problem — what did the author say?

I define reading as a message-gaining, problem-solving activity, which increases in power and flexibility the more it is practised. My definition states that *within the directional constraints of the printer's code, language and visual perception responses are purposefully directed in some integrated way to the problem of extracting meaning from cues in a text, in sequence, to yield a meaningful communication, conveying the author's specific message.*

The brain is not packed with visual images. It is not a library. It is not an encyclopaedia. The brain has a theory of the world, a complex theory of knowledge that works so well that we are not aware that it exists. We use that theory of the world, not in the present, not in the past, but in the future. We predict all the time and we do it very well. We only become aware of it when our predictions fail. Prediction is a method of asking questions, and a means of eliminating alternatives. We must encourage the child to ask himself questions and develop in him strategies for improving his predictions, (Smith, 1978).

All this applies to reading. You read with anticipation if you are to read with comprehension.

To help adults understand something of the way we actually behave when we read, researchers have from time to time produced strange reading tasks which reveal some of these reactions which we, as efficient readers, use. Here are some tasks like this.

*Take a piece of paper and number 1 to 20 twice. Read the first paragraph below and write down against each number*

- *what you look at*
- *where you search*
- *what you look for.*

*Do not write the words that are missing.*

- *The second time through, write down the missing words.*
- *Then read the second paragraph in the same way. First, observe your own behaviour, then try to get to the author's words.*

**Paragraph 1   An extract on TV for children.**
But school's out, and for
the next three hours it's
switch and mix according
to your age group. For how
_____ you talk of children's
_____ as an entity
_____ you mean pro-
_____ for children aged
_____ nine and twelve, for early
_____ and late adoles
_____ to say nothing of
_____ -from-work dads and
_____ grannies, each
_____ with a viewing pre-
_____ that may be an
_____ to the others.

**Paragraph 2   A comment on cartoons.**
Yet, as one who has, I
hope, survived unscathed
a youthful addiction to
comic _____ and _____ still
_____ secret _____ of _____ Flint-
stones, _____ like _____ think _____
children _____ every _____ as
capable _____ the _____ of _____ at
distinguishing _____
reality _____ harmless
_____ believe. And they _____ less
influenced _____ what _____
see _____ television _____ by
_____ example _____ the _____
of _____ elders _____
developing values.

**Missing words**
**1**   can; programmes; when; -grammes; six; teenagers; -cents; home; weary; group;
-ference; anathema.
**2**   papers; is; a; fan; the; I; to; that; are; bit; as; rest; us; between; and; make; are; by;
they; on; than; the; of; attitudes; their; in.

According to Frank Smith (1978) it is what the brain says to the eye that is so important in reading. The clever things you did in reading these paragraphs have been overlooked in many prescriptions about how we read and how we should teach reading. Instead programmes have concentrated on how we cope with strange and unknown words — *expialidocious, morphophonemic, superordinately-linked*. In doing so we have discovered at least 12 ways to make reading difficult (Smith, 1973).

Another way to observe the reading process is to have volunteers read unseen texts to a group of observers who do not have a copy of the text. Choose the texts carefully and you will break down the fluent reading skills of the best readers to reveal some of the processes they use. Some challenging texts would be

- an upside-down book
- a bad duplicate, typed or copied
- difficult handwriting
- a highly specialized scientific text
- a text in 'ita' (initial teaching alphabet) — I use a Churchill speech in this medium
- a text typed with very wide spacing between words
- a text typed with no spacing between words.

Have the observers write down what they notice about the reading of the performer. Talk about what the readers were trying to do and why it was necessary for them to all behave the way they did.

Few adults have occasion to think of the ways in which they identify words while reading. Their perception of words is usually automatic. What enables a mature reader to respond to most printed words accurately and quickly? What additional means may he use to identify an unfamiliar word when he meets one?

In efficient, rapid word perception the reader relies almost wholly on context clues and some minor features of the word's form. Awareness of sentence context (and often of general context) and a glance at the word enables the reader to respond instantly with the meaning the author had in mind when he wrote the word. This type of word perception occurs in most of the reading by experienced, mature readers. For example, you had no difficulty in perceiving the words in this and the preceding paragraph. You did not stop to study the form of separate words. Nor did you analyse words by consciously noting root words, prefixes, and suffixes or by 'sounding them out' syllable by syllable. It is highly unlikely that you consulted a dictionary for the pronunciation or the meaning of any word. Why not? Every word was familiar. You have used each one yourself in writing and have seen it in print thousands of times.

Observe your own behaviour as you read the next three selections.

- When he first came there she had resented him; after that she had gone on to ignore him. It had been clear enough at first that she did not like his being there. The companionship and the interest that he had there was with Stenning in their work and in the farm. She had a habit whenever they were in the house together of always interrupting Johnson when he spoke. She always helped him last at meal-times, so that it should be plain that he was their servant and not one of them.

- The making and breaking of chemical bonds is the job of a particular and very varied group of substances found in every living cell and in many body fluids such as saliva and gastric juices —the enzymes. These compounds speed up the forming or decomposing of polymers and other complex substances by making or breaking the chemical bonds between the various parts of these giant molecules. Any one enzyme can usually act on only one particular bond, say, for example, the bond between two glucose molecules in a starch chain. Thus every different chemical reaction needs its own enzyme.

● From the brain the *circumoesophageal commissures* pass around the gut to the suboesophageal ganglion lying ventrally in the head. Nerves arising from here inner-vate the mouth parts. From the suboesophageal ganglion paired connectives pass back to the pro-thoracic ganglion in the floor of the *prothorax*. Then follow the next two thoracic ganglia. The ganglia supplying the first two abdominal segments have proba-bly fused with the meta-thoracic ganglion.

The concept of precision teaching (accurate and exact teaching based on a scientific approach to instruction) seems inappropriate when applied to reading. Frank Smith says, we present the child with the problem — to work out how our oral language relates to our printed language — and we say to him, *go ahead, we cannot help you much, you work it out!* We delude ourselves if we claim to know what the child has to learn to do. That is why no reading programme is foolproof and each produces some reading failure. Teachers of experience tend to produce fewer problems. Like the child who succeeds they have an inner knowledge of what is required that supple-ments the rather sparse articulate statements we make about the teaching of reading.

# The Need To Look More Closely and Think More Clearly

A text on beginning reading or a teachers guide will provide descriptions of skills to be developed, usually couched in general terms. Some examples can be quoted:

| SKILL | WE DO THIS — |
|---|---|
| **LEFT TO RIGHT EYE MOVEMENT** | By example and by giving specific instruction at all appropriate times on <br> ● where to start <br> ● what way to go <br> ● where to finish <br> ● beginnings and endings of stories and sentences. |

This statement may be sufficient for teachers who work with children who learn easily and quickly but by referring to the chapters in this book on *Learning about Direction* and *Visual Features of Print* the reader will find that the statement above does not describe clearly what has to be learned. It is not sufficiently precise to lead teachers to the detection of the particular problems of individual children.

Another example is:

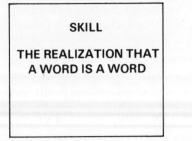

| SKILL | WE DO THIS — |
|---|---|
| THE REALIZATION THAT A WORD IS A WORD | By encouraging children to read known stories and poems, matching the voice in one-to-one correspondence with the word. |

And when encouragement fails to produce the required integration, what then? By thinking more clearly about what reading is the teacher may be able to aid the child who cannot 'get his ducklings all in a row', to make his responding effective.

Three concepts that developed to increase our understanding of children's progress in learning to read have become insurmountable barriers, blocking the development of early intervention programmes. These concepts are reading age, reading readiness, and the belief that 'intelligence will out'.

# The Concept of Reading Age

A child's level of performance on a reading test is usually expressed as a reading age. A reading age tells nothing about the child's reading skills; one has to interpret it. The reading age unit as such does not describe the skills a child has, or the skills he has yet to be taught. The major criticism of a reading age concept for the early identification of reading failure is that it tends to force us to delay for several years. Because tests involve test error, small differences in scores cannot be considered significant. They may have occurred by chance. If we have to rely on reading tests to select our failing readers then only a sizeable difference between reading age and chronological age can ever be reliable. It is commonly recommended that a difference of two years indicates that special tuition is necessary.

By such a criterion reading failure might be detected at 7:0 if the child began school at 5:0 (Kellmer Pringle. Butler, Davie, 1966), but in fact, the child is likely to be 8:0 with 3 years of failure behind him before special help is considered in the form of complementary or compensatory teaching. And yet, in all probability, classroom teachers have always classified these children as bottom group readers.

Another problem with a reading age concept is that classroom teachers tend to teach according to a particular, prescribed or preferred method, and to evaluate progress according to an easy-to-administer standardized test. The main criterion for a test's selection is that it does not take too much time. When the test isolates a failing child there is no ready means of translating the test score into the classroom practices of that teacher.

# The Concept of Reading Readiness

School entry is not the beginning of development or of education in its broadest sense, but it is the beginning of society's formal attempts to instruct all children, in groups, in skills that are considered important. It is supposed to coincide with a state of reading readiness in the average child, although studies of preschool children who have taught themselves to read have been reported. Despite lip service to a developmental concept of reading readiness there remains the cultural anomaly which allows New Zealand and British children to face reading at 5:0, American children at 6:0, and Swedish or Russian children at 7:0.

One version of the readiness concept states that children become ready for formal reading at different times as a result of different rates of maturing. It is rarely clear what is thought to be 'maturing'.

Another view of the readiness period is that it is a transition extending over several months during which time the child gradually changes from a non-reader to a beginning reader. In this case the readiness programme couples the child's past learning with new learning and brings the child, gradually, through the transition. The child's old ways of responding are modified so that they can be applied to the new task. For example, the preschooler who has learnt to look at picture books will scan the objects and colours back and forth in irregular patterns extracting meaning from the picture. We do not see a picture as a whole but rather our eyes focus and move, focus again and move around the picture. In the early stages of learning to read, the new entrant to school must confine this free-ranging, scanning behaviour to a particular directional pattern suitable for moving across lines of print.

Thus, the child's old response undergoes a transformation when the child develops new expectations about the links between oral and printed language. This transformation cannot occur with three-dimensional blocks and shapes, nor with two-dimensional picture materials. These materials will certainly have value for the child, whose preschool life has been barren of experiences, to develop visual perception. But the transformation at the early reading stage takes place only in the presence of print and when the child actively seeks to discover how oral and written language are related.

Although visual perception and language behaviour were patterned in intricate ways during the preschool years they are linked to later progress in reading by a reorganization or transformation that takes place when the child is introduced to printed language. This creates a kind of developmental discontinuity.

Reading instruction places new demands on the child. He must use his old preschool ways of responding in novel situations and he must discover or invent new coordinations. The initiative for this active learning comes from the child and it bears no relation to the 'growth from within' maturational concept of readiness.

The preschool child can respond to print as a source of messages and can use the kind of language and thought processes that he will use in reading later on. He acquires a control over the more formal language of books or book dialect if he is read to. Yet the formal instruction situation presents the child with a new set of problems and places him under some pressure to get them solved. However slight the pressure and however positive and enjoyable the experience the demands of school create a discontinuity with his past experience. For something between a year and three years he must struggle with a new and complex problem — how to act on several things he knows relating one to another to predict, and check on, the messages he finds in print.

It follows that a child may have developed good visual perception for forms and shapes and yet fail to learn to read because he thinks the task depends on visual memory for particular letters or forms, and does not appreciate that his power to produce language has anything to do with it. Similarly, a child with good language skills may be unsuccessful in applying these to reading because he does not pay the visual cues sufficient attention.

It is the need to transform preschool skills into new ways of responding that creates the developmental discontinuity, makes the early reading behaviour a matter of learning, and discredits the 'growth from within' concept of readiness. In this book the new entrant stage of being introduced to printed language will be referred to as the 'early reading behaviour stage', and the terms 'preparation for reading' or 'reading readiness training' or 'pre-reading' will be avoided.

This concept of the early reading period as a time of transition which transmutes preschool behaviour into new forms, suggests that there will be wide variations in the patterns of progress one might find among children during their first year at school.

*The Fast Learners.* A few children, well-prepared by their preschool experiences, will learn the early reading skills quickly under conditions of good instruction and pass on within weeks to basic books.

*The Average Learners.* Many children will need to extend their preschool experiences as well as learn transitional skills but the dual task can be accomplished by the average child within the first six months at school.

*The Slow Learners 1.* Some children might be unable to progress during the first year at school because teachers were not able to reach and build on to their limited preschool skills. (Cultural and linguistic differences could create such a situation.)

*The Slow Learners 2.* Other children might be unable to read because their experiences during their first year at school had tied their previously adequate responses into tangles of cognitive confusion, overlaid with emotional reactions to failure. Confusion was observed in children close to 6 years who sometimes moved from right to left or bottom to top across a page of print, or who still confused the concept of a letter with the concept of a word, or who claimed 'I can read this book without looking at it'. Such learning tangles can all too readily occur during the early reading stage in the best classrooms, but when they are detected they can be overcome.

To relax and wait for 'maturation' when there are many concepts and skills to be developed would appear to be deliberately retarding the child in relation to what is usual in his culture. To fail to observe that this early reading behaviour is blocked either by inadequate prior learning or by current confusion, and to omit to provide the required complementary activities, must be poor teaching (Malmquist, 1970).

After six months of 'normal' programme, children making slow progress require special and intensive efforts to establish the early reading behaviours.

# 'Intelligence Will Out'

There is an unbounded optimism among teachers that children who are late in start-ing will indeed catch up. Given time, something will happen! A temporary backward-ness will eventually be relieved by suitable teaching and children may even grow out of it themselves! In particular, there is a belief that the intelligent child who fails to learn to read will catch up to his intelligent classmates once he has made a start. Do we have any evidence of accelerated progress in late starters? There may be isolated examples which support this hope, but correlations from a follow-up study of 100 children two and three years after school entry lead me to state rather dogmatically that where a child stood in relation to his age-mates at the end of his first year at school was roughly where one could expect to find him at 7:0 or 8:0. This is what one would expect if learning to read is dependent on the acquisition and practice of a com-plex set of learned behaviours, and not the product of sudden insights.

# In Summary

Reading is a process by which the child can, on the run, extract a sequence of cues from printed texts and relate these, one to another, so that he understands the precise message of the text. The child continues to gain in this skill throughout his entire education, interpreting statements of ever-increasing complexity.

What then is a 'problem' reader? Presumably he has much more difficulty than the average child in coping with the day-to-day lessons in reading, and therefore he ac-cumulates this skill at a slower rate than the average child, slipping further and further behind. This kind of definition allows us to escape from having to state how far behind the child is. He does not have to be two years retarded to be a problem reader. He is simply a child whose rate of learning in this particular task is much slower than that of an average child of the same stage or level.

The concepts of reading age, reading readiness and an optimism that intelligence will eventually win out, tend to operate as barriers to the early identification of children with reading difficulties. Better descriptions of reading behaviour are needed both to avoid and to identify early reading failures; in particular, descriptions are needed of the early reading behaviours to be learned in the transitional period. Assuming that different programmes stress different aspects of the reading process at different times, descriptions are needed of the sequential accumulation of skills under different methods and programmes.

# References and Further Reading

Clarke, Margaret M., *Reading Difficulties in Schools*, Penguin, London, 1970.

Kellmer Pringle, M.L., Butler, M.R. and David, R., *11,000 Seven Year Olds: Studies in Child Development*, Longmans, London, 1966.

Malmquist, E., 'Diagnostic and predictive measures in the teaching of reading in Sweden', in W.K. Durr (Ed.), *Reading Difficulties. Diagnosis, Correction and Remediation*, International Reading Association, Newark, Delaware, 1970.

Smith, F., *Psycholinguistics and Reading*, Holt, Rhinehart and Winston, New York, 1978.

Smith, F., *Understanding Reading*, (2nd Edn.), Holt, Rhinehart and Winston, New York, 1978.

# Exploring Further

**Carefully observe your own reading behaviour on the texts provided in this chapter.**

# 2 One Day He Will Go to School

## Literacy Background

When a child enters school he has a private frame of reference which stems from his past experiences. The new entrant's teacher encourages him at first to use his personal repertoire of behaviour, then to extend it so that gradually he comes to share responses with other members of a group who will begin reading instruction together. What have these new entrants learnt in their preschool years that may help or hinder their progress in reading?

Children who learn to read slowly, fall into two main types. First, there are children with limited language skills, and secondly there are children whose visual analysis of complex shapes is poorly developed. Cases of the first type may have been slow to acquire speech and although spoken language difficulties may appear to be overcome before school age, there can be residual effects which are not obvious, like poor auditory discrimination of sounds, words and sentence structure. In learning to read, these children have particular difficulty in breaking up language into its parts or in synthesizing separate sounds into whole words, and sometimes they have difficulties with comprehension. Such children have usually not mastered many of the sentence structures used in English, and therefore are unable to anticipate what may happen next in the sentences of their reading text. It is, of course, not surprising that children with retarded language should have difficulty with reading. Reading is, after all, a language activity.

Reading is also an activity which demands the analysis of complex visual stimuli. What does this mean? It means searching a picture or text, with the eye and with the brain, to note details which one can interpret. Children can be retarded in their ability to scan and analyse pictures, geometric forms and letters merely because they have neglected to pay this kind of material significant attention during their preschool years. So they arrive at school with far less skill in analysing two-dimensional space than other children who have been practising this skill for some time.

These two aspects of the reading process have to be related to each other. There has to develop a facility for associating speech sounds with printed shapes. The child may find it difficult to link the visual and auditory stimuli or, more precisely, to match the flow of spoken language rhythms coming to his ear, with the flow of visual patterns across the page of his text. He may have trouble relating auditory experience to visual experience. Or more specifically, he may have trouble in relating the timing of the auditory experience to the spacing of the visual experience.

Now there is one particular feature about these visual skills in reading. Until he reaches school, the child has been free to scan objects, people, scenes, pictures, even books, in any direction that he chose, and he has not been required to limit his pattern of search in any way. Immediately he becomes a candidate for reading, he must learn that in the printed text situation there is only one appropriate direction in which he can proceed. That is, he must learn to go from a top left position across to the right and then to return to the next top left position and go again across to the right. For the 5-year-old school entrant of average ability that is a difficult piece of learning. We have for too long underestimated the magnitude of this particular task, and its particular relevance to subsequent success in learning to read. This directional behaviour, moving in a controlled way across a line of print, is related to motor behaviour or movement. This then is a fourth area in which a child may have difficulty. If his muscular coordinations are not well developed, if he has not gained good control over his hand and eye movements, this particular aspect of learning to read may be difficult for him, and so his attempts to relate what he hears to what he sees may fail because of his inability to move in appropriate ways across print.

So we have analysed the reading process and some of the abilities required for success in it.

- The child must have good control of oral language.
- He must have developed skills of visual perception.
- He must have reached the level of brain maturity and experience which enables him to coordinate what he hears in language with what he sees in print.
- He must have enough movement flexibility, or motor coordination of hand and eye so that he can learn the controlled, directional movement patterns required for reading.

# Problems the Child May Take to School

## Sensory losses

Reading involves vision, hearing, and senses associated with movement (which we may call kinaesthetic sensation). A child with sensory losses in any of these areas will inevitably have deficits in his experience. A blind child will have to learn to read in a different way to compensate for his handicap. A deaf child will have considerable problems with learning to read, but this is because he does not develop the control of language which the average child uses in reading. In fact, the deaf child may have to learn much of his language though his eyes and may have to be taught to read early in order to develop facility in oral language. The child with cerebral palsy, or some physical disability, may have his movement experience in preschool years limited, and this may affect both his control over movement (which may affect the reading process) and the development of his visual scanning behaviour. However, while the extreme cases of sensory loss will probably be located and special provision made for them in their preschool years, other children may enter school with slight or undetected losses in each of these areas. Mild degrees of visual defect do not usually handicap the child in learning to read unless he has frequently avoided visual experiences in his preschool years. On the other hand, mild degrees of hearing loss, particularly intermittent ear trouble during the 2 to 4-year period, can have severe effects in limiting the richness of oral language which the child develops and also limiting the experiences he has to bring to bear on understanding the stories in books. Least obvious are the motor incoordinations which make it particularly difficult for the child to learn a specific motor pattern such as the directional movements in reading. These children are least likely to be noticed and given extra encouragement in their preschool years.

## Deficiencies in experience

A second reason why children may not have the skills that are necessary for good progress in reading when they enter school is that they have not had adequate experiences in their preschool years. Their homes may not have provided a good range of interesting experiences appropriate to their developmental needs. More specifically, the child who has not had many opportunities to converse with adults will have limited language skills and will have difficulty in reading. The child who has not lived in a home where adults share books with children will have less skill in the perception of two-dimensional space than the average child. More than this, the child who has not learned that books contain interesting ideas, and that the language which he listens to is related in some way to the story in the book, has missed some valuable learning experience. The child who has had limited experience to run around, to climb, to use his body effectively in activities which demand gross motor skill, will not be ready for the finer adjustments that are required in the motor skills of eye movement and hand/eye coordination in school activities. A child severely deprived in this way could be one who had spent most of the preschool years in bed or in hospital.

## Emotional disturbance

Every child must feel that he is important, that he is wanted, and that he can accomplish things. Many children get these feelings effortlessly through the process of growing up. Some do not. Feelings of security and adequacy play an important role in achievement. The children who start school having acquired positive views of self are fortunate, because they have been accepted and taught how to succeed. A positive view of self can be learned, and preschool teachers can help if they create a climate where each child is respected for his uniqueness, and where children are listened to, as well as spoken to.

Another reason why emotional disturbance can interfere with reading progress is that learning to read requires a great deal of personal initiative and a willingness to take risks, which the insecure child is unwilling to take. It is easier for him to apply to the new learning tasks of school his old emotional reactions of withdrawing, or attacking, distorting or ignoring, and so, by applying old habits to the new situation, causing himself to fail again.

## Physical disorder or impairment

A group of possible causes of reading difficulty lies in the neurological or physical makeup of the individual. Sometimes genetic or hereditary factors could be involved, but we can only suspect and rarely prove this, and always we are left with the task of teaching the child to read in spite of them! Various kinds of brain injury might interfere either with the visual side of the reading task or with the auditory side or with the relating of visual and auditory stimuli, or with the extracting of meaning from these signals. Brain injury often implies in addition other symptoms which can interfere with the learning process. The child may find it difficult to attend for long periods of time, or he may attend too much to detail and be unable to tolerate the complexity of the reading task. A neurological condition may make him a hyperactive child who flits from task to task assimilating little with each new learning experience. It is possible that nutritional or chemical imbalance or metabolic disorders may influence the child's intellectual functioning, or sensory efficiency, and so contribute to inadequate preparation for reading.

Another possible area of difficulty is described as a 'developmental lag', a notion which implies that to some extent maturation in the brain and in the nervous system is going on continually and that there is a steady increase in capacity to deal with information from the environment. For some children it is suspected that this unfolding of learning potential proceeds at a slower rate than in other children, although their ceiling capacity may not in the end differ. This is easy to understand when one thinks of the child's height. One child may grow very fast at an early age and then his growth pattern levels off, and another child slow to grow at first, has his growth spurt at a later age, but finishes with the same height as the first child. Applying this concept to development of the nervous system and its ability to handle learning experience, we can see that one child could be at a disadvantage compared with another if an activity like reading were introduced at the same age to both children. As far as prevention of reading failure is concerned, there are no specific signs that we can observe. Although we may look at a child and say that his behaviour suggests an immaturity which could be a developmental lag, it might just as easily be a limitation in his previous experience that caused the very same behaviour.

Brain damage accounts for only a very small part of learning disorders encountered. Many disabilities in learning tasks are related to inappropriate experience, rather than to impaired structures.

# The Prevention of Reading Problems

This analysis has uncovered four areas of preschool development which are critical for progress in reading. If we were able to ensure that the child who entered school had rich and adequate experience in these areas, we might be able to drop from our list of reading problems those that arise from the limitation of experience.

The child's ability to control his own behaviour, and in particular the movement patterns of his body, is related to early reading progress. His ability to learn from his sensory interchanges with his environment, and to relate this sensory input of information to the output in language or movement activities, is an important foundation for the input of reading experience and the output in understanding or activity.

The preschool child's language development is vital for his progress in reading. We are concerned not only with the development of his vocabulary, or his articulation of his sounds, but with the range and flexibility of the patterns of English sentences which he is able to control. His development in this behaviour depends almost entirely on the opportunities he gets to converse with an adult. The more of this experience he enjoys, the more mature his language will be on entering school. Children, like adults, like to talk about themselves, their possessions, their home, their family, their pets, their friends, their neighbours, their relatives, their trips. Invite children to talk.

In the area of auditory discrimination, important learning must take place. Long before the child enters schol, he has learned to discriminate between vocal sounds sufficiently to differentiate words one from another. Auditory discrimination activities can aim to have children perceive likenesses and differences in non-vocal sounds, and to perceive the sound of recurring rhyming words in language games, favourite stories, poems and songs. This should prepare them to hear the words that rhyme and contrast them with the words that do not rhyme, and to recognize that spoken words can begin with the same consonant sound when they begin to read. In developing such skill with rhymes, provide activities that permit frequent and varied repetition and capture the ear with rhythmic movement, alliteration and voice modulation.

It is not easy to observe the third area of importance, that is, visual perception behaviour, and yet just as there is gradually increasing control over language in the preschool years, and over movement and body control, so there is a similar continuing increase in ability to scan new material, organize one's perception of it, remember it, perhaps refer to it by some label, or assign meaning in some other way. The child gains this experience in play, in conversation with people who point out features of objects and pictures to the child, and in contact with books.

However, the preschool 'seeing' experiences tend to differ considerably from school experiences. In preschool days, children are constantly looking upon a wide view, viewing much and seeing little. This causes some children to observe far less than they could. Seeing must go beyond just looking; it must become a systematic search for precise information and an ability to structure a mental representation of the forms that are seen. Schoolwork requires near-point vision and the development of new and precise focussing skills.

What child starting school does not experience mixed feelings about school and about home? Security, self-confidence, acceptance, tolerance and a sense of belonging are a foundation for attitudes that encourage participation in effective learning experiences. Happy, relaxed, stimulating relationships between children and between child and teacher, promote growth of personality which in turn advances achievement. Some important guidelines for parents and teachers which could encourage the young child's self-acceptance could be:

- Recognize the individuality of each child.
- Listen to, respect and use the child's opinions.
- Accept his feelings.
- Accept the aggressive, rough and tumble play of an exuberant youngster.
- Plan work and play so that he can use his particular abilities.
- Give time and thought to him and his needs.
- Allow opportunities for him to be with his friends.
- Participate with him in pleasurable activities.
- Make it rewarding for the child to enter into activities which seem to be his weakness.

In a report on children who read before they entered school, Dolores Durkin (1966) describes the families of the children. Certain assets were apparent. The parents and siblings of these children had a high regard for reading. The children had been read to regularly at home and, in some instances, from the age of two. Someone in each family took the time not only to read to the children but also to answer their questions about words and about reading. It is in these situations of sharing books with children that the child learns to bring language and visual analysis to bear upon the task of extracting messages from books (White, 1956). Before he enters school, he can be found composing his own stories, stimulated by the pictures, producing within the limits of his language a story for that particular book. A child who does not have books in his home (suitable books, which are read with him) will have missed experiences with bookish kinds of language, with concepts that are found only in books, and with picture exploration, and he will lack practice in coordinating language and visual perception in a way that facilitates progress with reading after entry into school.

# Reading Begins at Home

The most valuable preschool preparation for school learning is to love books, and to know that there is a world of interesting ideas in them (Butler and Clay, 1979). Parents who love to share books with children transmit their feelings, their understanding and their language patterns to their little listeners. Some books enrich children's thinking from their plots, their ideas or their language. The books that are very, very simple are the ones that call children's attention to print. The Carrot Seed (Kraus) is one example of a tremendously simple but exciting text for a preschooler's story time.

Reading to preschoolers teaches them more than this general feeling for the worth of written language. The child who asks 'What's that say?' in response to a television advertisement shows his awareness that language messages can be written down. The child who charges his parent with having read his favourite story incorrectly because he missed part of the story has a basic awareness that there is an exact message to be decoded and that sequence is very important. When such children are given their first books in school they already understand that the captions bear some relation to the picture and to the sort of things they can say about the picture.

If a child shows an interest in words and in print any parent would do well to respond to that interest for it is wisdom to enrich the child's experience. Sometimes parents wonder whether they should try to teach their preschoolers to read. Some parents are concerned lest they 'spoil' the unspoilt child for the teacher. Others are rather too anxious to prove something to themselves about their children's abilities. It is folly to kill interest with over-instruction. In recent years, research has established that under special conditions children can teach themselves to read. They can certainly be taught to read letters and words, if this can be called reading. I think that reading is better described as a sequential activity in which a message is extracted from a continuous text.

But there are several counts against over-zealous efforts by parents. The process of learning to read is a slow-growing skill, which usually takes the 'average' child four years to master. An earlier start results in an even slower accumulation of learning for the 'average' preschooler, who may be satisfied — but may not. One mother-teacher writes (Begg and Clay, 1968): 'There were times when the boy did love to learn to read and the reading appeared to be a considerable satisfaction and pleasure, but there were times when he seemed to resent reading and showed discouragement and behavioural difficulties. It seemed that he finally regarded his reading experiences as a task in which he had failed rather than as the source of enjoyment and satisfaction it had been in the early stages.' This 3-year-old child of superior intelligence was taught to read as well as children who were 5 years of age, in school, and of the same superior intelligence level. The programme was intensive (to fit the mother's research schedule) which was less desirable than a more relaxed one would have been. The child's loss of skill when the lessons stopped for three months was almost total, although perhaps he was able to relearn these skills more quickly when he started school. The quality of the child's learning differed from that of the 5-year-olds in certain ways, particularly in the area of spatial relationships and the visual perception of print, where his development lagged behind the older group. A careful comparison of this 3-year-old child with two 'normal' school entrants showed that while word recognition and book reading in the basal series were the same for the preschooler aged 3:9 and the new entrants aged 5:6, the preschooler's performance on visual perception activities like spatial drawing, letter identification and knowing the conventions of written language, was inferior to that of the older children. This suggests that a school entrant who can already read may need to develop further his control over the motor, spatial and visual perception aspects of the task despite his apparent control over the reading process. A serious limitation for the child studied seemed to be his inability to use several sources of cues, as the older child does. He tended to focus on one type of information which often led him to false conclusions. (Piaget's theory would predict this.)

But perhaps most important of all, the reading progress and the mother-child relationship became intermingled and thrived or suffered conjointly. When an older child struggles with learning to read at school, failure is bad enough, but an accepting mother at home is a refuge from that failure. If the preschool child, who is taught by mother at home is allowed to feel he is failing when his mother becomes irritated or comments negatively on his efforts this is an earlier encounter with failure in a much more intense relationship with a much more fundamental person. Just as too much attention to the correction of efforts to talk can be very detrimental to language development, so the child's early attempts to read can be inhibited by over-correction and an urge to 'put him right'. Parents who respond with enthusiasm to the child's attempts to discover things about print for himself are providing a richer foundation for schooling than those parents who generate tension and stress as they instruct the child.

# Individual Differences

Here is a brief account of the behaviour of four children in a test situation five weeks before they entered school. They came together in my home for their first experience of a school-like situation. They were given a booklet of pictures and were asked to mark certain pictures according to instructions. The task was the New Zealand edition of the *Metropolitan Reading Readiness Test* (1943).

Simon found the situation challenging. He frequently called for help and was often unable to make decisions on his own. He would respond to part of the instructions rather than wait for the whole sentence. The only letter he could write was 'S' and yet he could recite the spelling of his surname which his older brother had taught him. At first he could not find his way around a page but he overcame this later. He was not confident but his attitude could be summed up as 'Give-it-a-go-and-don't-worry-too-much.'

For Peter the test period proved too long. He had been told by his mother that good children had been chosen to do this task and he was over-impressed, reluctant to try in case he failed and wanted to escape to outdoor play. He had great trouble finding his way around a page and locating lines of pictures. When uncertain of an answer he would scan two pages of pictures with a random wandering gaze and would have to be brought gently back to the test item row. He had not established any habits of left-to-right, top-to-bottom or left-page-before-right-page survey and he showed no improvement during the hour's testing. This boy could also write one letter, 'e' but seemed unchallenged by paper and pencil work.

Sally had directional problems for the first two subtests but learned to find her way around the book as the task proceeded. On difficult tasks she looked for guidance and reassurance. She made each choice hesitantly, revised it and revised it again. She was willing to try but was not particularly satisfied with her efforts. Overall, she was average in performance, in confidence and assurance. She knew her limits, was prepared to ask for help but was also willing to try to adapt without guidance. 'S' was the only letter she could write.

Joan had no problems locating the rows of pictures and surveying them systematically. She attempted everything without encouragement sorting out an answer for those items she did not know. Although not confident she saw it as a task to be completed, something for which she accepted responsibility. She was self-sufficient, adaptive, found her work challenging and worked with little assistance. She could write the four letters of her name.

Two years later the children's reading progress was ranked in the order Joan, Peter, Sally, Simon. Peter's progress was interesting. Despite his unpromising performance in the preliminary test situation his caution had been turned by good teaching to a careful approach to work, and his love of outdoor life to a love of stories (life beyond the present). Extracts from diaries kept by Peter's and Simon's mothers illustrate the development of the two boys' interest in books.

> *At bedtime tonight Peter said he would read me a story. It was one of his brother's books about cowboys. I told him the words he didn't know and was very surprised at the words he knew like 'cowboy', 'few', 'boys', 'horse', 'pony', 'Dusty'. He reads very confidently, looks hard at any new word he doesn't know and tries to sound it out.* (Peter's mother's diary at 5:9)

> *His printing has improved and he reads 'The Cat in The Hat' backwards and forwards. It is a book with real appeal to him — he loves it. He reads it at night, alone and very loudly.* (Simon's mother's diary at 6:0)

It is important to emphasize that new entrants differ markedly. Those who talk fluently have different vocabularies. Those with rich preschool experiences have different concepts — of farms or cities, animals or machines, poetry or people. Once at school they have to make different adjustments to the physical environment and to the teachers. There are intricate differences in their oral language patterns which may help or hinder their progress in learning to read books and to write stories. They differ in patterns of attention and the mere task of sitting still demands tremendous concentration for the physically active child. Teachers of new entrants who are concerned with issues of class atmosphere and the work habits of groups must also heed Helen Garrett's caution that energy is not a cheap commodity to be scorned or punished.

The child's home background is not solely responsible for such differences. Two mothers who had been teachers wrote these descriptions of their 5-year-old sons.

> *Bruce reads stories to himself when he knows the stories by heart. In a new book he will work out a story from the pictures.*

> *William does not read or try to write. He spends his time playing outside or making things. He likes to have a story at bedtime.*
> Six months later:
> *I have not noticed that he has started to read anything yet.*

Children from homes that value education highly enter school with differences. And many other children come to school lacking the elementary skills upon which teachers would normally build a reading programme. They lack the concepts of up/down, above/below, first/last, same/different, and so on. They are inexperienced with crayon, pencil, chalk and paint. They speak in monosyllables, rather than in structured sentences and are unable to follow spoken directions.

The teacher of a new entrants class must be very skilful to handle such diversity. For what she is about to receive she must be truly thankful, and she must be careful that the skills and confidence which the children already have when they enter school have not been destroyed before she has finished her early reading programme.

# Preschoolers are Different

Individual differences can be an asset rather than a liability. Ample evidence is available to show that differences do exist. It is reported that tests of different aspects of maturity show a range of five years at the early reading stage. A constellation of physical, mental, social and emotional factors will affect the child's preparation for school. The patterning of individual life experiences will be particular for any one child, even in the same family Preschool experiences should develop the individuality of children, enriching them in areas of strength and interest, fostering their weaknesses and the activities they avoid, building confident children who feel adequate.

It then becomes the responsibility of the school to arrange the early reading programme in ways that do not require all 5-year-olds to fit a single-size shoe. One cannot expect them to move into a narrowly-conceived, preselected sequence of learning. Because the individuality of new entrants and a belief in group instruction are, initially, out of step, an important quality in a good teacher of new entrants will be an ability to use diverse responses in her pupils.

# References and Further Reading

Beadle, Muriel, *A Child's Mind*, Doubleday & Co., New York, 1970.

Begg, Judith A., and Clay, Marie M., A note on teaching a preschooler to read: Some problems of evaluation. *N.Z. Journal of Educational Studies*, 3, (2), 1968, 171-174.

Butler, Dorothy, and Clay, Marie M., *Reading Begins At Home*, Heinemann Educational Books, Auckland, 1979.

Clark, Margaret, *Young Fluent Readers*, Heinemann Educational Books, London, 1976.

Dept. of Educ., *On The Way To Reading*, Wellington, 1978.

Durkin, Dolores, *Children Who Read Early*, Teachers' College Press, New York, 1966.

Holt, J., *How Children Learn*, Pelican, London, 1970.

Kraus, Ruth, *The Carrot Seed*, Harper and Row, 1945.

Metropolitan Reading Readiness Test. N.Z. Council For Educational Research, Wellington, 1943.

Pines, Maya, *Revolution in Learning*, Harper & Row, New York, 1967.

Todd, Vivian, and Heffernon, Helen, *The Years Before School: Building Preschool Children*, Macmillan, London, 1970.

White, Dorothy Neal, *Books Before Five*, N.Z.C.E.R., Wellington, 1956.

# Exploring Further

Make a study of a preschool child. Consider the child's health, motor behaviour, confidence, language, book behaviour, story interest.

# 3 The Importance of School Entry

Important changes take place in the character of learning around the age of five. One author says[1]

'the older child plans, the younger child does not.'

Another finds that[2]

'the older child's learning is mediated by words whereas that of the younger child is unmediated.'

And a third concludes that[3]

'the older child can deal with several features at a time and in some structured relationships while the younger child can only manage one aspect at a time and depends on the properties he can perceive rather than those he knows about.'

At about this age the child depends less on the association of things that have occurred together or responses that have produced contingent results and he is more likely to act upon the experience he has, trying to solve an incongruity, direct his thinking to some past event, organize his experiences in related categories, label things sensed, recall verbally experience observed, draw what he has heard about and so on. The child begins to organize and relate his information about the world — coding, categorizing, sorting, applying learned coding systems to new events. He has been doing all these things since he was an infant but now he does more of these things more deliberately.

This has been described in relation to memory. At 3 to 4 years the child at this age cannot yet set himself a goal to memorize or to recall. Memorizing, like recalling, is accomplished unintentionally at this age. The 3- to 4-year-old children mainly memorize and recall connections formed by constantly repeating spatial and temporal contiguity of impinging objects and phenomena.

A young child does much better in memorizing a connected text — poems, stories and fairy tales. In this case, along with a large number of repetitions, a number of conditions are present that favour memorizing:

- emotional content of the text (cf. Ashton-Warner)
- clear images
- evocation of empathy
- sonority and clear rhythm (facilitates construction of a verbal-motor image)
- rhythm of speech and rhythm of body movement.

[1]Zaporozhets  [2]Kendler  [3]Bruner

At 5 years behaviour is characterized by the appearance and gradual development of intentional memorizing and recalling. Note the single repetition of material that must be kept in memory and by 6 or 7 years the child, with improved efficiency, is able to

- analyse the material to be remembered
- group it
- establish logical connections
- systematize representations of the surrounding environment.

Experimental evidence suggests that the memory is not a copying device but a sort of construction process that uses what it already knows to construct the material that it is supposed to remember. The 5 to 7 year age group is a particularly interesting one for cognitive development. Piaget has described this as a period of transition from perceptual learning to the thinking operations of the child who can classify and consider inverse relationships. Writers who have criticized Piaget have emphasized that the effects of environment are greater than he allows and that a powerful teaching environment can accelerate development in limited areas. Russian child psychologists have described a transition from self-instructions, spoken aloud, to inner self-instructions in the 5 to 7 year period. Experimental studies of children's learning have suggested some interesting transitions taking place at this time which speed up the process of acquiring new skills or re-applying old ones. For example, the child can produce a whole new set of behaviour merely by applying the concept of 'opposite' to old learning. It is a period when the child learns strategies or ways of proceeding which help him to find his own way around new learning. He learns how to instruct himself.

# Adjustment to School

How different children are, even at 5 years old! Not only are they different in sex, boys and girls, and in style, pretty or perky, intelligent or sociable, but also they have learned quite different things from the environments they live in. They are complex beings whose behaviours are all tied up mysteriously into patterns we can sense but are not always able to describe. They are very different one from another.

Sometimes parents and teachers search for this or that single cause that might explain a particular child's behaviour. But every little incident in a child's day occurs against a backdrop of the whole context around him at that time. The impact of that incident is determined in one sense by all his experiences in life so far. The child, however young, is not just taking in experience. He is actively approaching or withdrawing, coping or failing. He brings his personal resources to bear on *his* life problems. Lois Murphy has called this learning to cope in the widening world of childhood (Murphy, 1962).

We should look from time to time at the balance sheet, to see whether a good life is emerging from the daily interchange of our children with the world around them.

'Depending on how we handle such daily interactions our children's personality and their relationship to life will take one of several courses. No single event need have specially great impact, but it is amazing how . . . little experiences make up, in the long run, a good life or a pretty miserable one. And all this occurs without anything terribly important having happened, good or bad.'

(Bettleheim, 1962)

So, children are complex, development is complex and we must observe carefully life's balance sheet as it is detailed for each individual child.

'There are many reasons why child and parents alike have butterflies in their stomachs on the first days of school. From the child's point of view, starting school means leaving the safety and comfort of home for a long time every day. He is still small physically, and the school building appears as a large and unfamiliar structure for him to investigate. The child has undoubtedly heard about school from siblings or other peers, and some of the butterflies must represent excitement at embarking on an adventure that is associated with growing up. While the school experience is anticipated with some knowledge, expectation, and excitement, there is still much about it that is unknown. The uncertainty about what really happens at school and the imaginative fantasies about what happens at mysterious places away from home are other sources of anxiety for the child.

From the parents' perspective, the beginning of school has a strong symbolic meaning. The first day is only the beginning of a long sequence of school-related experiences which have become incorporated into the adult's self-concept. The school represents external evaluation; opportunities for success and failure; the setting for peer group formation and social evaluation; and the initiation of a set of experiences which in adulthood may lead to advancement of socio-economic status. At a more immediate level, the school represents a new source of influence on the child beyond the family. Beliefs and practices which are followed in the home will come under the scrutiny and challenge of community norms and values. The personal hopes and aspirations which parents have for their children now will be tempered by the reality of performance.'

(Newman and Newman, 1975)

Tensions occur in many families at the time a child enters school. For the parents and the child it is a relatively sudden change. Many parents have an inner concern about some of the difficulties they think their children could encounter. For example they may fear physical attack, or criticism of the child. Some anticipate that the home will be criticized. Their concern runs like this. 'I've been spending five years doing my job. Now everyone will see whether I'm a success or not.' When the child enters school parents may feel relief and sadness at the same time. One mother asked 'Why do I feel so near to tears when I expected to feel relieved and happy that my child is growing up.' Such reactions to separation are not uncommon (Klein and Ross, 1958).

Children show signs of increased stress during the first few weeks of school and they express this in many different ways. Some show physical reactions with loss of appetite, fatigue and stomach upsets. Others return to old problems they had given up, like bedwetting, thumb-sucking, and dawdling. Irritability, fighting with brothers

and sisters, talkativeness or reticence, keyed-up behaviour, a worried expression —
all these behaviours have been reported by parents.

On the credit side there are often signs of growth as the children begin to feel that
they can manage the new classroom situation. These changes in the children come
from an increase in independent behaviours —

- acting like a 'big shot'
- not wanting to have a baby-sitter
- playing further from home
- visiting neighbours' homes more often

or from the feeling that they are more grown-up —

- more responsibility for self-help
- increased cooperation
- imitation of older children
- more responsible with younger brothers and sisters

or from new attitudes and interests —

- more interest in other children
- decrease in shyness
- new interest in music, and painting
- wanting to 'work' rather than 'play'.

Entry to school calls for a rapid transition from old adjustments to new ones for
both the child and his parents. Important feelings are involved and the child is not the
only one making the change. Going to school calls for adjustments by the parents
who may wonder —

- about the school as an authority
- how their child will measure up
- what is happening to the child for large parts of his day
- about the teacher's handling of problem behaviours.

A satisfactory transition to school will be important for the child in two ways. He
must feel able to grasp the new experiences and grow in the new environment. And,
for the continuing richness of his education in future years, his parents must weather
the transition so that they feel comfortable in their interaction with the school and the
teachers. Time spent on these two adjustments could be valuable.

# The Unlucky or Unusual Child

When the child enters school the teacher is in a privileged position for gathering significant information about him. Parents in interviews want to explain their child and
his past development to the teacher, the preschool can provide further background,
general practitioners will make themselves available to comment on the very unusual

child to ease his passage into formal education and school psychologists will be prepared to give guidance to teachers in order to prevent a pattern of failure.

Children who have been unfortunate in their early childhood experiences or whose development has been unusual for other reasons probably need quite *different* programmes. Their different behaviours at entry should trigger in the teacher an openness in observing their interaction with the new environment, and creative solutions for alternative activities when these are needed. To illustrate this I include a description of some rather older children who were 5:6 to 6:6 when a gifted young teacher was asked to reverse the failure pattern that was already evident. They were part of her class of thirty children.

### Grant
. . . brought problems to school from an emotionally disturbed home.

### Frank
. . . came from a Samoan home with the problem of learning English as a second language. He also had partial hearing in his left ear.

### Clive
. . . was an overactive child with a short attention span.

### Martin
. . . had a speech impediment. His speech was very nasal.

### David
. . . had defective eyesight that was only picked up at 6 years when he was found to have a 6/9 vision in left eye and 6/60 vision in the right eye. It was not until 6:7 that he actually had glasses. Then he broke them several times, had his good eye covered with sticking plaster to make the right eye work and subsequently had to have his left eye corrected by an operation for turning in. He could not see the detail of print.
● He had defective ears although they were operated on later.
● He had poor motor coordination. All his eye-hand learning had been handicapped.
● While he was having his good eye patched periodically, he would change writing hands with each switch. During his second year at school he changed from right to left and back to right. The following year he used his right hand.
● He was so tiny at school entry that he attended growth clinic. To compensate for his small size he was very aggressive and had frequent tantrums. In fact, he was called 'Tiger' in his first year. It was later found that David had an allergy to wheat which could account for him being over-emotional.

### Len
. . . came from a Samoan background with little English spoken at home. He was an adopted child and there was a negative attitude to him at home. Before he arrived at school he had a reputation for being naughty and had received severe punishments. He found great difficulty handling excitement or any change in his home or school environment. He became extremely difficult in the middle term when his mother went to work, and an older cousin came with an aunt to stay at home. This occurred at the same time as a change of class and teacher at school. He had a very negative attitude to himself. His motor coordination was very poor. He had a very short atten-

tion span and was extremely easily distracted. He was not able to listen to all of a story read to the class.

In retrospect, it is easy to see that *the school should be flexible enough to adjust itself to the needs of such different children.* But to take a stand fairly and squarely on the side of prevention the school must orient itself to such special needs close to the time that the child enters school. The special needs must be matched as far as is possible with mitigating programmes so that the child is brought to common ground for group instruction — but by different programmes or at least different emphases within the programmes.

## Settling in

So, the passage is not always a smooth one and anxiety must be minimized because it interferes with learning. The welcome is important. This is one teacher's account of her practices.

Reading ability often depends on whether the child settles easily into the school routine and so it is most important that he comes into a pleasant, friendly room.
In fact most children are given the opportunity to visit the school before they turn five. They come on regular visits with playcentre or kindergarten groups or if they do not attend either of these they come with mother to sit in for an hour or so. Most mothers with older children at school bring the little ones into the infant room several times before their fifth birthday. On entry the child finds many interesting pictures, captions, wall stories and exhibits to look at and plenty of activities in the reading, maths and science corners to occupy him.
He finds that the teacher has arranged her work so that she is free to talk to him when he arrives at school each morning. This is often the only time that shy children will talk.
He must be made to feel secure and as routine helps this feeling of security the sooner he becomes familiar with the class routine the better.

# The Unresponsive Child

Once in a while a reception class teacher finds a child who will not offer any responses. The teaching process is impotent if no interaction with the child can be established. The child who is emotionally upset by leaving home, by the crowd of other children or by the impact of newness and strangeness in his environment will sometimes over-react, and sometimes take refuge in neutrality. But as the teacher wins him over to the new setting he normally begins to participate eagerly, a little at first and later wholeheartedly, almost in spite of himself.
There is another type of child who seems to be more afraid to perform than he is emotionally upset in the new environment. Perhaps he is afraid to be wrong; his reticence sometimes seems to be related to a lack of confidence in his own ability; on other occasions it seems to stem from a vague awareness that he is 'no good' at a par-

ticular activity. Someone or something in his past experience has made him feel this way. For example after six months at school one boy put a caption book on the observer's table and stood motionless and speechless. Both child and observer waited. The observer read the title aloud and ran her finger across the text. The child offered no response despite encouragement and several patient invitations. The observer read several pages of the book. Slowly the child moved his finger towards the print and in an approximate way traced left to right and right to left across the print as the book was read. He was not totally unresponsive; he could be coaxed to move in the reading situation, making a global, tentative response to print in a situation that was relaxed and unhurried.

Another child was quite happy to say the text, repeating what he heard, but refused to point, to move his hand, to put a response of his body or hand into the situation. For six months one little boy maintained, 'I'll read to you but I won't write my name!' 'Won't' really meant 'Can't', and his stance was a defensive one protecting himself from criticism and failure.

A child who is reluctant to point, refuses to speak, or will not look searchingly at print, is like a child out for a walk with his group but limping with an injured leg. The reading process will be learned haltingly, until he is confident enough to respond in the troublesome area. Coaxing that is not carping, support that is not demanding, confidence in him that does not deny the reality of his inadequacy, these are the fine distinctions that must determine the teacher's behaviour and attitude towards the unresponsive child.

# Individuality and Change

A child's first five years have been peopled with attentive human beings. How does he see them? How does he draw them? (Harris, 1963.)

## Primitive messages

One 5-year-old girl drew a lady with a baby. She pointed out the lady's hand, arms, body and leg (one only) and the baby, a much smaller figure, alongside.

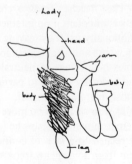

A 5-year-old boy of superior intelligence produced an equally odd man with a body (centre line), legs (side lines), arms, and fingers, toes, hair, eyes, and nose. The ideas were clear in his mind. It is the transformation into a statement on paper that is difficult, not unlike the ease with which I recognize the face of a friend but the difficulty I would have in painting her portrait.

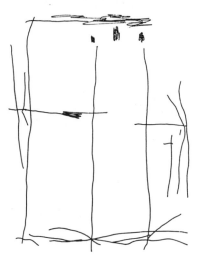

This primitive creature was produced by a 5-year-old boy of above average ability who became an excellent reader within the year. His ability to transmit what he knew into a clear statement on paper was very limited at entry to school. One thing is fairly certain. He had had limited opportunity to explore a two-dimensional paper and pencil world.

## What a variety!

New entrants differ more, one from another, than at any other time for the next few years. This is because, in their preschool years, they have had very different kinds of experiences, whereas in school they have many shared opportunities to learn. So, at the point of entering school, children express their ideas in very individual ways.

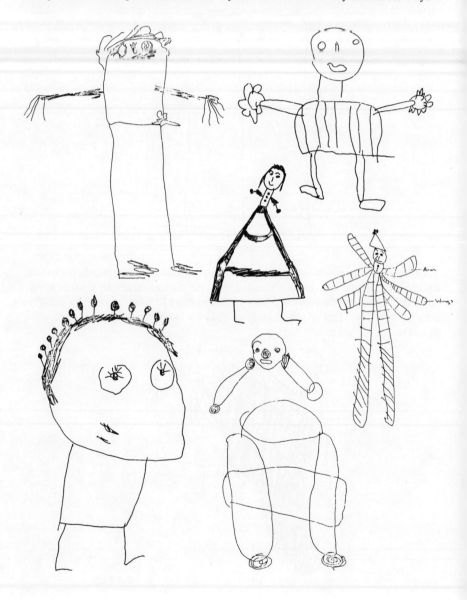

## Not haphazard

But if you save several drawings made by one particular child over two or three weeks you will often find that he is working to a basic plan. His ideas are organized and he produces the same pattern or scheme again and again.

It seems as if the child has learned a plan of action which produces the pattern or schema. This gives the child enough control over pencil and paper to play with variations, which often leads to new discoveries.

## Even twins are individuals

Fraternal twins are like brothers and sisters. They do not have identical heredity but they have been reared in the same home and are likely to have had similar preschool experiences. At 5 years one might expect them to do similar kinds of things but at that age their drawings are often very different. This underlines the fact that they are individuals, making different use of similar experiences.

## What does 'big' mean?

When children were asked to draw a man or a lady and to 'make it big', this was intended to avoid the miniscule creatures that they sometimes draw in one corner of a page. But 5-year-olds found some interesting ways to make the human figure 'big'.

Even common words have different meanings for young children who tend to focus on one aspect of a problem at a time.

## Rapid change

Some children's drawings change very greatly within six months, partly as a result of new experiences at school. Compare the drawings of 5-year-olds with their own productions six months later.

## Continuity

Yet underlying the changes one can often detect the persistence of a basic pattern reminding us that experience is cumulative and early experiences are the foundation upon which a child builds.

## Being asked the question

Racing commentators will often say, of the leading horse, that he is being asked the question — has he anything more to give? Education in the home, preschool or school, consists of asking such questions. We may accept the child's drawing on a particular day in its present stage of primitive thought, expressing his individuality, and limited to the features that have caught his attention for the moment. How do we know whether he has anything more to give? And if he has, how do we reach towards it?

If we present children with very simple tasks we do not have an opportunity to observe the great variety of individual differences that do exist because most of them perform successfully. Preschool and infant rooms must be rich in opportunities for the child to move beyond today's statement in the direction of personal growth. The foundation of personal success is to discover one's particular competencies.

An illustration may help to make this point. Four children, A, B, C, D, were asked to copy some shapes. All completed the circles well. Child A failed Item 2 but the other three succeeded, more or less. By Item 3 only children B and D could copy the master figure which was a triangle inside a circle. By Item 4 only child D succeeded in producing a divided diamond.

These examples suggest that a teacher must do more than provide the child with stimulating experiences and opportunities for growth. She must know which tasks will uncover his capacities and what records will best reveal the changes that are occurring.

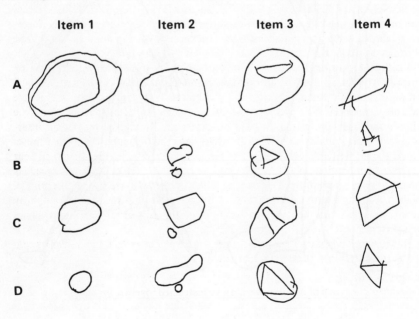

# On Entry to School

'When a child enters school he has a private frame of reference which stems from his personal preschool experiences.' His particular parents in his particular home have given him an opportunity to explore some things and not others so that he knows a great deal about a limited number of personal experiences. The language he uses mirrors his parents' language; the forms, idioms and dialect he uses reflect the language that his parents use most often as they speak with him. The child's feelings well up from inside him, the product of intense experiences he has had with significant adults in the past. If the new school experiences are strange, his feelings take vague and mysterious shape from half-comprehended comments overheard in his home or during play with other children.

From the challenges (and failures) of his first five years of growth the child brings to school a store of behaviour patterns for meeting new situations. Some of these responses are his strengths and the observer labels them mature. Other responses are less effective, the product of unsuccessful attempts to cope in the past, and the observer labels these 'weaknesses'. All the child's past confidence may melt to a state of weak wonder as he tries to discover how his usual ways of doing things fit with the strange new situation in which he finds himself. Even adults face such 'newness shock' in strange situations.

A good teacher supports an individual child in finding his personal solution to coping with the new school situation. After he has come to terms, in his own way, with the new place and the new people the teacher encourages him to share experiences with other members of the group. A good teacher of new entrants needs this important quality of being able to use the unique background of each pupil so that in time he comes to share common experiences with his learning group.

A different approach is possible. A teacher can decide upon a sequence of learning which the child must master. She can programme his progress step by step, teaching and observing. With many children she will be successful because they are flexible and able to re-orient their previous learning to the teacher's demands. But for some children the first steps of the teacher's pre-determined sequences may be an insurmountable barrier which turns them off into a side-road of failure. If a teacher thinks a child should write his name before he begins a caption book, the child with poor eye/hand coordination may be handicapped whereas he could have learnt to read his name and gone on from there. If naming letters is an early step in the programme, children who could have used their control of sentences to support their learning may become confused with the large and incomprehensible task of learning funny names for many symbols.

This is a problem of translation. How can the behaviours which the child does control be translated into behaviours that are

● useful in reading
● common to a group of children who can be instructed together.

Common ground for group instruction will probably be achieved more rapidly by translating the child's available responses into appropriate reading responses than by insisting upon a preselected sequence of learning which the teacher has chosen. This argument favours an 'experience' emphasis to beginning reading rather than an emphasis on learning a sequence of skills. The question of what to observe in new entrant behaviour is therefore important.

What kind of person is this child? What does his preschool teacher remember about him? Was he active? Slow-moving? Was he talkative or quiet? Was he usually contented or miserable? More specifically, what gave him a feeling of mastery and assurance? What did he dislike or avoid? How did he use his eyes to explore things? His language to communicate to people? His curiosity to seek new understanding? To what does a particular child give his attention? Is he reaching out for language experiences? Is he eager to explore the written symbol? Is he oriented to manipulative movement in his play world? He will not attend exclusively to one mode rather than the other, but will often show a preference.

When his parents enrol him they will want to meet the people in charge of his school as well as his class teacher to whom they are transferring the care of their child. Can one assess how his mother is feeling about this moment of enrolment? What do you think she may have said to the child to prepare him for this experience? What does this particular parent expect for her child and for herself from the school?

A school would do well to send a parent away confident that her child's individuality will be respected, that his weaknesses will find support and that his family will not be blamed for his failures. If the parent has some responsibilities like supplying equipment or coming to school to collect the child or to participate in parent discussions, these should be explained. An invitation to come and discuss the child's settling period after four to six weeks could be extended at this time.

Children who are to move confidently into reading must feel happy and comfortable in their new classroom and school. Fearful children will be inarticulate, unable to listen, awed by the teacher, and withdrawing into their old competencies rather than reaching out for new ones. One way to increase children's confidence is to have child and parent visit the class and take part in activities some weeks before he is enrolled at the school.

## The fast learner

Many of the well-prepared children have already had experiences in their preschools and homes which have fostered early reading behaviours and motivated them to begin to solve the reading puzzle (Clark, 1976).

Improved liaison with kindergartens and play centres will help teachers to identify the children who are showing an early interest in reading. Discussion with parents in the first few weeks of school will provide additional information.

The fast learners will soon indicate their interest in books and they will move quickly into writing words and learning early book skills. When the teacher has had sufficient opportunity to observe the child's response to books she has two or three options for the placement of the fast learning child. She may provide an individualized programme using a vast and varied supply of story books and lots of opportunity for the child to write stories. She might consider promotion to a slightly older group of children whose reading needs are close to those of this child. Or she may use the opportunities of flexible grouping in the new entrant class or the Open Plan classroom to group this child appropriately for reading. If this fast learner enters a school where most children have had enriched preschool opportunities then most of his classmates will be starting school with similar advantages and compared to them, this child will be an average learner.

## The slow learner

Some children, who have responded well to their opportunities in the preschool years are nonetheless slow to profit from the school programme. There are many different reasons for this, but one major reason is that our intelligence determines to some extent the rate at which we learn. Some school entrants will be slower than others at responding to instruction. Flexible grouping helps here as it did with the fast learner; the child is moved with groups of other children whose responses to new learning are more or less keeping pace with his own.

For the slow learner it takes longer to get adjusted to the new place and new people. He does not find very many familiar tasks around him. He joins in the group activities but when the teacher asks questions he does not know what to say. Perhaps he is not keen on talking anyway. If she is hard to understand he tunes out. He does not notice many of the things that are going on around him.

If all goes well the teacher establishes a good relationship with the slow learner and he begins to respond to some of the early reading tasks. From time to time he is joined by smaller and younger children who have reached his stage but they may pass on before he is ready to move.

The teacher's task during that first year is to get the slow child responsive to instruction, happy to try and to discover for himself, steadily accumulating the early reading behaviours and not losing his buoyancy and bounce. Most slow learners, gaining confidence in this way are ready for book reading by the beginning of their second year at school. If they are not, whatever their intelligence, the school might well take out an insurance against expenditure of effort in later years and provide the child with individual tutoring in a reading recovery programme (Clay, 1979).

A world authority on reading and on early prevention programmes, Eve Malmquist, urges teachers, parents and pupils to have a little patience at the beginning of instruction.

Growth in reading cannot be hurried without some undesirable and even damaging effects on some children. Yet dalliance can mean the consolidation and habituation at best of low-order processing habits which resist reorganization at later stages of instruction; at worst the training in of erroneous concepts and handicapping procedures.

It pays to waste time, to start easily, by introducing a variety of reading readiness experiences, and using materials on a difficulty level far below the capacity level of many children. This make-haste slowly policy permeates the teaching of reading with emphasis on interest and easily-won achievement.

. . . when it is time to begin instruction in the various reading skills the teacher is urged to use materials systematized as to sequence so that the child is steadily challenged to raise his level of performance.

(Malmquist, 1973)

# References and Further Reading

Ashton-Warner, Sylvia, *Teacher*, Secker and Warburg, London, 1963

Bettleheim, B., *Dialogues with Mothers*, Free Press of Glencoe, New York, 1962.

Bloom, B.S., *Stability and Change in Human Characteristics*, Wiley, New York, 1964.

Butler, Dorothy, and Clay, Marie M., *Reading Begins At Home*, Heinemann Educational Books, Auckland, 1979.

Clark, Margaret, *Young Fluent Readers*, Heinemann Educational Books, London, 1973.

Clay, Marie M., *The Early Detection of Reading Difficulties: A Diagnostic Survey with Recovery Procedures*, Heinemann Educational Books, Auckland, 1979.

Durkin, Dolores, *Reading And The Kindergarten: An Annotated Bibliography*, International Reading Association, Newark, Delaware, 1969.

Harris, D., *Children's Drawings As Measures of Intellectual Maturity*, New York, Harcourt Brace, 1963.

Klein, D.C., and Ross, A., Kindergarten entry: a study of role transition. Morris Krugman (Ed.), *Orthopsychiatry and the School*. Amer. Orthopsychiatric Association, New York, 1958.

Levin, Esther, 'Beginning reading — a personal affair', *Elementary School Journal* 67, 1966, pp. 67-71.

Malmquist, E., Sweden. In Downing, J., *Comparative Reading*, Macmillan, New York, 1973, 466-487.

Murphy, Lois, *The Widening World of Childhood*, Basic Books, New York, 1962.

Newman, B.M., and Newman, P.R., *Development Through Life*, The Dorsey Press, Homewood, Illinois, 1975.

White, Dorothy Neal, *Books Before Five*, N.Z. Council for Educational Research, Wellington, 1956.

# Exploring Further

**Observe a child on his first day at school. What individual differences can you capture by asking children to draw a simple object or person for you?**

# Part 2

# Early Reading Skills

# 4   A Tale of Success

Before I begin to partition the developmental process of learning to read let me recount from my observation records, taken at one or two week intervals, the progress of one successful child. One of the problems that teachers, parents and theorists have with observing the very rapid progress made by the young child in his first year at school is in trying to pull together all the evidence over a long period of time and make sense of it. Looking back over well-kept records it is easy to see patterns emerging in a child's particular experiences.

This history of one child's first year at school illustrates that a child at risk can be brought into profitable interaction with instruction by good teaching.

John's score on a reading readiness test (Metropolitan, NZCER, 1943) at entry to school in 1964 showed him to be poorly prepared for instruction. *He had a lower score than 95 percent of school entrants.* At the end of one year of instruction he was in the top progress group with the best 25 percent of a research sample from five schools. John was a child of average intelligence from a working class home which did not provide much support for what he was trying to learn in school. His progress is worthy of attention.

| | RECORD | LOOKING BACK ON IT |
|---|---|---|
| **TERM 1** | | |
| **Feb. 3** | Enters school at 5:0 on the first day of the school year. | John was alert and friendly but was not well-prepared by his home for school. |
| **Mar. 10** **(D₀)** | Dictates a caption for his picture. *I saw boxing on TV.* **Points R-to-L and bottom-to-top as he rereads the teacher's print.** | |
| **Apr. 7** | Brings me a caption book. Tries but cannot respond to it. Does not seem to know what is required of him. | It has been two months before he was judged ready for a caption book and he had no immediate success. |
| **Apr. 14** **(D₁)** | He makes up the text of another caption book, *What Goes Fast.* He is almost word perfect. He moves in the correct direction using either hand to point. | One week later he had grasped the essential nature of book reading. He spent the next two months reading one and two line sentences in simple books with picture clues. |

| Apr. 21 (D2) | New book *My Games,* **less accurate, correct direction, whispers, reluctant to point.** | |
| Apr. 28 (D3) | New book *Every Day,* **correct direction except for one lapse bottom to top. Text not word perfect.** | |

**TERM 2**

| June 2 (D4) | New book *What Can Jump,* **correct direction, very fast, not locating words as he says them.** | |
| June 9 | Promoted to new class. New book *Mother and Father.* **Uses correct direction, the first word in a line, memory for text, and picture cues. There was evidence of this in the running record of reading behaviour.** | John was beginning to use a variety of cues to prompt him. |
| June 16 | Now on a prereader *Come Here* **(McKee) with a high error rate, one error in 2 or 3 words.** | Good teaching for him for the last two months had brought him to his first reader. He struggled for a month. |
| June 23 (D5) | **As for last week, and on the first page he went R-to-L.** | |
| July 7 | **As before but is gaining control over some words.** | |
| July 14 | **Read 12 pages of this book with 94 percent accuracy and 2 self-corrections.** | He was now able to coordinate all the behaviour he needed to read a very simple book. |
| July 28 | **Read *Wake Up Father* (R1 level) with 90 percent accuracy, 1 self-correction in 9 errors. Feels the effort of the task and reacts to the last page with 'Oh! it's a lot of words.'** | He was reading with effort not without error but with effective self-correction at times. |

**Aug. 4, 11**   As above with 100 percent accuracy and 4 self-corrections.

**Aug. 18**   Read *Early in the Morning* **(R1\* level) with 95 percent accuracy.**

**TERM 3**

**Sept. 15**   Reads *The Fire Engine* (Red 3 level) with 100 percent accuracy and self-correction.

After 8 months at school he was well-prepared for successful reading and began an unusually fast but successful run through the reading series plus many supplementary readers and some story books.

**Sept. 22**   R2 level 98 percent
R3 level 96 percent

**Sept. 29**   Y2 level 98 percent
Y3 level 97 percent

**Oct. 13**   Y3 level 97 percent
**(D6)**   Showed incipient pointing behaviour marking a difficulty

**Oct. 27**   B1 level 100 percent

**Nov. 2**   B3 level 98 percent

**Nov. 17**   G1 level 99 percent

**Dec. 1**   G2 level 100 percent

**Feb. 4**   G2 level 95 percent

This is a slight drop in control over the long vacation and no gain. There may have been little at home to advance his lively interest in words.

---

\* The early reading books in the *Ready to Read* series (Department of Education, 1969) are colour coded and numbered. The difficulty sequence is Red, Yellow, Blue, Green. There are three books in the graded series at each colour level. Many supplementary books are available at each level.

From July 28 when John moved onto the basic reading series my recorded observation sessions showed that John had

- read 2 888 words to me
- made 85 errors or 1 in every 34
- an average rate of 1.04 seconds per word.

John's progress was exceptional, and it is only possible to guess at why this was. It was certainly facilitated by the fact that nine months after entry *John became a commentator on the code.* He was interested in words and their possibilities and was actively verbalizing his comparisons of what he saw with what he remembered, noting features that did and did not fit with certain ways of categorizing words. For example, he would say –

'Look!
If you cover up *painting* you get *paint.*
If you cover up *shed* you get *she.*
If you cover *o* in *No* you don't get anything.
*I've* is like *drive* but it's *have.*
That looks like *Will* but it's *William.*'

John's is not a record which clarifies the problems of learning the directional constraints of printed language but there are some features worth noting. At points indicated in his record he –

$D_0$   moved right to left and bottom to top
$D_1$   used either hand for correct directional pointing
$D_2$   was reluctant to point
$D_3$   made one lapse going bottom to top
$D_4$   used correct direction but not matched word by word
$D_5$   made one lapse going right to left
$D_6$   used incipient pointing at difficulties.·

The record captured the stage of directional fluctuation as correct responses came and went, even for a child making excellent progress. After $D_5$ in his record, direction, pointing and matching get no further mention which means he had no further difficulties until $D_6$. The note 'incipient pointing at difficulties' means that he is reading by eye scan alone but as he works on the cues of a difficult part of the text his hand comes into action, remote from the page, fingers moving slightly as if to assist eye and brain in marking the significant cues. In terms of the Russian psychologists who have made a special study of such behaviours this is an outward sign of an inner programme for proceeding that has become a matter of brain attention rather than hand movement. Learned in action, the pattern has become a recipe for attending but it is easy to return to the full action schema if need be.

At 6:0 John can guide his copying with a high degree of control but his immaturity lingers, shown in his attempt to *produce* both his names from his own mental representation of them.

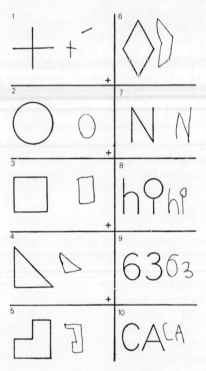

There is behaviour of interest in this early reading period which we will now examine in more detail.

# Exploring Further

**Keep a record of one child's reading progress over two or three months or longer. (Clay, 1979.)**

# 5 Early Reading Behaviour and Language Development

One translation we expect the 5-year-old to make is from spoken to written communication. Adults require some understanding of language development so that they can listen closely to children's spoken language.

Between the ages of 2 and 3 years very interesting things happen in language development for the average child. He has at first a 'private' language which not even his mother understands at times. But at this time a child usually has his mother constantly with him. She is emotionally responsive to the child's big efforts and she takes the trouble to try to understand his private references. She shepherds him through this stage to a 3-year-old level of language that is comprehensible to the outsider. The child with no mother or with many mothers may miss out on this shepherding — an orphanage child, a hospitalized child, a child handed over to his sisters to be minded. He needs somebody who will study his private frame of reference. When the child cannot make himself understood the communication process breaks down because when the listener does not reply the child's efforts are not rewarded. For continuing development towards mature language we have to keep the child talking, whatever his limitations. Our efforts should never make him reluctant to offer up his ungrammatical but expressive attempts to construct sentences. As we talk with a child he revises and refines his language, experimenting, making funny errors but gaining all the while in control over the expressiveness and the complexity of the language.

Every sentence the child constructs is an hypothesis about language. If he is understood, his hypothesis is confirmed — the idea could be expressed that way. When a listener is puzzled, the hypothesis is rejected and a different sentence is formed. In this process the term 'mother-tongue' is well chosen because the parents' role is so important. The child is deprived without the close, understanding, warm, readily-available listener, talker and speech model. If the child's language development seems to be lagging it is misplaced sympathy to do his talking for him. Instead, put your ear closer, concentrate more sharply, smile more rewardingly and spend more time in genuine conversation, difficult though it is. To foster children's language development, create opportunities for them to talk, and then talk with them (not at them).

Questions may be exasperating but they are sometimes used by the child in a systematic search for information about language. 'What's that?' questions draw a list of nouns. 'Why?' questions usually require answers with 'because' and 'if' and therefore introduce the child to the more complex structures of the language, and to the qualifications of thought.

# Adults Provide the Language Model

For the first five years the child's language growth is entirely dependent on what people say to him — on how much they speak to him, about what things, in what dialect or mother-tongue, and in what manner, whether gentle and explaining or peremptory and imperative.

We have known for a long time that conversation in the company of an adult is the best tutorial situation in which to raise the child's language functioning to a high level. Descriptive studies of language development gave us sliding scales of proficiency from 'only' children at the highest levels of maturity, to those in small families, to those in large families, to twins or triplets, to institution children and to deaf children — an apparent correlation between the amount of 'mature conversation' the child has with adults and the maturity of language used by the child. Adults have been shown to be effective models in this role. Other children do not provide such satisfactory models.

What is it in the adult's behaviour that fosters increased maturity in the child's language? So far research has provided some interesting leads but no clear answers. When adults are not sure of whether they have understood a young child they often repeat the child's language, a kind of imitation in reverse. The adult echoes the child. But children's sentences often leave out important words or inflections and parents, in their imitation, replace the missing parts and give a completely grammatical version of what the child wanted to say. Adults do this to check their understanding of what the child said. This process has been called 'expansion'. In normal conversation the child's sentences, particularly his questions, are reformulated in some way in the answers, an immediate feedback of correct information. 'That a boy?' 'Yes that's a boy.'

Some parents are convinced that children have something to say that is worthy of attention. Parents who are not child-centred will spend less time expanding their child's speech. This would leave the child to struggle with the rules of English language from the haphazard flow of difficult speech around him. When adults speak with children they usually adapt or simplify their language but their conversation among themselves is more complex in construction. From this the child isolates words, or short phrases but does not learn sentence patterns. Children need frequent opportunities to test the rules of the language they are discovering. These opportunities arise on many occasions because children like to hold an adult's attention with a little conversation about the spontaneous activities they engage in.

A correcting or tutoring approach to language development is fraught with dangers. If a child's language gets attention only when it is in error, will he understand that all the other things he says are approved of? Or will he come to feel that his speech is defective? All children make errors in speech. It is a sign of remarkable progress when the child says 'bringed, throwed, writed.' He has acquired a rule for past tense verb endings that is regularly applied in English. That he has applied it to irregular verbs is of little concern in a young child because the regularities are mastered before the irregularities in the language. Parents may be disconcerted to find that a child's language which at three years is apparently error-free and highly grammatical, becomes full of errors a year later. But research has shown that this often indicates progress. At each successive stage the child masters a limited range of simple structures. When he tries to use more complicated structures to deal with his more complicated thinking, his attempts again become hypotheses which are again tested by whether he is understood or not. 'Can you say it this way?' At each successive stage the child makes errors, but only because he is trying to use more and more of the available possibilities of the English language.

Children learn the language of their parents and their playmates — that is, they learn the dialect or usage of a particular group. A dialect may differ from the language of education in sounds, accent or intonation, in vocabulary, in the grammatical forms and in the type and range of sentence forms used. My favourite example comes from an English county dialect where two children playing together ignored the call of a third child's mother, saying, 'Her b'aint a-calling we; us don't belong-a she.' If you study this example you will find that every pronoun is used differently in this dialect from its use in standard English. The children are not making errors; they have learned to use the rules that their parents use in their home dialect.

In the preschool years almost all children acquire the sounds and structures of the local dialect. Some children acquire through parents and neighbourhood what can be called a non-standard' dialect. It is an intimate possession, understood by loved ones. It reflects their membership of a particular speech group and identifies them with that group. It is personal and valuable and not just an incorrect version of the standard.

A good teacher would not destroy this first language that children use so fluently. She would try to add to their speech a dialect for standard English to be used in some oral situations, and to open the world of books to them. She would leave them their first dialect for family and friends. This poses two real problems for the teacher. She must first establish communication with the child despite the fact that she may speak a strange and unusual dialect. Beyond this she must train the child in the new dialect, knowing that for most of his waking life he is going to live and speak among people who use his home dialect.

How easy it would be for the child in this situation not to speak more than is necessary in the classroom where the standard dialect is used; to choose instead the self-limiting strategy of opting out, instead of increasing his efforts.

For every child, entry to school places heavy demands on his language skills to store the new information needed for educational success. At 5 years the child's language learning is still open to influence but the years of preschool learning are valuable ones. The provision of stimulating preschool environments does not necessarily boost language learning. Interesting play and work activities may be of great value in themselves and still not produce much language behaviour. Does the play activity bring the child into conversational exchange with a mature language model? What opportunities are there for one-to-one conversational exchanges with an adult who understands the child's frame of reference and so shapes up the word and grammar skills of a particular individual? When we try to provide experiences that will compensate for poor language backgrounds we must go beyond the usual bounds of spontaneous learning in a free play situation or group learning from one teacher. The child's spontaneous wish to communicate about something which interests him at one particular moment should have priority and he must have adults who will talk with him, in simple, varied and grammatical language. We should arrange for language-producing activities — activities where adult and child must communicate in order to cooperate.

Compensatory programmes in language acquisition for school entrants whose development has been limited and slow must bear the same principles in mind. Scheduled periods of close interaction with a familiar adult are needed and activities should stimulate a flow of ideas from the child and personal responses from the helper or teacher.

# Some Changes That Occur

The speech which a child uses when he enters school will be unlike the language of his books. Firstly we do not speak as we write. Oral language sentences are often ungrammatical; the usage is conversational or casual. Secondly, the child's language shows immaturity and ignorance of some formal features of his language which he will learn later. As the child becomes familiar with the language of books that are read aloud his attempts at reading become more 'book-like'. Gradually he begins to produce sentences which replicate those of his book.

There are three major directions in which the language changes during the first six months at school for the 5-year-old entrant.

● Firstly, there is an increasing ability in the child to understand speakers who speak differently from the 'people at home' and to make himself understood by teachers and peers who do not know his particular individual frame of reference. This is not merely a matter of the accuracy with which he uses the language, but also the flexibility with which he can adapt his language and rephrase his utterance so that his listeners understand.

● Secondly, there is continuing development and increasing precision in the use of the sound system, the vocabulary, the sentence patterns and the rules for combining words and for making them agree, and a growing richness in the way he puts his meanings into words.

● Thirdly, the child begins to acquire a feeling for the kinds of language that he can expect to find in books. Some of his oral language is unlikely to be found in books, some will be found and some new features that occur in books will be very rarely or never heard in his speech.

Being in school and having to communicate provides opportunities for such development. Each of the three trends is open-ended so that at whatever level the child functions on entry to school there is always room for further differentiation, flexibility, and new applications of skill. There is always something more to be learned.

As a speaker or a listener, in instruction or in play, the child learns language. He tries to construct a message that will be understood and he learns something about his effort if it is understood. He listens to a speaker and if he 'catches the drift' he has matched the input to the correct meanings. Failing as a speaker or listener is disconcerting if not upsetting and the child is usually willing to struggle to be understood or to reach the meaning of another speaker. Progress results successively from such brief tussles in moments of not quite understanding.

The teacher's lessons provide one opportunity for drawing the child's attention to those three lines of development, to flexibility in communication, control over linguistic features and an awareness of book languages. How can the teacher find out about the child's control of the English language?

# Observing Language

## Observe the child in conversation

If the child can carry on a pleasant conversation with the teacher then each is using a flexibility of language that is suitable for a good communication to take place. The child who does not like to talk with the teacher or who has some difficulty in understanding what the teacher is saying may be a child at risk.

Be strong-minded about talking with the child with whom it is difficult to hold a conversation. The human reaction is not to talk much to him or her. The educator's reaction is to create *more* opportunities for talking.

## Language tests

A second approach to language observation is to use language observation tests which permit teachers to identify the lower third of their new entrants group who could be at risk within their teaching programme.

### Sentence structure

When a child is asked to imitate a set of carefully selected sentences and his responses are recorded one can observe how he phrases a sentence compared with what he was asked to repeat. *The Record of Oral Language* (Clay et al, 1976) is such a set of sentences, specially designed for use with 5- to 6-year-old children. It is possible to notice what change has occurred between two administrations of this record. Children's oral language differs markedly from one district to another and from school to school. However, a good programme will be directed to the kinds of children who enter a particular school and the lower third of any class in oral language performance could benefit from extra help.

## Vocabulary

The *Peabody Picture Vocabulary Test* (Dunn, 1965) is used by some junior class teachers in New Zealand as an assessment of children's language ability. It can only be used as an *estimate of intelligence* when a child's mother tongue is English, but it can be used more widely as an estimate of vocabulary control in English.

## Rules about inflections

Children's ability to add appropriate endings and inflections to plurals and verbs (Clay, 1974) is thought to relate to reading progress in that the child who does not use appropriate endings is going to have great difficulty in locating and using the printed form of these as cues in his reading. The child with high skills in handling inflections should be able to use this in his error correction behaviour whereas the child with low skills in these may in fact generate more reading errors because he is not noticing in-flection errors in his reading. Such learning is not a matter of memorization in the preschool years. It has been shown to be a process of learning rules for forming plurals, for forming verb tenses, for relating verb forms to the person who is speak-ing, and for applying appropriate pronouns. Children in the first year of school are continuing to consolidate their rules for using inflections.

## Articulation

We've looked at speech production, at vocabulary, at the rules for changing the end-ings of words, and now it is appropriate to look at the child's control of the articula-tion of sounds. Research has demonstrated the progress that is made in learning to pronounce sounds. It documents a shift in the distribution of scores from those shown by 5:6-year-olds through to those shown by 6-year-olds although there is con-siderable overlap between 5:6- and 6-year-olds (Robinson, 1973). Articulation moves gradually towards perfect control of the sounds in English. We would expect most children to end up with perfect scores before they had been at school very long. But there are 6-year-olds who are low scorers on this test as well as 5-year-olds. A child needs to be able to produce most of the sounds which he is trying to use in his reading in order that he may link them to clusters of letters. And the articulation of a word or sentence clarifies the sequence of its sounds (Elkonin, 1971). We have also found that good articulation is associated with early progress with writing vocabulary and poor articulation with limited progress (Robinson, 1973). My reaction to a low scoring child on an articulation test would be to observe carefully whether this appeared to be impeding his reaction to printed text, because it might not. If it was, I would want to minimize the attention to letter-sound relationships in reading for the time being. Then I would give individual instruction to that child at any point where confusion over articulation seemed to be interfering with the reading process.

## The stories they dictate

A third way to observe children's language is to listen carefully to the stories they dic-tate for the teacher to write under their pictures. At first the teacher should be an ac-curate scribe and record exactly what the child says. As the child moves towards book reading the teacher should be able to notice an increasing control over simple English sentences for those children who began at a rather low level of sentence-forming skill. The stories that the child dictates may have language that is —

**Grammatical**
The yacht is sailing in the water.

**Flexible (in that he changes the story as he re-reads it)**
This is the yacht sailing in the water.

**Ungrammatical**
Them together ride the bike.
The mans are boxing on.

**Like spontaneous speech**
It's a house
and then all colours of the sun
and then that there's
all ledges around

**Like formal statements**
I saw boxing on T.V.

**Full of the excitement of telling**
They all chuckeded him out orv bed!

**Trimmed to a caption-like text**
Tall tree

## A record of language production

If a child is asked to tell a story about a picture, can that story be used to tell something about his language development? Robinson (1974) used a set of four rating scales. The child's story is rated on a seven-point scale for its content, imagination, structure and grammar. It is quite difficult to analyse the language a child uses, as Mark's example shows.

**Mark** (5:6 years)
And then when he's got a carrot he left the door open so he's he got out and escapted to school.
That one is . . . he's far away from his really home and he's going to a farm.
It looks like he's gonna be caught by going through the farm.
He meets chickens and hens and then sun goes down and he sleeps.
Then it's morning.
When he wakes up all of a sudden he's at school.

Robinson (1973) found that tallies for grammatical and structural features produced reliable scores (.83 and .72) but that content and imagination were not reliable measures. The child, retested, tended to score differently on the second occasion when content and imagination were scored.

## Language used for early reading books

Perhaps the observation situation which is closest to the reading task is when the teacher listens closely to the sentences that the child generates as he attempts to read the caption books or instant readers of the early reading stage. As the child progresses the sentences which he produces become more and more like the sentences which occur in the text. He produces the same kinds of sentences, he uses the same kinds of vocabulary and although he doesn't get his text precisely correct he moves toward an accuracy level of about 80 percent correct.

How close does the child get to the text of his first little books? It is possible to take a record of the language he uses in response to a text.

● Write down the text.
● Record above the text exactly what the child says.
● Count the sentences or the captions in the text.

Now consider these questions.

Good structure    *Were his responses well-formed sentences?*

● How many were grammatical?
● What percentage was that?

For example    *Child:* | The dog is little.
              Text:  | A puppy can run.

Exact copy of     *Was his sentence a copy of the structure or form of the text*
structure         *sentence?*

● Did he copy the form of the text sentence more or less exactly?
● What percentage of his sentences were close copies?
● This shows that the child can invent book-like sentences or that he can remember them because he heard someone else read them.

For example    *Child:* | The dog can jump.
              Text:  | A puppy can run.

Self-correction    *Did he revise his response without prompting?*

● Did the child alter his response
— from ungrammatical to grammatical?
— from his own sentence to the text model?
— in some other way?

For example    *Child:* | *The dog/puppy can run* (Self-correction)
              Text:  | A puppy

This is different from mere remembering. The child is reconstructing the sentence out of *its component parts.*

# 'Talking Like a Book'

Before they go to school many preschoolers will 'read' books by inventing the text. The 4-year-old reads to grandfather and the older preschooler to the younger one by memorizing the text exactly, or by inventing it, or by a little of each. Some will confidently believe that this is reading while others show more insight. One child 'read' to himself in bed while his mother bathed the younger children. He said, *'I wish I could really truly read this book for myself.'* Probably he recognized that the sentences he was producing were not the same as those he had heard read to him. Another child 'expressed it well when he said, *'I can't read all the words but I know what they say'.* He understood the message but he could not read the words.

Our use of the language when we speak differs from our use in written form. With or without a special dialect the child's own speech habits must be modified so that he can produce sentences like those in his reading books.

A new school entrant came home from school and announced that he had a new book to read to mother. He took it out of his bag and 'read' to his mother, making up a story for each page. Then he asked his mother to read it. He changed and went to play but later that evening read the book again, this time using the correct sentence beginning *'Here is a . . .'* for each page. This illustrates a shift from sheer inventing from the pictures to the more controlled behaviour of 'talking like a book'. After all, who says *'Here is a . . .'* in 'real' speech?

At the stage of early reading behaviour this transition to 'talking like a book' is a very important step in learning. While absolute correctness of the text may not be the aim of reading at this stage the child learns some of these important concepts:

- Print can be turned into speech.
- There is a message recorded.
- The picture is a rough guide to that message.
- Some language units are more likely to occur than others.
- There is a particular message, of particular words in a particular order.
- Memory, or what the ear remembers, helps.

Gradually, with tactful guidance, children can be prompted to develop and apply these concepts to the language of books in a sequence roughly like the following:

*Stage 1: Print can be turned into speech.* The child invents a sentence which could describe a picture. Or he writes a simple word (*is*) and proudly names it something else (*Tip*). Print and spoken language are equated.

The 5-year-old's speech can be heard in the ungrammatical sentences he invents for caption texts:

*I having a bath.*
*Here is blue flowers.*
*I sailing a boat.*
*Him is going.*
*Here rocket go up fast.*

and in some examples of correct colloquial style which do not match the reading text:

*'Father's here,'*
*. . . says Mother.*
*'I'm hungry.'*
*'Paul's sitting on the seat.'*

---

**EXAMPLE OF STAGE I**
**Print Can De Turned Into Speech**

*Reads:* 'Tip' in wall story
*Draws:* Tip stuck in a rabbit hole
*Writes:*     I S     and reads it as Tip
(After 9 weeks at school)

---

*Stage 2: A special type of talking.* The child begins to use a special type of talking found only in books (Here is a . . ., Mother said '. . .'). He has a psychological set to use only particular kinds of language structures.

*Stage 3: The picture is a guide to the message.* The child invents a statement which is appropriate to the picture but which is not an exact rendering of the text.

---

**EXAMPLE OF STAGE 3**
**The Picture is a Guide To The Message**

*Draws:*     Giraffe
*Dictates:*  Here is Johnny the Giraffe eating the tree.
*Reads:*     Johnny the Giraffe is eating the tree.
(After 25 weeks at school)

---

*Stage 4: Some sentences from the text are almost memorized.* A child at this stage reads a caption book relying on what his ear remembers of the text, prompted by the pictures, and usually in sentences. His responses more or less convey the message of the text.

Phillipa 'read' this question in *Snow White* getting the words almost perfectly:

*Tell me mirror, tell me* $\dfrac{mirror}{true}$
*Of all the ladies in the land*
*Who is the fairest, tell me who?*

With a little more experience the child alters his language because he remembers hearing something from this book or one like it.

|  | **1st Attempt** | **2nd Attempt** |
|---|---|---|
| *Child:* | A puppy | *See the little dog.* |
| Text: | Little dog | |

Then he gets very close to 'reading' or saying exactly what is in his book, but he does it as if hearing it, or remembering it. The texts in the example below occur as one line per page in a caption book.

---

### EXAMPLE OF STAGE 4
#### Some Sentences Are Almost Memorized

| Text | Response |
|---|---|
| I like my dolls. | I like — dolls. |
| I like my doll's pram. | I like my doll's —. |
| I like the Wendy house. | (No response) |
| I like my kitten. | I like my kitten. |
| I like puppies, too. | I like puppies — |
| I like ballet girls. | and ballet girls. |
| I like pretty dresses | I like pretty dresses |
| best of all. | best of all. |
| Can you make a book | Can you make a book |
| about what you like? | about what you like? |

---

A child with a 'good' ear for language may come to depend upon recalling what someone else has read. From his viewpoint this is using his strengths. From his teacher's perspective it is a strategy with considerable risks involved if it interferes with the development of visual strategies.

Paul followed his sister's reading of a repetitive story.

*Little furry mouse*
*scampered round the kitchen.*
*But he ran back home*
*before the cat passed by.*

He had a good memory for context and was fairly accurate in retelling the story. He repeated the words rapidly, remembering the repeated lines, stopping for help, expecting it on each phrase that was new on each new page. He paid little attention to the print even when encouraged to look at the words.

*Stage 5: Constructing the sentences.* Now there comes an important transition which it takes some experience to observe  The child combines his ability to produce sentences, his half memories for the text, the picture clues to meaning, and visual cues from letters. Putting all those together in a sequence of actions he seems to compose his response word by word.

Her mother pointed out that the name read 'Toys, For Girls And Boys.' *She followed this along with her finger repeating the words and locating them more or less correctly.* She repeated this without further help seven hours later to her father, getting the sequence and pointing correct.

Suppose, in a controlled vocabulary text the child has learned that there are a limited number of words that can occur — Janet, John, come, look, the, up, jump, dog, here, little. The child may look at a text and pay no attention to the distinctiveness of the printed forms. He optimistically draws a response from that limited pool of words. He is 'talking like a book'. In both the examples below the child uses some clue (probably from a picture) and composes the kind of sentences that he knows occur in his reading book. Given no more instruction than the teacher's negative attention (No!) he reformulates his response three and four times until he gets it correct. He would prefer not to have to search for better responses, but he is learning a vital link in early reading, to search, check, reformulate, correct and obtain some confirmation that he is right. He is not 'reading' but he is learning how to process language information.

---

## EXAMPLE OF STAGE 5

### Building A Sentence Word By Word

| | | | | |
|---|---|---|---|---|
| *Text:* | Little dog | | *Text:* | Janet, look |
| *Child:* | See the little dog | | *Child:* | Look up, Janet |
| *Teacher:* | (No!) | | *Teacher:* | (No!) |
| *Child:* | Come and look | | *Child:* | Look |
| *Teacher:* | (No!) | | *Teacher:* | (No!) |
| *Child:* | Here | | *Child:* | Look |
| *Teacher:* | (No!) | | *Teacher:* | (No!) |
| *Child:* | Little dog | | *Child:* | Look up, Janet |

---

If a child reaches Stage 5 without paying attention to visual cues he may merely invent a book-like text.

| | | | |
|---|---|---|---|
| *Child:* | Come here, | Text: | Here, Red. |
| | Red, come. | | Here, Bill. |
| | Bill, Bill. | | Come here. |
| | Come here. | | Come here. |

But if he now begins to compose sentences word by word and to use visual cues then he can correct an error in mid-sentence, instead of having to depend on an auditory memory for the sentence.

The linguistically able child who is using his knowledge of language as a source of cues will make 'errors' but these will be both grammatical and meaningful. One girl was thinking about meaning when she insisted that her book should say 'The fish *under* the sea'. Language rather than print was guiding the response.

The child's everyday speech is linked to the fluency with which he will read. Certainly he has to learn to decode new words and to predict what sounds are produced by which letter combinations. But such details can be discovered within the larger chunks of meaningful language. The child who already uses a wide range of English language features in a flexible manner, will find it easier to remember the sentence structures in his reading book. He simply has to select the appropriate structures from his speech repertoire. The child with rich experience of books will have greater understanding of bookish forms of language and more motivation to master the art of reading.

# Hearing Sounds in Sequence

Long before the child enters school, he can use and hear the difference between words like *cup* and *cut* in natural speech. But a child who hears and understands those words probably does not know that those words consist of several sounds and that the difference lies wholly in the last sound. This skill must be developed.

Do children differ in their response to learning about sounds in words? To find out what segments children could hear in words some researchers asked preschool, kindergarten, and first-grade children to tap out the number of segments they could hear in spoken words by tapping a dowel on a table. One group heard words of one, two and three syllables (*box, morning, anything*) and the other group heard words of one, two or three sounds (*/oo/, coo, cool*). Results showed that:

● The older children did better than the younger ones.
● Syllables were easier to 'hear' than the sound (phonemes).
● The analysis of words into sounds developed later than the analysis into syllables.
● Sharp age trends were observed for both tasks with these 4- to 7-year-old children (Liberman, I.Y., 1974).

One Auckland study showed a close relationship between high scores in articulation and high scores in writing vocabulary (Robinson, 1973). The child who can analyse his own words into their sounds seems better equipped to write those words for which he does not already know the spelling form.

The acoustic signals in the spoken word *cup* are not the same as the sounds it contains when they are spoken separately. In the spoken word the consonants seem to be collapsed in onto the vowel and the three sounds are recoded into a single syllabic utterance. For the child to discover that the single syllable which he hears really contains three different sounds requires learning. This learning is easier if you are older. The children cannot map the printed word *cup* which has three segments onto the spoken word *cup* unless they become explicitly aware that the spoken word consists of three segments. *In ordinary speech it does not.*

The sounds of speech are a very complex code, and a written alphabet is a simple substitution cipher. In speech

We organize the phonetic segments (b -a -g) into syllables like 'bag' and we *overlap the segments* that constitute the syllable and transmit them *'at the same time.'* This procedure is efficient in contrast to writing. In writing we must make the movements for one gesture and then the movements for the next . . . in speech we move muscles for several successive phonetic segments all at once . . . Not only are the articulatory movements made with great speed and accuracy but they are organized and overlapped in very complex ways. The essence of the (speech) code is that information about two or more successive phonetic segments is carried *simultaneously* on the same piece of sound.

(Liberman, A.M., 1974)

We do not articulate separate sounds one after the other the way we write them. If we make children do this we teach an analysis that is completely novel for them.

What, then, has phonics been throughout the years? Phonics are not immutable rules relating letters to sounds. They are tricks that work, sometimes called heuristic devices, rules for locating words already known to the ear.

For many years the teaching of sounds and phonic systems of decoding have been de-emphasized in New Zealand reading programmes. Single consonant sounds and other letter groups are introduced slowly in the first year of instruction but these do not receive the focal attention they are given in many published reading schemes. What have we done? We have minimized the explicit teaching of phonics. We have taught the child a variety of procedures for analysing words into sounds, during daily lessons in small groups eager to read the story for the day. We have provided massive opportunities for the child to make his own analysis by having him read large quantities of easy material giving him prompts that guide his word-solving. And we have encouraged children to write down their ideas, even new entrants. Under these conditions most children have slowly but surely categorized the complex relationship of letters with the sound forms of words.

Unfortunately these categories are hidden 'within the child'. If our classroom practices are not leading to a slow-growing network of rules which relate sound patterns to printed forms in some particular children the lack may be missed by the teacher who is not observing closely.

To explore this vexed question further we can refer to the work of two other authorities who worked independently and arrived at similar conclusions.

Charles Read (1971) made a study of preschool children who developed their own way of spelling English. From what they wrote he concluded that these children had made some kind of an analysis of the sounds of English before they had even encountered reading, and a year or more before they started school.

In the word D I K T R (doctor) for example, the child has recognized that the word has five segments that need to be represented.

The children's spellings deviated from the standard English forms but often there were regularities in these differences.

| | | | |
|---|---|---|---|
| **AS CHRAY** | (ash tray) | **CHRIE** | (try) |
| **CHRIBLS** | (troubles) | **CHRUCK** | (truck) |

The child who produces the words above and wants to spell truck with a *ch-* will not, according to Read, be enlightened by a teacher who tells him that *ch-* spells *'chu'* in 'chicken'. He already knows that. The close relationship between the first segments of 'truck' and 'chicken' as we articulate these sounds is what he has already discovered and what he is trying to represent. The child who spells brother without an *e*, liked with a *t*, or butter with a *d*, may be listening very sensitively to how people around him speak, and recording it exactly. A phonetician might make similar judgements.

These spontaneous preschool spellers were beginning to listen to these phonetic variations. They invented non-conventional ways of translating them into English spelling. However, Read's children were exceptional as most children do not spontaneously analyse their words into sounds, and some have problems even with analysing their sentences into words.

Russian psychologists have made a close study of the child's awareness of the sounds in words (Elkonin, 1973). A good reader in the schools of the USSR is 'one who knows how to create the correct sound form not only of a known word but also of any unknown word.' Elkonin believes that 'no matter how the written word is perceived visually, whether it be perceived as a whole, in syllables, or letter by letter, *the understanding is based on the sound formation of the word.*' Russian children are taught to hear the sound sequences of word forms *before* they are introduced to print.

New Zealand teachers would probably not wish to place such a heavy emphasis on sounds as the key to reading especially as their new entrants are only 5 years old. Russian children would be nearer to 7 years on entry to school. What is valuable in Elkonin's account of beginning reading in the USSR is the scheme he provides to train children to hear the sounds in the word.

In our schools reading activities would use the visual form of the word to teach the child about sounds. But according to Elkonin, this focusses the child's attention on the letters or characters. Like Liberman he believes that an alphabet is a very simplified code which does not represent the sounds of language very well. Elkonin insists that the child should learn to hear the sounds in words *before* he is exposed to letters.

In Elkonin's scheme the child is given pictures of objects. Below each picture is a rectangle divided into squares according to the number of *sounds* in the name of the object. The child is given some counters.

● The child utters the word aloud separating each successive sound with a drawled or stressed sound while placing a counter for each sound in the corresponding square of the diagram below the picture. The sounds of the word are separated and they are marked by counters.
● This activity is changed gradually during instruction. It becomes an oral analysis without the use of counters and squares.
● Later still the child is required to carry out the analysis silently.

This procedure was used in New Zealand with 6-year-old children who were not making good progress with learning to read (Clay, 1979). We found that many could not hear the sound sequences in words at the outset of our programme. With a training scheme like Elkonin's the children learned to analyse what sounds were in words and what the order or sequence of sounds were. The sequence of sounds is what Elkonin means by the sound form of words. From a limited number of words, say nine, consisting of a small number of sounds, say ten, many of our 6- to 7-year-olds who were 'at risk' as readers were able *to learn the strategy of sound sequence analysis* and generalize it to the analysis of new words.

Liberman demonstrated that the segmenting of words into sounds is a skill that improves from younger to older children. Elkonin describes how Russian children are taught to do this. Read showed that when children take the initiative they can invent spellings in systematic ways using knowledge that they have, such as alphabet names. What does this achieve? It forces children to carry out a splendid sound analysis of the words they want to write — a first to last segmenting of the sounds in the word. They pay attention to the sounds of words and search for a visual way of representing these.

Some failing readers are unable to analyse spoken words into sounds and many 5- to 6-year-olds need special help to learn this.

Does your programme encourage children to learn this skill? If it does they will have little trouble linking the sounds they hear to the letters they are learning to scan and to write.

Teachers may feel that the critical thing for the child to learn is his sounds, and provide an elaborate scheme for teaching that overrated aspect of reading known as phonics. They are teaching the child to go *from letters to sounds.* Current knowledge suggests that we may have to revise our thinking about the value of phonics. A strategy of analysing spoken words into sounds, and then going *from sounds to letters* may be a critical precursor of the ability to utilize the heuristic tricks of phonics. And many children may not need phonic instruction once they acquire and use a sound sequence analysis strategy.

What Read, Liberman and Elkonin are leading us towards is the insight that, given the limitations of alphabets, it is easier if you know the sound segment to find some letter or letter group which could be the written realization of that sound than vice versa.

We do not find it easy to examine our own speaking. Courtney Cazden says that 'the ability to *make language forms opaque* and attend to them of and for themselves is a special kind of language performance.' How can we get young children to want to hear the sound segments in words and to search for these on their own initiative.

Carol Chomsky has encouraged a discovery approach. She has suggested that children can write first and read later in school settings (1976) and she suggests that invented spelling could be easily introduced into classrooms where child-motivated activities are valued. She has experimented with encouraging nursery school, kindergarten and Grade 1 children to try to write before they read.

'Children who write in this way in their own invented spellings receive valuable practice in translating from sound to print. This practice and experience with letters and sounds form an excellent basis for reading *later on*. In addition the activity develops self-reliance in dealing with print, and contributes to a do-it-yourself attitude which carries over into learning to read.'

Carol Chomsky describes one first grade classroom where the approach which she favours has been on trial. I have selected some extracts which capture what I consider to be salient points.

● The teacher has been getting this message across to the children in her room with regard to spelling *Your judgement is good. Trust it. Figure out how the word sounds to you and write it down that way.'*

● She provides a bucketful of wooden and plastic letters, a diary for each child, and many *reasons* to write.

● She spends a great deal of time reading to her class, and discussing the sounds of words in the stories.

● They work on rhyme, beginning sounds, and end sounds.

● She gets across the idea of sequence: *'What comes first? Next?'* and so on through the word.

● The children's names are good to use for this kind of game, too. Names are clapped, changed and played with. In creative movement, the children move to their names.

● They need a *reason* for writing. Writing is real and interesting when children have a purpose, *their* purpose, for doing it. An outgrowth of this personal involvement is an independence on the child's part, so that he writes regardless of the teacher.

● Using plastic letters frees up some children who have handwriting trouble. They don't have to worry about the mechanics of letter formation, and they can put their energies into the message.

● When children do this writing, they quite naturally begin to read what they have written. They read what they themselves have written more easily than unfamiliar material.

● The children are expected to write from the start. Many can, but some are reluctant to try it out at first. Mrs Bailey, the teacher, says she knows fairly quickly which ones aren't ready, and allows them to dictate their stories. Some will prefer this for a month or more. But eventually they gain the confidence to go ahead and try spelling some words on their own, according to the way they sound. *'You see their mouths moving as they think their way through the word, and you know they're on to it,'* says Mrs Bailey.

The children's early attempts at their own spellings are often much more primitive than later productions. Here is one early story that requires some interesting interpretation:

I MED A SBOYDR WEB ON A BRENH AND AFTR I WHT THE FILM AND I LOT AT KRAFIH. (I made a spider web on a *branch* and after that I watched the film and I looked at crayfish.)

BRENH, WHT. The *ch* sound is spelled with an H. Why? Because the *ch* sound is in the name of the letter H: *aitch*. This child knew the letter name, was looking for a way to spell *ch*, and quite logically came upon *aitch*. This use of H for *ch* has been observed repeatedly in early invented spellings.

'This hypothesis construction is an active process taking the child far beyond the "rules" that can be offered him by the best of patterned, programmed or linguistic approaches. The more the child is prepared to do for himself, the better off he is. After such a programme they bring to reading, assumptions that they made about writing, an assurance that it is something that you work out for yourself, and a confidence to go ahead.'

(Chomsky 1976)

This aspect of preparation for reading has not been wholly neglected in the past. Textbooks have treated it under the 'readiness skill' of auditory discrimination. In a global approach to the whole area teachers have helped children:

● To perceive likenesses and differences in non-vocal sounds.
● To perceive the sound of recurring rhyming words.
● To hear the words that rhyme.
● To contrast them with the words that do not rhyme.
● To recognize that spoken words can begin with the same consonant sound.

This has provided many children with the opportunity to teach themselves a sound sequence analysis strategy. It has, in the past, left us guessing about some children whose reading skills do not increase despite the global auditory discrimination exercises. The Elkonin techniques make more explicit what is being learned.

It would be as well to point out that sound-to-letter analysis does not reign supreme in the hierarchy of skills required for very long. The child who has learnt only a small reading or writing vocabulary begins to generalize about letter-sound relationships. A kind of perceptual (visual) learning occurs for those simple clusters of letters which consistently represent certain sounds. This knowledge is transferred to unfamiliar material.

A child in the first stages of reading skill typically reads in short units but has already generalized certain regularities of spelling-to-sound correspondence, so that three-letter pseudo words (e.g. zif) which fit the rules are more easily read as units. As skill develops, span increases, and a similar difference can be observed for longer items. The longer items involve more complex conditional rules and longer clusters so that generalizations must increase in complexity.'

(Gibson, 1965)

When the child works out a new word from two words he already knows like *string* from *stop* and *ring* he is operating on the spelling-to-sound correspondences that Gibson has written about and he has already gone beyond the simple heuristics of phonic systems. But to do this he is still leaning on his skills in the sound segmentation of spoken words. They have wider application than the phonics on which we have spent so much instructional effort.

# Language Handicaps

The child who has a restricted control of English vocabulary or sentence structures will have a difficult learning task at this stage because he will have to learn a great many new things about language. After 10 repetitions one child was unable to imitate the sentence, 'He is kicking the football', because he did not control the verb pattern in his normal speech.

When children enter school with pronounced language deficiencies a dual attack on this problem is required. Firstly the child's language patterns are most rapidly improved by quantities of one-to-one conversation with an adult. Some means must be found of talking frequently with the child who has poor language patterns. Speech therapy is probably not enough. The teacher can help by keeping the child's need constantly in mind and making opportunities for conversation. But in addition she will need assistants, such as mother-helpers, to engage in talking sessions with small groups of three or four children. Teachers may also plan activities specifically to increase the amount of conversational interchange between adult and child. And guidance along similar lines can be given to parents. (See Davies, 1963.)

The teacher's words provide a good language model for the child to imitate but this is not enough. The child needs the opportunity to formulate his own statement, that is, to construct his own hypothesis that this is the way you can say it in English, to actually say it, and discover from the answer he gets whether he has been understood. If he is understood, his hypothesis has been supported.

A second modification of programme for the child who has language handicaps is to simplify the material that he is expected to read. Texts which are good for average or better children will contain language which is too complex for the child with language handicaps. Much simpler texts are required and the vocabulary should be very familiar. The sentences should be of the same kind in length and in construction as the ones the child uses in his speech. This means that the sentences would not be so drastically reduced as to be unfamiliar to him, as would be the 'Look, John, look,' or the 'See John run,' sentences.

It becomes obvious why the child's own dictated sentences or stories have frequently been recommended as remedial reading material. What the child can produce he can also anticipate. This provides a fluency that gives him time to attend to cues, and to relate several cues to one another. This is time that the retarded reader needs.

One question arises from such an approach. How will he ever learn to read texts which contain more complex structures unless he is required to attempt them? Perhaps he could improve his oral language by learning to read more complex constructions. Applied to the nonreader, or the beginning reader both these arguments are fallacious. For him, it is a question of the current learning goals. His task is to learn how to learn. This can be achieved with the simplest range of reading material. Only when the process is running smoothly should reading be considered a means of language learning. We do learn new linguistic forms from our reading of English. We can handle complex constructions which we would never speak. This excerpt from a daily newspaper is an example:

Smith, who appeared in Court from the cells and had been arrested on the count, was charged that, between 3 April 1969 and 30 October this year at Wellington, having received from . . . the sum of . . . in terms requiring him . . . did fraudulently omit to account for the same and thereby committed theft.

But we do this after we have learned to read. While learning to read, children match the text to what their ear remembers of the language. Much later they learn to understand a range of forms specific to written language. Sometimes you can hear the written language patterns in an older child's mispronunciation of unusual constructions learned from extensive reading.

For the nonreader, his own language patterns should be a guide to the type of text he should try to read until the reading process is well-established. Meantime, his oral control over language can receive attention so that it develops not from his reading but in parallel with it.

# References and Further Reading

Anderson, P. (ed.), *Linguistics In The Elementary School Classroom*, The Macmillan Co., New York, 1971.

Bar-Adon, A. and Leopold, W.F., *Child Language: A Book of Readings*, Prentice-Hall; Englewood Cliffs, New Jersey, 1971.

Bloom, L. and Lahey, M., *Language Development and Language Disorders*, Wiley, New York, 1978.

Cazden, C.B., Play with language and metalinguistic awareness: one dimension of language experience. Organization Mondial pour l'Education Prescolaire, 1974 6, 12-24.

Chomsky, C., Approaching reading through invented spelling. Resnick, L.B. and Weaver, P.A. (Eds.), *Theory and Practice of Early Reading*, Hillsdale, N.J. Erlbaum, In press.

Clay, Marie M., Gill, M., Glynn, E.L., McNaughton, A.H., Salmon, K., *Record of Oral Language*, Wellington, NZEI, 1976.

Clay, Marie M., The development of morphological rules in children with differing language backgrounds. *N.Z.J. Educ. Studies*, 9, 2, (November) 1974, 113-121.

Davies, M.R., 'Home deprivation and intellectual development', *Education*, 12, (March) 1963.

Dunn, L.M., *The Peabody Picture Vocabulary Test*, Americal Guidance Service, Minnesota, 1965.

Elkonin, D.B., USSR. In Downing, J. (Ed.). *Comparative Reading*. Macmillan, New York, 1973, 551-580.

Elkonin, D.B., Development of speech. In A.V. Zaporozhets and D.B. Elkonin (Eds.), *The Psychology of Preschool Children*, M.I.T. Press, Cambridge, Mass., 1971.

Fodor, J.A., Bever, T.G., Garrett, M.F., *The Psychology of Language*, McGraw-Hill, New York, 1974.

Gibson, E., Learning to read. *Science*, 148, 1965, 1066-1072.

Lefevre, C.A., *Linguistics And The Teaching of Reading*, McGraw-Hill Book Co., New York, 1964.

Liberman, A.M., The speech code. In Miller, G.A. (Ed.), *Psychology and Communication*, Voice of America, Forum Series, 1974.

Liberman, I.Y., Shankweller, D., Fischer, F.W. and Carter, B., Explicit syllable and phoneme segmentation in the young child. *Journal of Experimental Child Psychology* 18, 1974, 201-212.

Read, C., *Children's Categorization of Speech Sounds in English*, National Council of Teachers of English, Urbana, Illinois, 1975.

Robinson, Susan M., 'Predicting Early Reading Progress', Unpubl. M.A. Thesis, Univ. Auckland, 1973.

# Exploring Further

**Observe language behaviour. There are many different ways of recording language behaviour recommended in this chapter. You might use** *The Record of Oral Language* **to observe language differences in several children.**

# 6 An Introduction to Print

## Before School

Some children are fascinated by big words on billboard advertisements, on television or on a packet of breakfast cereal. Words in favourite story books which are well-spaced and repeated are sometimes recognized. A few children spend considerable effort in writing their names, or letters to grandmother. And some push their parents into helping them to read.

Such high levels of attention to the detail of print are unusual rather than common.

Many children have listened to a book shared at bed-time and have looked at the pictures, but the hieroglyphics across the pages have had no particular significance. These average children are only vaguely aware that the words which express the idea occur in the books.

At the opposite extreme there are children who have never had the opportunity to see and hear someone reading. They have no children's books in their home and the paper, if read, is silently devoured by parents remote behind its pages. Pencils and paper are rarely available in these homes. It is easy to believe that a child from such a background might take weeks to understand that the words spoken by children and teachers have anything at all to do with the marks in books.

### Visual searching

A lookout in a sailing ship scans the horizon for sight of another ship or of land. Parents, searching the beach for a lost shoe scan the ground for sight of a colour or shape cue to the shoe's location. The eyes of an adult, viewing a large painting at an art exhibition, rove over the canvas fixing on one feature after another, flicking back to trace or check a relationship or a similarity and after moments of survey, producing in the mind of the observer an impression, an understanding or a reaction for or against the painting. If the adult who once knew a little Russian or French is presented with a magazine in either language he will scan a page of print in much the same way that the observer looks at a painting, picking up a cue here and a half-understanding there and trying to link these fragments into a meaningful message. Rarely can this 'reader' get sufficient information from the text to confirm whether he is right or wrong.

The child who has looked at books from 2 years of age will have learned to scan pictures for meaningful messages, slowly learning how to look at books and building up an efficiency over many hundreds of contacts. Parents will recall that a familiar story-book is read quickly because the child expects to see the familiar pictures, comments on them quickly, and turns the page. In contrast an unfamiliar book takes longer to scan. Looking takes longer, understanding takes longer and labelling is a slower business. This contrast illustrates the marked difference that exists between seeing the unexpected and seeing the familiar.

The unfamiliar picture could be scanned by the child as the adult scans a large painting. Some features draw the attention while others remain in the background unnoticed. If something in this background is attended to the child may focus on it for a moment or two. At the next reading that newly noticed feature may be included in the scanning pattern.

With the familiar story book the child begins with memories of what is in the book and each page triggers more memories. Some brain response is already alerted before the page is turned and so the response is made more quickly. This anticipation of what may follow creates a pleasing tension — a puzzle to be solved. It is related to a skill that will be needed in reading as the child anticipates the structure of the sentence and the next step in the story. But the preschooler can already anticipate oral language.

Betty aged 5 years is listening to her brother reading a Standard One journal. He stumbles over 'he never makes mis———.' Betty from the other side of the room, mutters 'mistakes'.

What the beginning reader has yet to do is to build anticipation of the visual patterns that are likely to follow in written language.

A picture must be scanned to gather information and it may be scanned in any direction, by complex tracking and back-tracking. A printed message must be scanned in a different manner; its meaning is dependent upon scanning in a particular way dictated by the directionality conventions of written language.

Reading demands the analysis of a complex text by the eye and by the brain to note details which one can interpret. Some children arrive at school with far less experience in analysing two-dimensional space than other children who have had opportunities to practise this skill for some time.

As a preschooler the child responded to and used oral language, learning 'by ear'. The new activity of reading demands that he use his eyes to scan and analyse the printed text. The language and the visual aspects of a reading task now have to be related. There has to be an association of the analysed speech with the analysed shapes. This is a third area in which the child may have difficulty — pairing the visual and auditory stimuli. He may find it difficult to match the flow of auditory signals coming to his ear, with the order of visual patterns on the page of his text. Specifically, he may have trouble in relating the timing of the language behaviour to the spacing of visual experience.

Until he reached school, the child was free to scan objects, people, scenes, pictures, and even books, in any direction that he chose. Immediately he became a candidate for reading, he had to learn that in the printed text situation there was an inflexible set of directions for proceeding across print. There are one-way routes to be learned. He must learn to go from a top left position across to the right and then to return to the next top left position and go again across to the right. For the 5-year-old school entrant of average ability that is a *difficult piece of learning*. We have often underestimated the magnitude of that particular task, and its particular relevance for subsequent success in learning to read. This directional behaviour moving in a controlled way across a line of print depends upon learning something about movement. For some children whose muscular coordinations are not well developed, or who have not gained good control over linking hand and eye movements, this particular aspect of learning to read may be difficult. Any attempt to relate what is said with what is seen may fall at the hurdle of not moving in appropriate ways across print.

# As New Entrants

It is interesting to note that in New Zealand schools, children are enrolled on their fifth birthday, rarely before (because of insurance laws) and rarely afterwards (because of cultural practice). Children are not required by law to attend school until their sixth birthday but almost no family waits until then. In other countries children may start school at a younger age, or at a much older age. In several countries there is a movement towards earlier entry into formal school and an interest in entry at any time in the school year. Until a few years ago, however New Zealand was the only country where all children start school on a particular birthday and no reason can be found in historical documents for this practice (Birch & Birch 1970). There are advantages in starting school on the fifth birthday: except for a clutch of children who enter after vacations, individual children are admitted at any time during the year and for a period each has the status of 'the new child'. The teacher's attention tends to be drawn to that child, and his particular individuality, which increases the teacher's opportunities to observe the child's strengths and weaknesses and his adjustment to school. In such circumstances readiness tests, although available, have not been used to predict reading progress. They are presumably of greater use when large numbers of children are admitted to school and must be grouped into classes according to abilities. This admission policy has emphasized the importance of individualized instruction with flexible grouping and regrouping of children according to their learning needs. If John and Mary enter school one day in March, by June John may have learned all the early reading behaviour and be promoted to the basic reading series, whereas Mary may have mastered only some of the skills and need further work on caption books and language experience texts.

Such a school entry procedure means that each school-year classes grow slowly from small groups of 5 to 10 children to an ideal number of 20 to 25, but regrettably it is often not possible to limit the numbers to this level. However, as this practice of flexible grouping within the class has been established for many years, teachers of new entrant classes manage four or more groups of children at different stages of the transition to reading with great skill. Flexible grouping at this level is the best compromise to meet the needs of individual differences found among large classes of school entrants who enter on their fifth birthdays.

Could instruction be tailored to the individual needs of each child and opportunities created for the teacher to develop one-to-one teacher and child learning situations whenever learning in a group is difficult for a particular child? That would be ideal.

If we had better descriptions of the ways that behaviour changes as the child moves into reading, teachers would be able to make frequent, and more accurate observations of his progress. Such an approach is called 'diagnostic teaching'. It calls for a teaching programme which includes time specially scheduled for observation by a well-trained teacher. Using simple discovery procedures, good record-keeping and vigilance the teacher can retrieve the child smartly from any by-ways into which he strays (Strang, 1969).

Another important feature of such a preventive or diagnostic approach, is the reinforcement that is provided for the child's early tentative and inefficient efforts. When the teacher shows pleasure at the child's interest in books, his behaviour has been generally reinforced. But there is no certainty that as a result the child's verbal responses to the texts will become more accurate. For the behaviour to be shaped into accurate responses the teacher must check closely on the individual child as he reads.

It is not uncommon in classrooms for teachers to be generally approving in the early stages and to pay closer attention and become more specific as the child moves into the basic reading books. That emphasis is wrong. While the child is vague about the nature of the reading process, the teacher's carefully delivered approval can sharpen his concepts and help him to discover what reading is really about. Once he becomes 'a reader' and has learned to search for cues and check on his own responses the basis of reinforcement shifts from the teacher, to the child's own judgments of 'being correct' or 'making sense of the story'.

# Observing Behaviour

The behaviour that should be observed on entry to school depends on several factors — among them the individual child's past development, the programme provided in the classroom, and the type of reading programme for which the child is being prepared. There is certainly no single set sequence of skills required for beginning reading because different programmes demand different skills. Even within one programme there is no particular developmental sequence that all children will necessarily pass through. Fast learners with rich preschool experiences will hop, step and jump through the preparation stages while average-to-slow learners will halt or become stranded at many points on the way. Despite such diversity, some systematic records of the tentative beginnings of reading behaviour can and should be made.

Do you know how children learn to read? Whether the answer is 'yes' or 'no' you should observe children closely to check on your intuitions. Have a group of teachers or a class of older children come into the beginners' class and take them individually for caption book reading. Wander around and listen closely to the children and observe exactly what they are doing and saying. Try to record all that you see and hear for several interesting children. If you are a good observer you will soon find you are unable to record all that a single child is doing. Yet each teacher must observe very carefully what her pupils are doing and particularly what they are confusing. The younger the age of school entry the more important this observation becomes.

At first, the child's performance is varied and fluctuating. Responses do not become stable from their first appearance. They come, and go. They are used at first without confidence, and later, perhaps, with overconfidence. A further learning challenge may cause the child to lose his grasp on one of his newest accomplishments. Adequate responses appear one day and disappear the next. Slowly the responses become more controlled and accurate, but it is not always the most appropriate behaviour that finally becomes habitual. Bad habits are learned by repetition in the same way that good responses are learned, which is something we frequently forget. The teacher has to know whether any change is taking place in the child's behaviour and whether each change is, in some gross manner, pointing in the direction of progress. Southgate Booth (1968) states three important requirements if young children are to learn to read in classrooms where the atmosphere and working conditions are free and relatively unstructured:

● The teacher should know in detail the various stages which the child must master in order to acquire this skill; in other words, she needs a master plan.
● The reading materials should be so structured as to form parts of this plan.
● The teacher needs to keep meticulous records of individual learning so that each child's progress in the different spheres of reading can be guided and aided.

Southgate emphasizes that meticulous planning is not synonymous with formalized instruction. Rather, the more informal the programme the more imperative it is that the environment should be structured to facilitate reading.

# Print Tells the Story

Does the child know that print (and not the picture) tells the story? On entry to school the general concept that print rather than a picture tells the story was understood by two-thirds of the children in two research studies (Clay 1966, Clay 1970). But, according to Diack's simile (1960, p.130), the child probably has no clearer visual image of the print marks than an adult who looks at the pattern of the branches of a tree momentarily silhouetted against the sky. Within six months 90 percent of new entrants understood that print contained the message. But 2 percent still confused print and pictures as the source of the story at 6 and 6:6 years, and this was fatal for progress in learning to read. One confused child (aged 5:10) brought his book to the author and recited the text from memory as he turned the pages. He repeated the act with the text covered and only the pictures as cues. Then he said, confidentially, ' *I can read that book with it closed,*' and he did! His confusion had gone undetected and no-one had taught him that a picture is only a rough guide to the message of a book, that print carries a precise message, and that to read means to discover the precise messages in print. He thought that reading was reciting a memorized text, cued by the picture, and he was quietly proud of his achievement. That is an early by-way into which some children stray. While picture cues can be a source of extra information in reading, in this case they were a source of misconception. (The boy's intelligence was above average.)

A sensitive and observant remedial teacher has reported some unusual reactions in a minority group of her clinic cases. They had unusual difficulty reading black print on white paper. The black marks seemed to become the background and the white spaces were attended to. As one little boy said amid tears *'It's all the little white rivers . . .'* (Meares, 1972). If this were occurring (and how would we know if it was) the reading task would be extraordinarily difficult.

Some children become aware that print carries messages before they have had formal instruction.

Let us take an example from a well-prepared child who was to enter school in two weeks. Penny was 4:11 and had not learned to read. She could write her name and several single letters. Yet she was quite certain that her writing conveyed messages. , The postman brought her an invitation to Mary's party. She whipped it out of her mother's hand, retreated to her bedroom and then brought it back *displaying the writing in the centre.* Her mother read it to her. She was, for the time being, satisfied.

After her bath that night she asked for paper, saying *'I want to write to Mary'.* There had been no suggestion made that a reply was necessary. She complained about the first piece of paper she was offered. *'Too scrappy!'* Obviously this was a very important letter. *'How do you write "come"?'* she asked after she was given a more elegant piece of paper. *'What do you want to say?'* she was asked. *'I would like* (pause) *to come to your party.' 'Don't you want to know "I" and "would"?'* her mother inquired. *'But I will have to write 'come',*' she shrilled in excited irritation. *Come* was the significant message: it was the first thing she wanted to write. She went to the newspaper cupboard and tore off an edge strip for her mother to write the copy on. When asked *'What do you want to say?'* she repeated the message. It was written and she was asked to read it — *the first time she had been asked to read words in sequence, in a sentence.* She did this word for word. (Remember, it was *her* message and she had already stated it twice.) She began to write 'I' at the *top right* corner of the page. *'That's the wrong side,'* Mother corrected. She then copied the words carefully and correctly with good spacing because she could copy letters quite well. No further help was given until she realized she had skipped the second 'to' and asked for help. She completed the task and then asked for 'from Penny'. She was only given 'from' and insisted on getting Penny although she could write her name. Was this because she could not delineate the sequential relationship of one word to the other? She asked for an envelope, and copied Miss Mary B . . . . . . on it putting the surname on the next line. Her mother was quite satisfied but Penny seemed to be searching for a word — *'Put* (pause) *the address.'* She got a copy of this and added it to the envelope, showing concern when she thought the line would clash with the previous one.

This seems to be a milestone. It is the first request for a coherent message to be conveyed in words to someone else, and was in response to receiving a verbal invitation. Two promptings were given, one as to the order of words in the message and one as to the placing of the first word on the page. The episode demonstrated a skill for letter by letter copying, maintaining direction once it is established, spacing words and keeping somewhat in lines. Although she could re-tell the message accurately there was no clear awareness of 'reading each word', no evidence that she knew that each grouping of letters had an equivalent word. There were few errors and no frustration, and the request for the address surprised her mother. The emotional tone was not one of achievement; she did not think to display this to the family, but treated it rather as an important social task, like the reply to a question.

The example illustrates some of the concepts which children master in the early reading period. She knew

● that messages can be written.
● that within the message was an important word, *come*.
● how to speak the message.
● that the copy she asked for was the message which she could retell on request.
● that letter follows letter left to right in copying and spaces are important.
● the pattern of directional movement across two lines of print.
● that one can check and correct when an error has occurred.
● that letters to people have addresses.

The episode also showed that she did not know several things

● that words in a sentence have an order; 'I would like to *come*'.
● that the starting position on a page is on the left.
● that the visual forms of her writing had some systematic correlation with her oral message, that is, she could not read it.

Children come to such concepts in different ways and at different times, but much of this preparation depends upon the child's opportunities to share book experiences with adults in the preschool years, and to try his hand at written language.

Theresa entered school with much less preparation than Penny and she learned about messages during her first year at school. When she tried to make a statement by scribbling, creating her own mock writing, she showed that she knew that messages can be written down. Theresa at 5:0 could not copy her name but she produced her own form of writing.

**5:0 (Copy)**

What the child writes is also a rough indicator of how he views printed language. To him it may be funny marks, a string of letters, or words with special meaning like his name. By the time Theresa was 5:6 she wrote her name as two letters without regard to order or sequence.

**5:6 (No copy)**

When she had a model to copy she produced a string of odd letters, more or less in correct sequence.

**5:6 (Copy)**

By the time she was 6:0 she produced this signature without a copy. It is a word with a known sequence of well-formed letters.

**6:0 (No copy)**   T h e r e s a

Theresa's last example illustrates that she now uses successfully the concepts of 'message to be written', letters, letter order, particular letters needed for a particular word, and even the use of a capital letter for a name. After one year at school Theresa has reached the same control over her name that Penny already had two weeks before she came to school. These are examples of the individual differences in preparation for reading that the new entrant teacher needs to recognize. Although the examples given are examples of writing the concepts which they illustrate also apply in reading. (These early responses to print are discussed in more detail in *What Did I Write?* Clay 1975.)

This ability to write one's name illustrates two important features of how the brain works. Firstly, the name-writing actions are a set of instructions or a programme which can lead to many different products. 'A man who knows how to write his name at all knows how to do so under a variety of circumstances and in a variety of ways. There is, for example, no-one who is able to write his name only in letters less than an inch high, or only with a pencil, or only on the blackboard ' (Fodor, 1974 ). Secondly, the information about how to write one's name is linked in complex ways to other information one has '. . . my knowledge of how to write my name connects with my knowledge of how to speak my name, with my knowledge of what my name is, and so on' (Fodor, 1974).

Such programmes for action, and systems of information determine the regular features of a behavioural response without prescribing its shape in rigid ways. The first programmes for action are learned slowly for the child is learning not only the specific programme, but also how to put such a set of instructions together, and how to remember them.

Similarly the first networks of related information — the spoken word, its letters, how you say it, what it looks like in capitals or small letters — these networks form slowly, but they teach the brain to build such information systems about print.

## Attending to print

Observe a group of children who have recently entered school aged 5:0 to 5:6. To what do they attend in the printed text?

The 5-year-old finds himself with opportunities to draw and paint and look at books. He is encouraged to talk about these activities. The teacher puts some marks on his drawings and these carry some message. The room is full of signs and messages among which he is sometimes able to locate a familiar one, his name.

$$H$$

**That says Douglas Homes!**

He is encouraged to make marks with chalk or pencil and soon finds that if he adds his name or some other marks to his drawing the teacher seems to be pleased with him. She may ask him to say what he has written. The importance of the written code seems to become more obvious to the child when he attempts to put his ideas into writing for someone else to receive, than when he tries to receive (read) someone else's ideas. Therefore it is important to foster the child's desire to communicate in writing.

A classroom for new entrants must be a planned environment in which the child becomes aware of the need for reading and writing in everyday life. At an early stage the child may know that print conveys messages without being sure what the message is. Dougie, who produced a drawing of letter-like forms (below) said to the author, *Give it to your children and learn them it, because it says a lot of fings.'* He hoped he had written an important message with the H's and O's on his page. He thought that his print conveyed messages but what they were he knew not. Dougie had acquired a basic concept, but this was a mere beginning.

On some days the child chooses not to draw, is not inspired to print, or to point, or to talk about his work. Individual children may refuse to participate in these activities for several months because of some inner sense of irrelevance or personal inadequacy. *I don't want to do any writing today,'* is a complaint, especially from boys who are reluctant attenders to print.

## Position is important

Does the child show a preference for a certain position or posture when he reads or writes? Perhaps he should be allowed some flexibility at first, to do what is required in the manner he finds easiest.

New entrants draw pictures and talk about what they are doing. They can be asked to point to their work as they speak about it. Sometimes this is done on the blackboard but more often in today's classroom this is paper, pencil and crayon work. The 'paper on the desk' is similar to the 'book on the desk' for a young inflexible child who has problems with direction. At first the upright position of the blackboard might seem to him to be quite a different task, especially if he has to turn his body round to copy a model from the teacher's board.

## Names

Can the child read or write his name? Teachers write the child's name on his work and this labelling of his drawing, of his coat-peg, of his lunch-tin, calls his attention to the distinctiveness of a name which distinguishes him from other children, and impresses him with the fact that there is a need to choose between names. It enhances his security and his self-image giving him a feeling of importance. In more than one place in the class he should have his own name on a card with big black print. He can hold it, run his finger along it, from left to right preferably, trace over it, try to copy it and contrast it with other children's names. When he begins to reproduce some features of it at home his parents will be very responsive. These primitive productions of his name have the very personal nature of a signature, his sign, which expands and develops in detail during the year, and yet is as constant as an adult's signature in some respects. Children with long names have a bigger problem.

| HCIOOIOHH | BENIIIIe | CLTPOIU |
|---|---|---|
| CHRISTINE | BRENT | CHRISTOPHER |

Some teachers find ways of including both first names and surnames for average and better children because this introduces the child to a phrase-like structure with two component words separated in space and in sound — several important concepts.

The use of children's names in a class activity is a useful way of developing letter knowledge. Children will use their knowledge of letters in family names, or classmates' names at later stages as part of their analysis of new words. Usually it is the initial letters that catch the attention.

## A Plan For Action

With some examples from children's writing it may be possible to illustrate how the early responses which children make to the features of print become programmatic in the sense that they provide a plan or scheme from which many variations can be generated.

To start at the zero point, some children cannot put pencil to paper either to produce 'writing' or to copy it. They seem frozen unable to move in any direction.

Then at the 'funny marks' stage they may produce formless scribble,

or repetitive forms

or variations on letter-like forms.

Early letter forms which the child controls are often found in his name.

**SUZANNE**                                                    **TONY**

Throughout the first year of instruction what the child spontaneously writes tends to be a fair reflection of what he has learned to look at in the detail of print. For example this child's control over letter forms in his own spontaneously-produced pattern

l i l i l i l i l

can be contrasted with his attempt to copy the word Indian on the same day.

What the child generates or produces himself tends to tell us what aspects of print he has under his own control. What he copies incorrectly may tell us what is new to him.

Theresa's examples showed how difficult it is for some children to copy letters and how slowly this skill is acquired by some. There is another gap which closes as the child acquires control over letters and words. It is easily observed. When children are asked to 'Write your name' and are coaxed to produce 'some of it' they can then be given a copy and be asked to write it again.

**Task 1**  Write your name
**Task 2**  Copy your name

For the competent child there is almost no difference.

For the slowest children there is little difference.

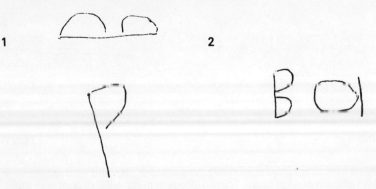

But between the stages of no skill and competence differences are clearly observed between the products of these two tasks.

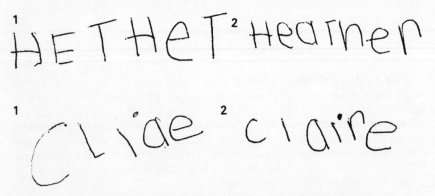

Progress is noted as the gap between production and competent copying narrows. To emphasize this point Bernard's attempts to write his name at 5:0 and again at 6:0 are given below. At 5:0 he made no attempt to produce his name and he copied without much regard for the letter order. His letters are scattered on the page.

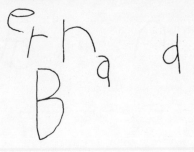

5:0 (Copy)

At 6:0 he is very conscious of the first letters in his attempt to produce both his names

**6:0 (No copy)**

and his copying demonstrates his progress.

**6:0 (Copy)**

## The principle of order

At 6 years of age Henry was coaxed and urged to write all the words he knew. Slowly, effortfully, but with confidence he wrote 't' and then to the left of it wrote 'a'.

$$\begin{matrix} a & t \\ 2 & 1 \end{matrix}$$

No further attempt of visible language could be extracted from him. A tentative and very limited set of behaviours after 12 months of school!

Extra help earlier than this would have been more advisable. Henry's example reminds us that the child does not necessarily produce or copy letters in the correct order from left to right. It depends at first on what letters are salient and later upon whether he accepts the ordering principle.

The child may learn quite a lot about words before the ordering principle is established. One little girl wrote 'the word we had at school today' for her mother. It was *little*. She produced the letters in this order

1  t t          2  e          3  ll i

but her final product looked like this.

Ilitte

It showed a commendable visual memory for a new word form but her order for remembering it was not the expected one.

Obviously in writing attention to letter order or sequencing must await some control over letters themselves. Familiar or salient letters will be recalled easily and first the child who accepts the ordering principle must hold back his response to the familiar while he searches for initial letters rather than salient letters.

It is often easy to overlook how industrious a child has been. Despite the illegibility of the child's story at first glance (see below), it can be seen that, with great effort he has attempted to copy the story letter by letter. His control of letter forms is effortful as yet, but he has a firm grasp of the ordering principle.

**Written sample**

**My Daddy is a builder.**

# Observing Responses to Print

Drawing is one way of expressing ideas in two-dimensional space, and children are easily led to this. The same ideas can be explained to the teacher in words. When the teacher acts as a scribe to record the message in words the child has two permanent records of his ideas, the drawing and the written message. His task is to discover from these examples the correlation between the ideas in the drawing, the messages he dictated and the rules of the written language game. If the child also traces or copies the message it is modelled in motor activity and this forces the child to explore more of the detail of the print with his eyes.

One message in the mind of the child and four modes of analysing it — drawing, saying, tracing, scanning. The action sequence has been — ideas, drawing, telling or dictating, teacher writing, child copying after some further analysing. If the child returns to the teacher she may say 'read it to me' and he will recast his ideas in another dictated message. Or the teacher may make a more difficult demand, 'read it *with your finger*. Then she is demanding an integration of several responses. She is saying, 'remember the ideas, retell them, find them in print and move correctly across print'. That integration is the heart of early reading success. From time to time the child may lose the ideas, stumble with the language, be superficial or neglectful in his looking, or clumsy and in error in his directional movement. Only when all these activities are under *his* control and can be deliberately adjusted *by him* during the on-going process of getting a precise message from the printed page will he become a reader.

Although the child is interested in books and is having stories read to him the *earliest* reading behaviours can be *observed* best in relation to his drawings. A teacher should take a record from time to time and that record should include comments under the headings below.

What can a teacher of new entrants find to say about these early efforts? Some things to watch for can be listed.

## Draws

Observe the sophistication of the child's drawing. How complicated is it or how primitive? If he has been at school for a period are his drawings becoming more detailed (see Chapter 2)? I will not try to trace progressions in children's drawings that might be related to reading progress although they undoubtedly exist. Let us assume that the drawing is a creative enjoyable activity which brings the ideas to be verbalized bubbling to the surface, and direct our attention to the emergence of visible language.

## Produces writing

The new entrant draws and before long he writes something. It may be limited but it provides a starting point against which later progress can be checked. It should be noted even a record which shows nothing — no writing — is a record with which later progress can be compared.

## Dictates

Ask the child to tell you a story about his picture and write it down for him.

## Copies

If you send the child away to write some of the text note the sophistication-level of his writing. Is he just scribbling? ignoring the story? tracing over your story? trying to copy some of the story underneath? Or can he transcribe a story at a distance, for example from the blackboard?

## Retells

Have the child read the story to you after a lapse of several minutes. Record exactly what he says as he 'reads' to you. Notice whether he has a memory for the story which he dictated. Listen to his language. Does he flexibly recast the identical story in another sentence? How close to reading his dictated story is he?

## Points

When you ask the child to read his story to you ask him to read it with his finger. Then you have the observation of directional behaviour available to you.

These activities provide opportunities
- for observing the child's ability to represent ideas in two-dimensional form
- for the child to relate language to these ideas
- for the child to try to write language which indicates his knowledge of letter forms
- for the child to read the story to you which indicates how well he remembers the text and how flexibly he handles sentences
- for the child to point to it as he reads which indicates his control over directional behaviour.

The effort and industry that is applied by the child to his products and actions at this stage marks the importance of the learning.

## Observation task summary

The child draws a picture. He dictates a story which you write down. You ask him to go away and write the story himself (trace, copy, add to it). When he brings this back ask him to read his story *with his finger*.

Make a record of these behaviours and contrast the child's performance one, two or three months apart.

| | |
|---|---|
| **Draws** | (Ideas) |
| **Produces writing** | (Generates written messages) |
| **Dictates** | (Language) |
| **Copies (or traces)** | (Visual analysis) (Motor control) |
| **Re-tells** | (Integration) |
| **Points and re-tells** | (Directional movement) |

The next examples are from children who could not yet perform in all these areas.

---

Deborah drew a house, a girl and flowers in the garden.
She dictated: 'The girl is going in the house' but she could not trace
or copy this.

---

Sam drew a truck and dictated: Truck.
The teacher wrote: The truck tips the dirt.
Sam could not read that back.

---

If the teacher has introduced a story or a shared experience she will not be surprised if Tony draws a crab instead of Goldilocks and dictates a story that interests him, rather than the one that interested her.

# Thoughts in Writing

What did the child actually say about his picture? At the time when children are learning to read their names they can be encouraged to speak in complete sentences about their colourful pictures. They pour out a story so fast and so idiomatically that the teacher has some difficulty in making an accurate record. From this spontaneous description the teacher writes down one or two sentences. How does she select what she will write?

It must not be too long, as the teacher's time is limited.

Should she copy the child's speech 'It's a Daddy' or should she transform it into book-like language (This is Father)? It depends upon the child's stage of progress. If the child is expected to read the text back accurately the teacher should write down exactly what he says. This is particularly important at the stage where the child is trying to establish the link between oral and written language. And if we want the child to feel good about talking, recording his language as he uses it avoids the risk of making him feel we reject it. On the other hand, to move a child closer to book reading, the teacher might change the child's statement a little, read it for him, and reinforce him for 'reading' her version.

Should the teacher write down ungrammatical speech? 'He get a truck.' Yes, if . . . and there are at least three 'ifs'. The teacher must decide what is the most important thing for this child to learn at this moment:

● If it is to talk more often in English he may be threatened by drastic remoulding of his sentence and lose confidence in offering his inadequate sentences.

● If the teaching point for a particular child is to re-read with 100 percent accuracy what the teacher has written, then he will do this more readily if she writes what he says, despite his inadequate grammar.

● If the important teaching point is not talking or reading but English grammar, only then may the teacher make a teaching point of his error.

A general rule at this level is to stay very close to what the child actually said. This will encourage fluency in reproduction and shows respect for the child's individuality.

## Captions and reading

In the preparation period the teacher adds captions and sentences to pictures the children have painted, to things they have made in activity or developmental sessions, or to photographs of themselves on some class outing. The activity which involved the child himself in some total way sparks a spontaneity of thought so that words that are expressive of the occasion come welling up within him. Children may bring a toy to school and a wall chart may be constructed which says 'Look at Richard's train', 'Look at Keith's book.'

A child can read a text like this with very little teacher guidance if the illustrations are opposite the text.

**A house is big.**
**A tree is big.**
**A truck is big.**
**A ship is big.**
**An aeroplane is big.**
**An elephant is big**
**and a whale is very big.**

Many teachers have a drawing time during the day when children put ideas into a two-dimensional statement as a painting, or for more detail in crayon or pencil. Then the teacher accepts a dictated story from the child, and, acting as his scribe, records it under his picture.

**There was a tree.**
**It was growing so big**
**and they couldn't get**
**any vegetable off it.**
**It was a vegetable tree.**

One little girl produced the recurrent house-and-flower picture but her story excused her from drawing 'Mother'

**Mother is around the back**
**watering the flowers.**

The child may trace or copy the story or merely add his name or a primitive signature. At first he focusses on minute and detached details of print but this activity helps him to find his way around.

Efforts to copy the teacher's words under the painting or drawing are lavishly reinforced by praise for progressive gains, and opportunities for teaching points about letter formation are numerous.

I prefer this 'whole story or idea' approach rather than giving the child his favourite words on cards, but many teachers have used some modification of this approach advocated by Sylvia Ashton-Warner (1963).

Class activities of various kinds often lead to the production of large brown paper books. The children may produce a series of drawings. They may devise a set of sentences telling about 'things that go up'. They may see how many different things they can begin with a particular word like 'we' — 'we go', 'we look', 'we stop', etc, etc., or a phrase like 'I am. . . .' They may illustrate a repetitive story like *The Gingerbread Man*, although some would consider that such delightful stories are spoiled by the drastic reduction that is necessary. When the teacher wants some particular feature of language to be brought to the child's attention, she may create interest in a book which stresses that feature, like a new 'sentence starter' ('Here is a . . .') or plurals ('One boy, two boys . . .').

Having created her big books the wise teacher will re-introduce them often to the group so that they become familiar to a point just short of perfect memory. She will hang them in accessible places so that a child may browse at his leisure or take a favourite one from the hook, and, flinging himself on the floor, read aloud to himself, pounding out the words with his hand, across the two-foot wide page. Cooperative effort is also seen as one child shows another what he can do. One child's less than perfect knowledge supplements the other's, so that between them they manage fairly well. A wise teacher would be available to use this moment of intense pre-occupation to highlight a new feature that one or both pupils were missing, or to discuss a point of disagreement.

Captions can be used to call the children from one task to another — 'Come and look', 'Put away the blocks', 'Sit on the mat', 'Pack up the toys'.

In all these single-line captions a demand for left-to-right movement of finger running under the reading is appropriate. The first specific thing for the child to learn about print is the movement, and the layout of stories can influence this learning. As each child speaks, his name can be written on a chart (after the manner of a dramatic script) and what he dictates can be written beside it.

| | |
|---|---|
| *Peter:* | I've got a car. |
| *John:* | Mummy went sick. |

What each child said can also be set off in quotation marks.

| | |
|---|---|
| *Alan said,* | 'I ate a big, big apple.' |
| *Betty said,* | 'I don't ever like dogs.' |

As the teacher reads each introduction, 'Betty said', she runs her finger under the words, and Betty, being quite clear (more or less) of what she said, can finish the sentence. This activity may be a child's first attempt to read a sentence — a whole utterance in its entirety.

# Words in Writing

Can the child read in isolation any words from such simple sentences? Words are smaller units than children are used to dealing with. Their preschool conversation was in ideas. They can, with benefit, be asked if they would like to learn a word, watch it being written on their own card, tell why they wanted that word, and place it in their own envelope of words. As new words are added to the child's collection day by day, those that he remembers can be left with him, those he forgets discarded. The words that individual children choose are personal, positive and picturesque.

# Caption Books

Before long the child is given a little picture book with black marks on it and he finds he is expected to say something as the teacher turns the pages. He may take this book home and say these things to his parents. When the teacher is pleased with his talking she puts him in a group of children and they talk about a book together. He becomes aware that the book contains specific messages which match the pictures. As he looks and talks he locates some of the marks with which he has become familiar in his printing. These seem to signal special words. He is now paying attention to particular cues in the print. His attention is to some very specific signs which are important to him — his name, his 'word' for the day, the three or four letters he really knows, or the one or two words.

The enthusiasm of a child for a home reader at this stage was captured in this mother's diary record (Michael — 5:5).

> Given a reading book called 'Are you my mother?' with pictures and a few words printed alongside. Michael loves this and keeps it at the top of his bed and always reads it when he wakes up. Knows about 4 pages mostly by guesswork but tries to make a story to fit the picture. Spends a lot of time with books.

What is a 'caption book?' It is a picture book with simple, short language captions very closely related to simple pictures. It has a limited range of vocabulary and sentence structures, and often has a repetitive theme. Each of these features make it easier for the child to invent sentences that closely approximate the actual text. He

## INTRODUCTION TO PRINT

When a group of teachers listed the activities in their introductory programmes *in order of importance* this was the combined result their statement.

| Activity | Examples |
|---|---|
| 1. Books made by individual children. | Scrap books, own drawings, photos of self or own family. |
| 2. Children's own names. Instruction captions. | Used in various ways. Please have your milk. Pack up now. 3 more minutes. |
| Class books made by children. | From a class outing (sports, zoo) or a story that was enjoyed, like *The Three Bears*. |
| Book table, reading corner or library. | Good children's books with simple texts. |
| 3. Easy introductory books. | Teacher-made monster versions of caption books. |
| 4. Labels or Sentence Captions. | On children's work, nature table displays. 'Peter's train' or 'A tree is big.' |
| 5. Wall stories. | Single sentence captions given by children. Similar sentence beginnings given by teacher and finished by children: 'A balloon goes up. A plane goes up.' |
| 6. Alphabet names. | Used incidentally by the teacher. Used with children's names, or for grouping words of same initial letter, or picture alphabets. |
| 7. Learning letter-sound correspondence. | Group pictures by initial sounds, say children's names and listen to first sound. |

practises directional movement and discovers basic concepts about print as his quasi-reading moves closer and closer towards real reading. Ideas, stimulated by the pictures, are translated into sentences. A response may be a long distance from the actual text.

Child: | Here is some cups, and a jug and a kettle.
Text: | Jane's tea set.

Or it may be almost correct:

Child: | Here is Jane's tea set
Text: | Jane's tea set.

Predicting or guessing how a text is likely to continue is related to what the advanced reader will do when he anticipates what the text will say next as a first step in fast, fluent reading. What the child must learn is to attend to the patterns of black letters and extract specific cues from these in sequence. Creative inventing is not satisfactory unless it leads gradually to the use of visual cues.

Although a teaching programme of wide scope would use language experience charts, caption books and simple story books I would select a simple caption book for the periodic observations of reading behaviour that should be made.

## Discovering cues to a precise meaning

Does the child respond to any specific cues in the print? He can be invited to be more specific. Ask a child to 'read' something and when he invents the caption pay him the compliment of having discovered something, and say, 'How did you know?' Either he can tell you or you have invited him to look for some reason for his choice.

'Which one says we?'
'How did you know?'
'Where is the beginning of we?'

A teacher with a group paying more specific attention to words says:

'Find Go. Find another one around the room.'

This appeals to the child's preference for early learning to have a fixed location — he learns a specific thing in a specific position. Only slowly does he relate other instances to that initial knowledge and arrive at knowing a word in isolation. Some children cannot recognize recurrences. They read as if every printed mark were individual.

'This is ride'.
'Does it look like go?' continues the teacher.
'Does it look like ride?'
'Have a good look at stop.'
'Do you think you can find it somewhere else?'
'Clap when you see stop', and she runs her hand along under the text.

This is a time for studying words in isolation, but it aims to train search and check behaviour, and perceptual scanning for cues. The emphasis on memorizing sight vocabulary has lost some of its imperativeness. How to look and how to scan rather than how to remember, is the emphasis.

# Home Readers

When simple books are sent home parents require some guide of what the child is expected to know. Unless they have this their demand of the child may well be unreasonable and may confuse him. One teacher sent the following note home:

> *The purpose of the Home Reader is to develop the child's interest and confidence in the reading of books. We send home only those books which have already been taken in school. At first your child is not expected to know every word. However, if he looks and says the word while you are pointing to it, he will gradually begin to learn those words which are repeated over and over again in other books.*

A note for families where English is not the mother tongue must necessarily be briefer. Its text might be:

> *Read this book to your child.*
> *Let him read it to you.*
> *Praise him when he tries.*
> *He does not yet know many words.*

## Notes by parents

Some parents who kept diaries made these remarks about home readers:

> *Returned from school with a caption book. Read it at once for mother, then again for mother, then told the story to his younger brother. Read it again at bed-time after mother had read his bed-time story.*

> *Michael has just gone through 'The Gingerbread Man' and he made up the words to match the pictures. Has obviously been learning this at school.*

> *While I was preparing tea, Todd came in saying 'Here — I'll read my book again for you'. Then he did, quite confidently. He wants to put 'got' into the story — 'Mother has got a red coat' and other 'has' stories.*

# The Teacher and the Parent

Here are some answers by teachers to questions about the value of home activities in reading and writing:

*What writing do children take home?*
- Drawings and paintings with captions under them.
- Stories they have written.
- Individual books they have made.
- Written expression when books are completed.

*What reading do they take home?*
- Individual books with captions.
- Drawings with captions.
- Commercial caption books.
- Supplementary readers.
- Basic reading books (only after they have been completed with the teacher in school).

*Why are these activities sent home?*
- Motivation   — for interest
  - — because the children like it
  - — to give children a feeling of accomplishment
  - — to enlist parent interest and help
- Learning   — to foster reading habits at home
  - — to strengthen the links between print and speech
  - — to practise directional behaviour
  - — to reinforce work done at school
  - — to strengthen vocabulary

*One teacher's comment:* 'I doubt if parent-help is very effective at this level. They think of reading as confined to word recognition from "hard" printed books.' But the practice continues as if it is felt to have some intrinsic merit.

Teachers should discuss the merits of home activities in reading and should design them to achieve particular learning objectives.

## Visual Scanning: Is it developing? Can you observe it?

It is easy to pick up from the turn of the head and the shift of the eyes whether the child is scanning the picture to gather meaning before he gives a word response to the text.

To check on directional scanning of the text ask the child to read with his finger. If he moves his finger in anything but the appropriate direction at any time one can feel fairly certain that
- his eyes are scanning in the inappropriate direction
- there is a conflict between what his eyes are trying to do and how his hand and body respond to the text.

Some special tasks are needed to discover whether the child is mastering later steps in visual scanning of words and letters.

Some questions for the observant Reception Class Teacher to ask are these:

● Does this child understand that print conveys messages?
● Does this child have any (mental) programme for producing a printed message (word or part-word)?
● What can I learn by contrasting this child's attempt to write his name with his attempt to copy his name?
● Does the child respect the principle of letter order in his productions? (Unless you watch him write it you may not be able to tell.)
● What can I observe in the daily *'draw a picture — write a message'* period? Would a cut-up story help my observation?
● What samples should I keep to check on progress?
● Is today's product any advance on his previous work?
● In what ways has this child's learning changed?
● Is he practising any handicapping strategy and over-learning it?

# References and Further Reading

Ashton-Warner, Sylvia, *Teacher*, Secker and Warburg, London, 1963.

Birch, J.W. and Birch, J.R., *Preschool Education And School Admission Practices In New Zealand*, University Centre For International Studies, Pittsburgh, 1970.

Clay, Marie M., 'Emergent Reading Behaviour', Unpubl. doctoral dissertation, University of Auckland Library, 1966.

Clay, Marie M., Exploring with a pencil. *Theory Into Practice.* 16, 5, 1977, 334-341.

Clay, Marie M., 'Language skills: A comparison of Maori, Samoan and Pakeha Children Aged 5 to 7 years'. N.Z.J. Educ. Studies, 1970, 153-162.

Diack, H., *Reading And The Psychology Of Perception*, Peter Skinner, Nottingham, 1960.

Gardner, Dorothy E.M. and Cass, Joan, *The Role Of The Teacher in The Infant And Nursery School*, Pergamon, London, 1965.

Southgate Booth, Vera, 'Structuring Reading materials for beginning reading', in R.C. Staiger and O. Andresen (eds.), *Reading: A Human Right and A Human Problem*, International Reading Association, Newark, Delaware, 1968.

Strang, Ruth, *The Diagnostic Teaching of Reading*, McGraw-Hill, New York, 1969.

# Exploring Further

Gather some examples of children's early writing behaviours. Consult *What Did I Write?* for some ideas about how to analyse them.

# 7 Directional Learning and Concepts About Print

In this chapter the learning of some early reading behaviours is discussed in some detail. Most children will have little difficulty in sorting out the conventions we use in writing our language. Yet, for a few children this is one area where reading progress for the next two years is crippled if the child makes a false set of assumptions which go unnoticed. The task for the teacher is to notice what is occurring.

Any complex movement like hitting a golf ball, playing a violin or reading a book must be organized or patterned. Study the letters in each of these blocks, close the book and write down the letters:

| | | | | | | | |
|---|---|---|---|---|---|---|---|
| t | d | | r | f | | s | w |
| v | m | | h | k | | l | g |

You have probably written the letters in an order which a large number of people would follow (tdvm; rfhk; swlg). Why should this be?

When you are travelling, do the road signs below cause you to look twice?

| | | |
|---|---|---|
| WAY | BRIDGE | AHEAD |
| GIVE | WAY | WAY |
| | ONE | GIVE |

Our reading habits tend to make us survey letter and word patterns from top left to top right and then return down left and repeat the pattern. This can be represented schematically as:

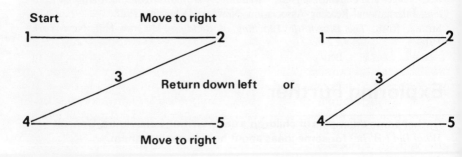

Children learn to sweep across the first part of the pattern, 1 to 2, rather easily. It takes them longer to consistently use the complete pattern in a way that is appropriate for scanning two or three lines of print.

Such movements are required by the quite arbitrary conventions we use in printing our language and the adult's perception has been trained to proceed within those particular constraints. The school entrant who has not learnt to read has not had his behaviour organized in this way. For him, such limits on visual scanning are quite different from any preschool experience he has had, except perhaps the experience he may have had with books. It is difficult to find a similar limitation on visual analysis in any other human behaviour (except reading music). Other language codes use a right to left, or a vertical directional pattern. All are arbitrary sytems.

There is a large motor coordination component in this learning, the significance of which probably varies with the age of learning to read. The younger the child, the more difficulty he is likely to have with this directional behaviour. The older he is the easier the motor or directional learning tasks will tend to be.

# Awareness of Left and Right Sides

A young child may scan the pictures as he scans the world, from a focal point of high interest in a criss-cross of 'open search' patterns as he links up ideas. By such a search he first locates the print of the text. Russian psychologists have been particularly interested in the development of eye and hand searching as young children explore novel stimuli (Zaporozhets and Elkonin, 1975). They found that children attended better to the stimuli before the age of 5 if they traced the new shapes with both hand and eye. Most older children were able to carry out effective exploration of new shapes with their eyes alone.

The child's experience has actually trained him in different habits from those he needs in reading. An orange, a dog, or mother must be recognized from any viewing angle. Meaning is constant when the object is small or large, is upside-down, back-to-front, or sideways to the viewer. The child has learned to recognize the constancy of objects despite their changing visual image. On entry to school he has to learn that in one particular situation, when he is faced with printed English, this flexibility is inappropriate. Now he must recognize some directional constraints.

Space around us becomes described with reference to our own body's position so that we locate things as up (above our head), down (at the feet end), before or behind, to this or that side. At 2 or 3 years the child has a basic awareness of his body when he names parts of it. Between 4 and 6 years research has shown that the child has an awareness that the two sides of the body are different from one another, although he cannot specify the difference in verbal terms. This is a sensory-postural awareness of one side as different from the other. Children with strong hand preference may distinguish their main hand side from the other side (Benton, 1959). This is all that is necessary to master the directional schema required in written English. If it is clearly demonstrated or modelled for the child, he can imitate the pattern, relating what he sees to his awareness of the sidedness of his own body. It is not necessary to have developed the verbal concepts of left and right *unless the teacher insists on talking about directional behaviour.*

# Orientation to the Open Book

Perhaps the first thing that the child learns is something about the placement of his body in relation to the open book, and he uses his hand to locate points of interest in the pictures. To read the printed messages (rather than the pictures) the child must locate the *left side* of the *first line of print.* How does he know where this starting point is? The placement of texts on pages changes in layout, and text may not always occur on a left page.

In the diagram below the arrows indicate some of the different actions that can occur when —

- either hand is used
- on either page
- in either of two horizontal directions
- and two vertical directions.

The child must come to use only those movements indicated by the solid lines and must not approach text by way of the dotted lines. It is more complicated than one would imagine (Clay, 1974).

Hand used to point to text. ■ = left hand;  ◯ = right hand,

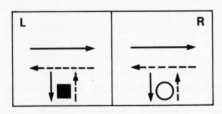 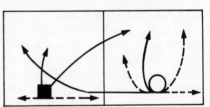

Help is provided by a signal indicating the starting point.

● **Tommy can ride**

and by a signal indicating the left hand side

↓ **Tommy can ride on his tricycle.**

The child should learn to do without such signals or cues as soon as he has gained stable control over starting position. He will be helped to such stability by a large measure of consistency in the books and blackboard texts he reads. Careful selection of materials can ensure that he gets practice with *a top-left, left page, starting point*.

On the other hand, he must encounter enough texts that are different to make him flexible in applying this directional learning to texts that begin in odd places on a page of print.

Finding one's place during a difficult visual task often involves locating and holding that place with the finger or hand, turning the head, scanning with the eyes, and locating with the finger. It is a coordinated set of movements in two-dimensional space. This pattern of behaviour is observable in most preschool children as they look at books. When they come to read the printed messages of books they must control both this set of behaviours and the directional rules.

If a child learns to be flexible about these inflexible rules in writing English he will have the problem of re-learning as David did.

David wrote *'I am a dog.'* His teacher wrote out the sentence on paper, cut it up into words and asked David to make the sentence again. She cut *dog* into separate letters to increase the difficulty of the task. David placed the cards this way —

**dgo a am I**
**654 3 2 1**

| | |
|---|---|
| T | *'Oh! Can you read it to me?'* |
| Ch | *'I am a dog.'* (moving right-to-left) |
| T | *'But you read it that way.'* |
| Ch | *'I know.'* |
| T | *'But you can't do that.'* |
| Ch | *'Why?'* |
| T | *'Because we always read that way.'* (left to right) |
| Ch | *'Why?'* |
| T | *'Because it's a rule.'* |
| Ch | *'Why?'* |
| T | *'Well if we didn't make a rule about reading and writing no one would know which way to start and which way to go and we'd get mixed up. Wouldn t we?'* |
| Ch | *'How?'* |
| T | (Picking up the book) *'If I didn't know that the person who wrote this story kept to the rules and wrote this way I might read the top line like this "Engine fire the at look."'* |
| Ch | (Long solemn look) — *'Ph.'* |
| T | *'Haven't you always been shown to read that way?'* |
| Ch | *'Ye — s. I didn't think it mattered.'* |
| T | *'You are absolutely not allowed to go the other way in reading or writing. Did you know that?'* |
| Ch | *'No!'* |

T   *'Well we will have to remember to go only one way and to stick to it. OK?'*

Ch   *'Yes, OK.'*

T   *'Where do we begin?'*
    Child points to the right.

T   *'Where is the beginning?'*
    Child points to the right and left and looks questioningly at T.

T   *'Where shall we start?'*

Ch   *'I don't know!'*

Both ends it would appear were legitimate. So now they start each reading lesson with a left-hand touch down.

Some children already have control over directional movement on entry to school, and some learn it easily during their first contacts with print. Other children have considerable difficulty in developing consistency in this behaviour for 6 to 12 months. Without it their efforts to read become a scrambled heap of cues which are impossible to untangle. To discover such children early, one needs to watch closely for specific signs of progress in learning the directional schema. It is possible that these directional skills are not given high priority by many teachers.

# Observing Directional Behaviour

In their first year at school most children learn all they need to know about the directional rules of written English. This is the time when we should observe their progress in mastering this facet of reading behaviour.

The first questions to ask are these:

● Does he expect to read a picture or to read print?
● Does he expect to read a left page before a right page?
● What consistency is there in his movements?

To check on the last question, ask the child to 'Read it with your finger.' If he moves his finger in anything but the appropriate direction at any time *note it down* and plan to observe him closely for the next few weeks. If it really was a momentary slip, caused by inattention or fatigue, pay it no further attention, but if it is a slip that recurs, treat it seriously and help the child to find a consistent and appropriate pattern of responding.

A teacher may suspect that the child's eyes are scanning in inappropriate directions or that there is a conflict between what his eyes are trying to scan and how his hand and body respond to the text. (The importance of visual scanning is discussed in Chapters 6 and 13.)

Sometimes teachers forbid pointing with a finger because authorities have associated this in older children with word by word reading and faulty reading habits. If directional behaviour is vitally important and pointing behaviour is forbidden, how is the teacher to know which way a child is surveying the page of print? She must arrange to observe such important behaviour at regular intervals, at the caption line and caption book stages. The instruction, 'Read it with your finger', provides a simple discovery technique for an observation test and reveals an amazing variety of behaviour. Shelly read a caption text with near-perfect accuracy;

Child: | *I made a fish pond*
Text: | We made a fish pond

but her finger travelled along the line from right to left as she read it!

Young children do not lack ingenuity in their attempts to find a track across print. They have been observed to point

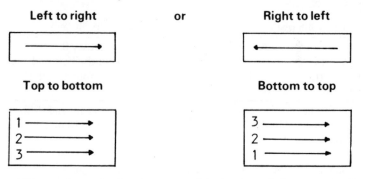

**Left to right**         or         **Right to left**

**Top to bottom**                **Bottom to top**

One child was observed using the centre of the book as his focus and reading out from the centre, right to left on a left hand page and left to right on a right hand page.

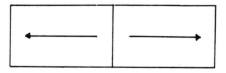

Snaking movements across a page are observed, in which one line is read left to right, the line below is read right to left, the next line left to right, and so on. This is really a very economical method, a line of least effort, for which there is a dictionary description — *boustrophedon* — or 'as the ox ploughs'.

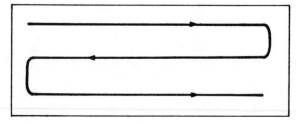

These behaviours fluctuate with increasing dominance of the appropriate move-ments but some children arrive at a consistency of the wrong habits. They become consistent in a right to left or bottom to top approach. This is critical.

# Examples of Directional Learning

Directional learning may have special importance in an instruction programme where children are attempting to respond to sentence texts without prior training on letter knowledge and word knowledge.

## Sally's success

On entry to school Sally dictated Story A and re-read it as Story B.

| ·Story A  The other day I went in the  bus with Naardi and saw  Mr Buffet's house. | Story B  I went up in the bus and I saw  Mr Buffet's house with Naardi  and a . . . . . |
|---|---|

She moved her finger across one line starting vaguely at *up* and drifting left to right beyond the end of the line. Her language patterns were advanced but her locat-ing behaviour was minimal.

Two months later she showed good control on an Instant Reader, *Round the House.* She was text-perfect (suggesting good memory for language). She consistently moved her right hand left to right across the text on either a left or right page. Because she had the idea that a letter equalled a word she became very confused try-ing to match this three-line text.

**This is  
the  
window.**

Three months after entry Sally's directional behaviour was securely established.

## Gordon's confusion

Gordon's confusion lasted a long time and he produced some unusual directional behaviour. Two weeks after entry to school he responded to *What Goes Up* by mov-ing his finger right to left across all five pages.

He usually read a right page before a left page, and pointed with his right hand. He was showing a consistent choice of 'right-sidedness'. After six weeks he 'read' text by matching a letter to a word and this time he pointed with his left hand. The numbers show the order in which he pointed to the words.

(2)   (3)   (4)   (5)   (1)

Two months after entry his Instant Reader was *Traffic*. He pointed left to right with his left hand, and remembered the text. He matched a letter to a word, looked surprised at what was left over but did nothing about it.

*Child:*  *Here is a car*
Text:     H  e  r  e  is a car.

On the same day he tried an unfamiliar caption book. First, he could not find the print. Then he began on a right page. On a two line text he read only the bottom line. He read the next page from right to left. At last, he gained control of the situation and read three pages from left to right with his left hand. He was learning something.

At the end of one term he gained a very low score on the Concepts About Print Test.

The first observation of Gordon in his second term at school showed the following movements over ten pages of Instant Reader text. What is unsettling about his record is that he is now beginning to follow some directional rules — *but they are his own rules*.

| | | |
|---|---|---|
| 1 ⟶ | one line | **His implicit rule is clear. On** |
| 2 ⟶ | one line | **a single line he moves left** |
| 3 ⟶ | one line | **to right. On a two line text** |
| 4 ⟸ | two lines | **he begins at the bottom** |
| 5 ⟶ | one line | **left, moves left to right and** |
| 6 ⟶ | one line | **returns moving right to left** |
| 7 ⟶ | one line | **along the top line.** |
| 8 ⟸ | two lines | |
| 9 ⟶ | one line | |
| 10 ⟸ | two lines | |

In another month some small measure of control emerged. He read *My Brother* with only one directional slip. Just before the end of his first year in school he read an early reading book *Wake Up Father* with 97 percent accuracy. He used the picture for cues, matched his saying and pointing, worked well at self-correcting, used his left hand to point. For all that, his movements were not smoothly coordinated. It is doubtful whether any instruction other than well-controlled individual tutoring could have reduced the time this learning took. Even with an individual programme a year may have been necessary for Gordon to put these elements of skill together.

## Jim's problem

Jim developed a reading problem. For nearly six months he seemed to have appropriate directional behaviour, but then he spent two months practising inappropriate directional habits on his first reading books.

After Jim had been at school a month, he painted a picture and dictated 'Jim is standing on Steven's head'. He located his name. He moved left to right and right to left across two lines.

Two weeks later he read a caption reader *Look at Me*. He used the pictures for cues (1). His voice slowed when he was asked to point (2) but he moved his finger left to right (3). This could be counted as *three steps forward*.

Next week some inappropriate behaviours were noticed. Once he moved bottom to top on a two line text; a second time he moved top to bottom. He gave a word response to a letter, and so could get no correspondence between what he said and what the text said. *Two steps back*.

In two weeks he read *Look At Me* again. The grammar was corrected and the search for the word segments in the sentence produced syllable breaks in run/ning, jump/ing. *Two steps forward*. This was repeated the next week with perfect memory for text.

After two months at school he was placed on the first reader *Early in the Morning* which he rendered with 94 percent accuracy, moving left to right but not matched. *Is* was the only word recognized. One week later this performance was repeated and the words recognized were *is* and *am*.

There was nothing exceptional about this pattern or progress.

After the term holidays this performance was repeated but the observer's comment now was that he 'cannot locate any words on a page'.

Jim moved to a supplementary reader, *Meet the Family*. He rendered the text with 80 percent accuracy and moved right to left. This was not satisfactory but he did read five words in isolation.

A week later he began right to left and returned left to right. In another week he moved consistently right to left, rendering the text with 86 percent accuracy. Directional behaviour was now a problem.

In the next two records, movement was consistently right to left and left to right across two lines, snaking.

For the next two months the observer noted that he could not learn anything new about words and responses until he learnt the appropriate directional approach.

He returned to *Early in the Morning* (*Ready to Read*, Red 1) using an erratic directional approach. Page by page his starting point was L, R, L, L, R, RRLL, LL, LL, R. He said "Mummy bought these books. I read to her last night. *She said I have to go backwards and forwards*'. He was aware that something was wrong in this area, that he must remember something but he was confused and could not verbalize what was wrong. The next week he had the directional schema under control and made only one lapse.

What is the final achievement towards which the child is working? He should move with consistency from a left hand starting point across a line of print, return down left, move left to right again, return down left and so on. With this directional movement it is important that he be able to match a word that he says with pointing to a word on the text in a coordinated manner as he moves left to right across print and returns down left.

Jim's records show that:

February to June he went ——————→
June to August he went ←—————     or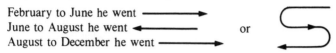
August to December he went ——————→

# There Are Different Reasons for Difficulties

One group of children who find directional learning difficult shows a general immaturity in motor behaviour which affects the learning of movement patterns.

Another group, unfamiliar with books, takes a long time to comprehend the concept that a sequence of print is related to a sequence of spoken words.

Some children settle into consistent but erroneous directional habits, (perhaps proceeding from right to left) hidden from the teacher's sight because they never point to their reading and rarely write on paper. Wrong responses can be learned and practised.

A small group of children practise error as frequently as they practise the correct pattern. Such alternating behaviour on a fifty-fifty basis either leaves the child confused or forces him to concentrate hard on the directional aspects of the task to the detriment of the visual and language aspects. In this case only close supervision will ensure that the left to right behaviour occurs more frequently than any lapses of right to left behaviour or other variant forms.

One study found beginning readers in U.S.A. so dominated by the left to right survey habit that they reported a series of pictured objects arranged along the sides of a triangle from left to right instead of in sequence around the triangle. This habit was relinquished a year later by good readers but not by poor readers. The authors, Elkind and Weiss (1967), suggest that the act of learning to read dominated the perceptual survey of all two-dimensional material in an exclusive way during the acquisition of the directional behaviour, although subsequently it is freed from this initial rigidity.

Children who taught themselves to read as 2- and 3-year-olds using computer-controlled typewriters had their behaviour controlled by a machine built to perform within the directional pattern of written English (Moore, 1961). The machine only moved towards the right and at the end of a line a simple control sent it sweeping back to the left side of the paper and down a space. A perceptual awareness of 'starting position, move to the right, return down left' would be learned by the child in a brief time and it was impossible to make any errors. The directional relationships were invariant, and the experience was consistent. These conditions should lead to rapid establishment of the motor habits and space orientation needed for reading. There are few classroom teachers fortunate enough to have computer-controlled electric typewriters so they must observe closely to see that the child programmes himself like a typewriter in his early contact with print. This means close supervision until the correct directional behaviour is firmly established. It is important that he knows when he is correct.

Teachers sometimes become concerned because a child writes from right to left with mirror-writing. Writing behaviour is only a gross cue to what the child is scanning with his eyes, and directional lapses in writing continue for much longer than they do in reading. Teachers should be much more concerned if the child of 6 years who has been taught reading for one year is still not behaving consistently in a left to right direction when he visually scans a page of print. These children must be reading failures. Their behaviour is disorganized. And only the invitation to 'read it with your finger' reveals this.

All children show some fluctuations in this behaviour. For how long is variability tolerable? Within a month of entry to school 40 to 50 percent of research 5-year-olds had mastered this schema in a test situation, and the average child was quite consistent within six months of school entry.

A teaching programme that assumed mastery of directional behaviour after a few weeks at school would only be appropriate for the well-prepared 5-year-olds. Obviously a sensitive teacher must be alert to the continuing confusions of many children with directional learning.

## CONSISTENT DIRECTIONAL MOVEMENT

### Percentage Pass at Five Age Levels

| Age | 5:0 | 5:6 | 6:0 | 6:6 | 7:0 |
|---|---|---|---|---|---|
| Study 1 (Europeans only) | 44 | 93 | 96 | — | — |
| Study 2 (different ethnic groups) | 53 | 77 | 84 | 99 | 99 |

## Changes in directional responses and aids to mastery

There is no one progression by which a child moves to control of the directional schema but there is a transition from early gross approximations to movements controlled by more and more of the detail in print.

## Page-matching

A text is usually page-matched at first in that a child directs his pointing and talking to a particular page, and to the print rather than the picture.

The child must be introduced to the marks he must attend to — black ones in his book, white ones on the blackboard. It seems impossible that a child should try to read the white lines in a book and 'the white rivers' on a page but some children attending reading clinic have reported this.

# Starting point

The left side of the print must be chosen as a starting point.

Until a school entrant orients himself to the arbitrary starting point of a printed line, he cannot begin to make the time-space transformation of his language skill into the location of important units in written language, no matter how skilled he is as a talker. As English print is read from left to right the child's first problem is to decide where to start. A child must locate left starting points rather than right ones with consistency.

The child may be able to become consistent in his choice of a correct starting position

● if he sees an adult modelling the movement pattern in the same position as he will produce it
● if he consistently uses one hand
● if the messages in his books always start in the same place
● if he learns some sign (like a 'green for go' sticker) which the teacher uses as a temporary prop, indicating starting position — and so on.

The control over direction must become the child's control but it may have to be exercised temporarily by the teacher.

# A helping hand

If the child has a firm preference for a particular hand it will be used to guide the eyes scanning the text. The preferred hand will be used on either a left or right page. Once the eyes have established their own left to right habit one might find the hand becomes of less importance in maintaining the response and either hand might be used to keep the place or to direct attention to some difficulty in reading.

If the child has no preference for one hand over the other, locating a starting point will be more difficult. The visual format of the pages might control his behaviour and he might be drawn to move hither and thither according to the design of pictures and print on the page.

It is clear from recent research that it is not necessary to know the names of 'left' and 'right' in order to respond successfully to the directional constraints of written English. Of course the child who knows this has an advantage as this preschooler demonstrates.

Putting on shoes says,
'Is this right?'
'Yes, right shoe on your right foot.'
'That is your right foot and the other is your left foot'.
Long pause.
'This, is my right hand'.

## Left to right across a line

A single word caption is easily located
**Me**

Two words are more difficult. There is the question of where to begin.
**My Father**

A one-line sentence provides some children with problems. Their first movements are a drift, or a sweep across a line, as the whole utterance is matched to the whole movement. Some children cannot even locate the end of the utterance.

The child may point to the letter or word at the left hand end of the line and make an uncertain movement somewhere to the right or the child may move very slowly over the first few letters or word and then sweep to the end of the line. He may move rather deliberately across most of the line and then somehow adapt to any little pieces he has over at the end.

An awareness of the right hand end of the line is often the next focal point to develop. Children are then able to locate the first word, sweep across the rest of the line and land upon the last word quite deliberately.

I *am a fireman.*

\* ─────▶ \*

## From inconsistency to flexibility

In the first approaches the child makes to printed text he might as well be scanning a picture for scattered points of interest. Records of his pointing reveal inconsistency. There is evidence to suggest that in the next stage of learning directional movements the child adopts a rigid pattern of using one particular hand to find his route across print. Gradually he becomes consistent, the lapses of direction disappear, his movements become surer and quicker and, we assume, more automatic. About this time he may begin to use either hand on either page of his book as the movement is quite easy for him and he can be flexible in his approach. To observe this transition the teacher might add another question to her record keeping.

*Which hand does the child use?* The progress of identical quadruplets was observed during their first year at school (Clay, 1974). One was left-handed, the other three were right-handed. For the first two to three weeks of school they each showed some inappropriate approaches to the printed page. Then for many weeks each adopted a preferred hand and always used it (see table below, weeks 4 to 9). One by one, they began to use either hand again. The change was in the direction of flexibility, away from a rigid routine. But the timing of this change was very different — 12, 26, 38 and 46 weeks after school entry. It is interesting that this order was perfectly related to their rank on reading achievement; the first to become flexible in the use of either hand was the first to make reading progress while the last to use either hand was the slowest to start reading. It is likely that attention, no longer needed as the sub-routine of directional behaviour could be given to other learning.

## HAND USED TO POINT TO TEXT

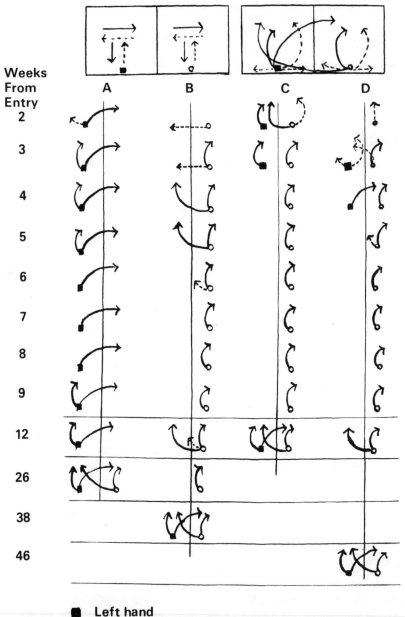

Weeks From Entry

|  | A | B | C | D |
|---|---|---|---|---|
| 2 | | | | |
| 3 | | | | |
| 4 | | | | |
| 5 | | | | |
| 6 | | | | |
| 7 | | | | |
| 8 | | | | |
| 9 | | | | |
| 12 | | | | |
| 26 | | | | |
| 38 | | | | |
| 46 | | | | |

■  Left hand
O  Right hand

## New challenges

The young learner who has established a fairly consistent habit is easily thrown by a new and unusual format and various other new factors that can enter into the reading situation. Because his directional habits are new they are easily thrown and he will be noted to lapse in his directional behaviour from time to time.

Although a young child of 5;6 years may have mastered the directional schema his teacher may notice one day that he is suddenly writing from right to left. There appear to be two reasons for this. One may be called 'the pancake effect' and the other may be called 'the pebble in the pond effect.'

## The pancake

David gives a clear example of his appreciation of the directional schema as prints his name.

ÞAV I
Þ

At this point of achievement it is easy for the child to flip the whole pattern over — to reverse it — and, choosing a top right starting point, to carry out the movements as a pattern with all the relationships reversed. The ease with which children accomplish this may be related to Bryant's discoveries that young children can be using the background (the framing of the paper shape) to guide their responding (see pages 217-218).

Translation of text copied from a basic reader:
' . . . but he liked the duck best of all.' Age 5:7.

Some visual guide to a starting point, like a coloured cross or a 'green light' sticker, in the top left-hand corner of a page should control this temporary variability. The error arises out of a measure of control over the directional pattern, and gentle coercion will 'turn the pancake' back. This behaviour is a sign of attainment.

## The pebble in the pond

The other disturbance is also a sign of growth. One by one the child masters elements of directional behaviour. One by one he encounters new problems with direction in his writing and reading. For example, although he controls the directional pattern in writing two or three lines, there comes a day when he runs out of page. With ingenuity and economy he often spreads his left-over letters in the remaining space, disregarding the directional constraints as the next illustration shows.

The layout of the story *Twice a Week* is a delightful solution to page arrangement problems. The child (age 5:1) who is not aware of the importance of space between words is content to begin page 4 with the last syllable of 'paper', continue with 'twice a week', and to put her last left-over word in any left-over space.

I colour my book
twice a week.

I draw on paper
twice a week.

Although the directional learning is well established, a new feature captures the child's attention for the moment and sends ripples of disturbance through his old habits. Given a little time the whole pattern will settle down again, incorporating this new feature in the old learning. (Spatial problems persist in writing for a longer period than in reading.)

This observation that new learning can create a disturbance in old responses which seemed to be well-established is not so strange when one thinks about it. If learning were only a matter of adding bits of knowledge to our old stores this would not happen. But when out skills are controlled by a pattern of movements or a complex set of brain reactions it is not really surprising that the whole set is disturbed by adding a new component to the pattern.

Questioned about directional errors, children will frequently be able to report what they have done. After 33 weeks at school Trevor read one page correctly. He turned the leaf, began to read at the left of the bottom line, continuing left to right and bottom to top without any other error. He then read six pages with correct directional behaviour. I turned back to the offending page and asked *What did you do wrong?* He answered without hesitation, *I read the bottom wrong* . These observations suggest that when directional behaviour is not quite a habit, and conscious attention is given to other aspects of the text, directional constraints can be overlooked. Perfect rendering of a text from bottom to top sounds an impossibility. Surely the story would not make sense! But in some controlled vocabulary tests the loss of meaning when incorrect direction is used is very slight!

## In summary

Good readers seem to learn a pattern of movements for the visual scanning of print. They must act within the constraints on movement imposed by our arbitrary ways of writing down our language. Children who learn to read from one-line sentences or captions acquire the left to right movement. Later, they become able to scan two or more lines. Into this general pattern they build the ability to search visually word by word in sequence, and, later still, the ability to search letter by letter, or cluster by cluster, but still in sequence. During the acquisition stage directional learning can be seriously disturbed by recurrent error. Its stability is also temporarily shaken when the child attempts to integrate some new learning (letter features, punctuation, sentences running over one line on to a second line) into the established pattern.

Evidence of the timing of such learning was provided in a longitudinal study of 100 children and test scores on these directional variables were highly correlated with reading attainment one, two and three years after school entry. For most children it is not difficult learning and perhaps the attention paid to it seems to stress it unduly. This is not so, if the reduction of reading failure is the aim of teachers. This directional learning and the total set for sequential processing that it implies is basic to successful and efficient reading. It is not, however, sufficient.

# One After the Other

Not only do children have to learn to move in a left-to-right direction but they also have to learn to observe words one after the other in faultless sequence. If we ask children of 5 years to count a row of objects one after the other, some children have difficulty. They have less difficulty with only three or four objects and this is one reason why a three or four word text is about right for the beginner's competence with one-to-one correspondence. In the sentence

### Here is Mother

the directional sequence is left-to-right and the motor sequencing one, two, three. Most children will manage the coordination correctly. The child who cannot point to three circles or blocks in sequence will not find groups of black symbols separated by white spaces any easier.

After he has achieved this one-to-one correspondence in pointing to objects guided by his eyes the child may still have a problem pointing to words on a page. After this second problem is solved he may have difficulty finding the words in his speech. He may clump words together, saying 'apastate' when he is trying to match with the text 'half past eight'. Or, he points to *the* and reads *the girls*. On the other hand, he might over-analyse into syllables and get two points in *pi - lot* or *laugh - ing*. Downing has explored this problem of knowing what is a word in oral language (Downing and Oliver, 1974). Other writers have called this portmanteau language. New difficulties of this kind continue to be met as texts become more difficult. There is a continuing challenge in matching new speech patterns to text layouts.

## Locating words

When a school entrant points to his reading text he is usually trying to match the time sequence of what he is saying with the visual survey of print in the book. He is trying to relate one form of notation (speaking) to another (writing). To help the child with this locating publishers have used larger print and increased the spacing between lines. Writers often place one sentence to a line in the early books, and reduce the amount of print on a page to a few lines.

How the learning proceeds on letters and words may be determined by the instruction programme. The child's attention may be directed primarily to letters, to words, to groups of letters, or to groups of words. There are two difficult concepts to be mastered. The first is the ordering principle of words arranged left-to-right, one after another. The other is the hierarchical principle that each word consists of letters which themselves have a left to right order.

Some children come to believe that each letter is matched to a word in speech. This is an early misconception.

Child A: | *Here is the cow.*
Child B: | *Here is the c----------ow.*
Text:    | H    e    r    e    is the cow.

Child A has not solved the problem of what to do with the left-over words. Child B has found an unsatisfactory solution; he draws out the rest of what he has to say as he runs his finger quickly along to the end of the line.

## Two or more lines

*Does the child match one line very well but lose control when he is faced with two lines?* The child should be introduced to:

● how to manage the return sweep on two or more lines
● how to move from top to bottom on two or more lines.

The fragility of the early learning can be demonstrated if a child who moves consistently across a single caption is faced with more than one line on a page.

**Come and play**                    **Grandad said, 'The**
**on the swings**                     **children are here'.**

The child may just ignore the problem and give the correct response to the top line or the bottom line only. He may be unable to return to the left hand end of the line. Perhaps no-one thought to prepare him for that item of learning. He may try to return from right to left discovering an approach that requires little effort. He may even be tempted to read a bottom line before the top line especially if no-one thought to prepare him for the top-to-bottom progression.

These difficulties have been demonstrated with 6-year-old readers receiving special instruction. A single sentence is written out on paper and cut into word units. The child locates words and reads with success the single line sentence. But when the same sentence is rearranged into two and three lines the children often show some difficulty in adapting correctly to these arrangements.

One child moved across two pages of print giving spoken responses that sounded correct until one noticed where the child was directing his attention.

| | | | | | |
|---|---|---|---|---|---|
| 3 | 2 | 1 | | 8 | 7 |
| Here | is | Peter | | Peter | has |
| 6 | 5 | 4 | | 9 | 10 |
| in | the | tree | | the | ball |

The memory for text was perfect; he read *Here is Peter in the tree. Peter has the ball* . Both the starting point and the return sweep are problems to this child on two lines of print but he controls the top-to-bottom movement.

## The match and mark task

A task which may be called 'Match and Mark' can be carried out to check the child's movement across print in this very early stage of acquiring directional behaviour.

Select a piece of tracing paper and pencil or clear plastic with a water based felt pen that will wash off. Say to the child *I want you to read this story for me and I want you to put marks to show what you are saying* . Help the child to understand how the marks can be made. Children will often be reticent to make marks on paper and will perhaps be uncertain as to what it is that you require. It is permissible to teach the child now to make marks on the page as he reads but it is not permissible to precisely mark up that particular text so that one mark falls under every word. This would be teaching the child who could then copy the teacher. What we want is a situation which will reveal what the child spontaneously and naturally does when faced with print. If you are satisfied that the child is not as familiar with the kind of task that you are asking him to perform, ask him to read two or three more pages of a caption reader saying the story and putting marks to show what he is saying. For the poorest children the marking will bear no relation to what the child is saying, and one might suspect that what he is attending to bears no relation to what the teacher is attending to as she reads it.

For example two children responding to the two-line text

**Big sister**
**is making the bed**

responded with 4 points and 16 points respectively.

| Text: | B   i   g     sister |
|-------|----------------------|
| Child: | Big sister |
| Finger: | * |

| Text: | is making the bed |
|-------|-------------------|
| Child: | making the bed |
| Finger: | *     *     * |

| Text: | Big sister |
|-------|------------|
| Child: | (Speech and pointing |
| Finger: | *****   *   ***   ***** |

| Text: | is making the bed |
|-------|-------------------|
| Child: | are not coordinated) |
| Finger: | *     * |

# Letters Within Words

Children need some help in understanding that a word is made up of a group of letters. Some teachers encourage children to cup their hands around words on the blackboard. Others find ways to help children to use the spaces as a cue to the word boundaries. A little attention to this *collection of letters* concept will assist the child to overcome the 'letter equals a word' problem.

At this early stage it is probably less important that the child be attending to specific letters within words. But in order to discriminate between words it will be necessary before long for the child to be paying attention to the left hand letter of a word as he proceeds word by word across the line. Later still it will be necessary for him to attend to the letters sequentially left to right across a word. And early writing directs attention to this.

The child who can write a few letters usually gains control of left to right sequencing in his own printing before he disciplines his approach to print on a book page. In writing *he* controls the complexity and variations; in a book the *author* and *printer* do this.

It seems likely that children taught in a programme that introduces them to word-learning or to sounding out three-letter words have less difficulty when the hierarchical relationships of several letters equal one word.

One tends to assume that the simple instructions, 'Look at the first letter of the word,' or 'Show me the first letter of the word,' are readily understood by children. To respond correctly one must understand:

● that a word is the pattern of marks, made up by letters.
● that a word must be approached from left to right.

## EXAMPLES OF DIRECTIONAL LEARNING
Children were asked to make marks with a pencil on transparent paper placed over the text of their caption book. What they said and where they pointed are recorded in these examples.

| | |
|---|---|
| My mother | A good beginning |
| Father is digging | Beginning, middle and end |
| Here is the horse | A letter is a word |
| I am a painter | More difficult than it need be |
| I am a nurse | Almost coordinated |
| I am a pilot | Coordinated speech and pointing |

But 5-year-olds will write letters and call them words or they may write a string of words and call them letters. What is a word? What is a letter? To make the correct generalization about these basic concepts, the child only has to know his name and two or three other words. However, many children make the wrong assumptions at first (Clay, 1975).

Ian failed to sort out his confusions about print throughout the whole of his first year at school. He claimed that his teacher, who wrote his name as 'Ian' could not spell it; it should be written 'IAN'. But in a bookshop he pointed to the title of a scrapbook, 'GIANT,' and said *There's my name,* unconcerned by the presence of extra letters.

What often happens is that the concepts of letter, word, and first letter become confused. For example, when one child was asked to read these words (in isolation) he responded with letter names:

Child: | a's    z     y's
Text:  | here   said   am

The ghost of a sound cue occurred when he responded with the letter 'z' to the word 'said'.

Another child demonstrated his concept of a word when he read his name, 'Stuart'. He was asked *'How do you know?'* As he pointed to the 's' he said, *'It begins like this — and goes as far as there!'* sliding his finger along under the word and ending at the final 't'.

In a test where the child had to slide two masking cards across a line of print to show the tester 'just one word', 'just one letter' and 'just the first letter of a word' (Clay, 1979) only 40 to 53 percent of 6-year-olds could pass these items after one year of instruction. Such scoring reflects partly a confusion of concepts, and partly the problem of establishing part-identities within wholes. Yet, the directional pattern was established in 84 percent of the group who could synchronize their pointing with their word by word reading of the text.

## THE ACQUISITION OF IMPORTANT CONCEPTS

| Task | Percentage Passing At Five Age Levels | | | | |
|---|---|---|---|---|---|
| | 5:0 | 5:6 | 6:0 | 6:6 | 7:0 |
| Matches word-space-word | 48 | 60 | 84 | 100 | 100 |
| Locates one letter | 34 | 47 | 53 | 56 | 84 |
| Locates one word | 22 | 16 | 47 | 53 | 91 |
| Locates first letter | 28 | 22 | 41 | 56 | 81 |

The young child does not have a concept of the spoken word that matches his teacher's concept. Up to the age of 8 years children confuse isolated sounds and syllables with words. Reid (1966) and Clay (1966) found children had limited understanding of a word or a letter and of the purposes of reading. Downing (1970) and Downing and Oliver (1974) demonstrated the child's confusion in distinguishing by ear the difference between a word and a sound or syllable in speech. Thirty children from 4:5 to 8:0 years confused isolated sounds and syllables with words. It is possible that these children thought that such sounds represented 'words' that they were not familiar with.

Children sometimes reject long words as words. Downing and Oliver suggest that short words of 3 to 5 letters are most likely to appear in their reading books and be associated with the teacher's label 'word'.

In learning to read a child must develop an understanding of such basic concepts as word, sound, letter, number, reading, and writing. Teachers cannot assume that beginning readers understand the terms they use or can isolate for attention the things the labels refer to. If they cannot, the teaching-learning interaction goes astray.

Hazel Francis (1971, 1973) at the University of Leeds confirmed Reid's and Downing's findings. She wished to trace the children's comprehension of terms teachers would use during instruction and their abilities to identify units in written and spoken language. Her study was longitudinal as she followed the same 50 children from 5:9 to 7:3. Children learned the concept of letter before word and word before sentence, the two latter concepts being mastered while children were already reading and derived from experience with written language. To the question *'What do we use words (sentences) for?'* almost nobody indicated an awareness of the use of words or sentences in the spoken language.

Let me illustrate the problems that the very young reader has in locating what he should be attending to.

Suppose a teacher has placed an attractive picture on the wall and has asked her children for a story which she will record under it. They offer the text 'Mother is cooking' which the teacher alters slightly to introduce some features she wishes to teach. She writes,

Mother said,
'I am baking.'

If she says 'Now look at our *story,'* 30 percent of the new entrant group will attend to the *picture.*

If she says, 'Look at the *words* and find some you know,' between 50 and 90 percent will be searching for *letters.* If she says, 'Can you see Mother?' most will agree that they can but some see her in the picture, some can locate 'M' and others will locate the word 'Mother'.

Perhaps the children read in unison 'Mother is . . . ' and the teacher tries to sort this out. Pointing to *said* she asks, 'Does this say *is?'* Half agree it does because it has 's' in it. *'What letter does it start with?'* Now the teacher is really in trouble. She assumes that children *know* that a word is built out of letters but 50 percent of children still confuse the verbal labels 'word' and 'letter' after six months of instruction. She also assumes that the children know that the left-hand letter following a space is the 'start' of a word. Often they do not. She says, 'Look at the *first* letter. It says s-s-s-s' and her pupils make s-noises. But Johnny who knows only 'Mother' and 'I' scans the text haphazardly for something relevant, sights the *comma* and makes s-noises!

Mother said,
'I am baking.

Teacher continues, 'What do you think Mother said? *Look at the next word* and tell me what it says.' That should be easy because most children learn 'I' early, but for a child who does not know the difference between a letter and a word *'the next word'* will often be the second letter in 'said'. For other children who have not established left to right movement with return sweep the next word may be 'gnikab' because they are returning right to left along the second line. Still others may be conscientiously striving to decode the commas or the inverted commas, before they get to 'I'.

The lesson continues and the class makes a final unison statement 'Mother said, "I am cooking".' Many have focussed on the quaint letter 'k' in the middle. The teacher says, 'Does it say cooking? Look carefully. Look at the beginning. Tell me what the first letter says.' Many children may not locate the first letter. 'Does it say c-c-c-c?' Children with an intuitive awareness of the phonic identity of 'k' agree heartily. The teacher has now reached the new information for which her lesson was designed. 'It says b-b-b-b-for baking.' Some of the class are surprised to find that the 'k' they are focussing says 'b' and others gain the impression that 'baking' says 'b'

An earnest child may be found reading the story to himself later in the day. Matching the number of word impulses he says, to the number of word patterns he sees we might hear him read *'Mother is cooking some cakes,'* and he could be very satisfied with his effort.

One could protest that if a good teacher was aware of such difficulties and was carefully pointing to letters and words as she spoke much of the confusion would be eliminated. But that assumes rather too much of group instruction where the young child's attention does fluctuate. If the teacher examines the things she says to her class, to small groups and to individual children she may find that she takes for granted insights which some children do not have. It was discovered that learning these concepts takes place slowly over the first year at school (Reid, 1958; Downing, 1965; Clay, 1979).

Young children lack a consciously analytic approach to speech. The use of the words *letter, word* and *sentence* in teaching was not so much a direct aid to instruction as a challenge to find their meaning.

A study at the kindergarten level carried out in Texas (Day K.C. and Day H.O., 1978) showed these children to have widely different abilities in concepts about print at the beginning of the year and to change markedly in twelve months in a traditional programme without reading instruction. They concluded 'One could suppose that when they enter first grade and begin formal reading instruction these children will be on different cognitive levels.'

In another part of U.S.A. teachers have developed a check-list using the concepts about print items to get information about children's readiness for their reading programme (McDonell and Osborne, 1978). The test was not intended as a predictor of progress but rather as a check during the first two years of an instruction programme. However, in the transfer of these ideas from New Zealand to U.S.A., a different educational setting, such a translation may be appropriate.

A set of masking cards or window cards can help children to segment the flow of print into patterns which are separated by spaces, (i.e. words) and into letters which make up words.

There is least room for confusion when the teacher asks a child about words which occur at the beginning of lines, and letters which occur at the beginning of those words. First words and first letters are 'portmanteau concepts' because they demand the understanding of two things at the same time, *word* and *first*. Final words and final letters will be easier than detail embedded in the middle of a sentence, but less useful than first letters and first words.

The puzzle in finding a word is to 'detach' that word from the whole utterance. Spaces help the child to segment the visual display of print and pauses help him to segment the aural flow of words in his speech. The two sources of information reinforce each other.

A similar task in segmentation relates to sounds. As a learning task this should probably follow after the child can effectively locate word units in what he says, but need not be delayed long for the linguistically able child. Listening for first sounds in words can then be related to segmenting first letters in print.

It is not self-evident to a child that left to right movement along a line, through a book, and across a word are related. And telling him that they are will not be sufficient. It is only through working with print, writing his own stories, reading and discovering things about printed texts, that he slowly consolidates the total network of relationships. For most children there is a gradual improvement with experience. On the other hand persisting confusions work against the teacher at every lesson, introducing noise or static into a process that should have a clear communication channel. These concepts could be mastered at the early reading stage with appropriate tuition, on the simplest line of print.

An example of the simplicity of this learning can be given: Peter learns to read and write the idea, 'Peter is here.' If his mind is working actively upon this experience he can learn these things:

**Peter is here**
'P' is important for my name but it is also for Paul.
(*There is a need to choose between words*)
Some more signs are needed. 'Peter' is not long enough.
(*There is a special pattern of signs*)
(*Signs can recur*)
'Is' is a little pattern.
'Here' is a longer pattern.
(*Size of pattern can be a cue*)
'Here' is like Peter but it is different, too.
(*Perhaps order is important*)
'P' is the first letter.
(*First letter at left end*)

Research has shown that children make gross discriminations before fine ones. They notice things about page layout before they notice features of words. Letter detail is noticed later still, but the letters near the spaces, first and last, are easier to analyse than those buried in the middle of words. The order of discrimination is roughly illustrated by Catherine's attempt to write her name.

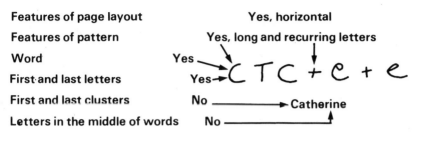

| Features of page layout | Yes, horizontal |
| Features of pattern | Yes, long and recurring letters |
| Word | Yes |
| First and last letters | Yes |
| First and last clusters | No |
| Letters in the middle of words | No |

Even a change in word size, or in its horizontal or vertical plane can be confusing to the young learner. Simon's Mother's diary (at 5:6):

> *Stood looking at Father's van for some time then asked if the large printed word 'SERVICE' on the side was the same as the smaller printed word on the front. He was correct.*

# Each Book Has Its Particular Difficulties

In order to explore the development of directional behaviour the teacher must make herself aware of the order in which her preferred texts introduce difficulties. This usually means an increase of 1, 2 or 3 lines, and any unusual arrangement of text. The teacher should also be aware that until the child gains control over the directional pattern it is easy for visual features of the text (such as colour, illustration, ornament) to draw his attention to a different starting point. Even the size of the white spaces may make him suddenly reverse his directional approach or start at the bottom of a page.

Teachers should check the early reading books that they present to children and make sure that when a new problem is introduced there is preparation for it. The teacher should give the children a slow deliberate demonstration of the movements needed so that all children 'get the feel of it'. She should be careful to place her body, book and arm in the same place or orientation that the children will use (otherwise as a model, she could confuse them).

Teachers will know from experience how the characteristics of layout and format in early reading books direct the attention of some children away from the print or make it difficult for the child to find a starting point. Distractions do not bother the competent child. It is the child who is unsure who can be confused in his code-breaking attempts by visual gimmicks which publishers could avoid. Teacher-made books can be planned to challenge a particular child.

# The Value of Writing

Painting with big brushes and bright paint may develop the artistic feelings of 4-year-olds but it should not replace paper and pencil or crayon and cardboard as additional media for preschoolers. These encourage the child to experiment with letter-like writing. He will often scribble at first, in imitation of his parents' cursive writing. He may want to write the names of his family members or send a letter to Nana. (Notice the double meaning of the word 'letter', which can be a source of confusion at this age!)

In writing, the child must construct his own words, letter by letter. The attention of eye and brain is directed to the elements of letters, to letter sequences and to spatial concepts. The child who writes a simple story is caught up in a process of synthesizing words and sentences. This building-up process is an excellent complement to the visual analysis of the text in his reading book, which is a breaking-down process. By these two processes the child comes to understand the hierarchical relationships of letters, words and utterances. He also confirms that the left-to-right constraint is applied to lines of print, to words within lines, and to letters within words. Although his knowledge of written language is severely limited, his early learning is patterned in a useful way and is not just scrambled (Clay, 1975).

Richards (1968) saw a particular value in this new control over writing. When the eye and the ear are jointly engaged in the management of a situation, each may be regarded as offering a check on the other. The acquisition of written language can give the learner a new power to check upon the language he has been saying and using. He can examine his speech in another form. He gains a new means of exploring and comparing segments of language.

# Learning Sequences in Writing

The comments which follow refer to a method of early writing instruction which uses a minimum of formal writing lessons. The child learns to write by tracing and copying stories written by his teacher at his dictation. The teacher gives an occasional group lesson on letter formation, perhaps once a week, but gives daily and individual guidance for the writing of *stories*. Each child, according to his own rate of progress, learns to print by passing through some or all the following stages:

● draw (and the teacher writes dictated captions)
● trace over the teacher's script
● copy captions and simple sentences
● remember words which are used often
● invent word forms (but not always correctly)
● write most of the words without help
● get a written copy of new or special words from the teacher.

Teachers often begin printing activities with the child's own name, a word of high interest which provides the insight that print conveys a message. The child who can write his name when he comes to school already knows that the message consists of:

- particular marks
- placed in a certain sequence
- which make a recognizable pattern.

In some vague idiosyncratic way the child knows that the name is constructed out of one particular set of letters.

---

*School holidays. David prints his name on anything available but does not write any other words.*

---

*Michael printed his name on blackboard quite legibly for first time. Needs something to copy but very proud of himself. Does it over again. Tries to write his name as soon as he is up in morning.*

---

If one examines early letters a sequence of concepts which may be detected are

- scribble
- mock hand-writing
- mock letters
- real letters plus inventions
- acceptable English letters.

**H ℮ ℗ℓ ϙ℘ ϒ**

**Keith**

At an early stage of letter differentiation one child had 'discovered' all these symbols:

Ƃ ⌒ Ọ I Ͱ ⊇ L ⊇ I ᵒᵖ   ƷI ⊃ ℗ ∮ ᣘ ﹤ ⊇α

When the child is attempting to write words his efforts may fit one of these descriptions. Words are

- invented
- traced
- copied incorrectly
- copied correctly
- written incorrectly without a copy
- written correctly without a copy.

The child may attempt to write groups of words. He may have learned that word groups

- can be invented
- go left to right without spaces
- go left to right with spaces
- go left to right with spaces and return down left.

It has been claimed that one advantage of an i.t.a. script is that a child can write his own stories much earlier. He can sound out the words and write them down without help. This produces more rapid progress with reading and writing in the early months, for the average and below average child, it is claimed. From observations of quite a different approach to early reading and writing I would claim that where the teacher individualizes her instruction and makes herself available to act as the child's scribe, the child can make very good progress with written expression without i t a and before he has a detailed knowledge of letter-sound correspondence.

On the other hand, I doubt whether building sentences out of words which have been printed for the child on cards, does more for him than build hazy word concepts, known only approximately. The details of words involve knowing precisely which letters occur in what order, and such discriminations and attention to sequence are consolidated by the acts of constructing these words in creative writing. Discrimination and an awareness of the sequential probabilities of letters and letter clusters in English are sharpened by the act of writing.

Children come gradually to understand these concepts about print; the slowest take the entire first year. Some write nothing but letters, others try words and the most advanced use groups of words to express whole ideas. First efforts are often invented, later ones copied, and later still the child can construct his own words, 'from within his head'. Writing is only a rough guide to the child's visual analysis skills for he may be able to see what his hand has not the skill to execute. But conversely, what he says is often a very misleading guide to what his eye really perceives. In many hard-core

---

## AN ILLUSTRATION OF THE COMPLEXITY OF THE TASK

Text:   **Butch is a dog**

Reads:   Butch is a do-o —— g

Sally has been at school three months. She had a correct starting point, a left to right movement across a line, and a correct finishing point. She used the correct words. The very large print of the text presented a new problem and she gave a word response to the first four letters so that further visual learning could not occur at this moment. When she had finished she said,

> That's *dog*, (pointing correctly)
> It's easy to spell.
> It begins with a *b* like *bed*
> and an *o* in *orange*.

Sally has many early reading skills. She needs to focus these skills in some integrated way so that they lead, in concert, to successful book reading.

reading problems the absence of a 'writing vocabulary' is a blatant sign that the visual perception of print has not been internally organized into programmes for producing words (see Chapter 13).

In one study (Robinson, 1973) it was found that the child's ability to write words was closely related to reading progress in the first year of instruction. In this study a child was asked to write down all the words he knew. He was encouraged to write his name, then he was asked, *'What other words do you know?'* If he ran out of ideas the tester prompted him using little words that he might be expected to know from his reading or writing vocabulary. Before five minutes were up most children had exhausted their store of writing vocabulary but the more competent children worked for up to 10 minutes before they had written 'all the words they knew'. A simple score for all the words correctly written (with letter formation readable and letter sequence correct) was closely related to the child's place compared with other members of his reading group.

# Is Pointing Good or Bad?

The answer to this question depends on the child's stage of reading progress.

'Should I sweep along the line of print as I read to my preschool child?' asked a journalist father. By all means, because a feeling for the direction in which one moves across print is hard to learn when the child is young and yet it must become a habit before book reading can be attempted.

Should you ask a child, 'Read with your finger'? Yes, if the teacher wishes to observe the child's directional behaviour, the pattern of his approach to lines of print. On most occasions a child will demonstrate an adequate directional pattern but sometimes he will produce surprising results. My favourite illustration comes from a child who was 5:9; he appeared to be ignoring many features of print:

|        | LINE 1      | LINE 2 | LINE 3    | LINE 4      |
|--------|-------------|--------|-----------|-------------|
| *Child:* | *Go go go go* | *Tim up* | *Up Tim*  | *Up up up*  |
| Text:  | Go Tim      | Go up  | Go up Tim | Go up up up |

In fact his reading was word perfect, but this was only discovered because he was asked to read it with his finger. If a teacher frowned on pointing, she would not discover this handicapping behaviour (which had probably been learned after entry to school).

A highly intelligent girl of 13 years was handed an infant story written in i.t.a. She read it slowly, pointing with her finger. An adult given a letter in illegible handwriting or a smudgy carbon copy would be quite likely to locate the difficult parts by peering for a closer look or by pointing. Even good readers locate their difficulties in a decoding task by pointing. It is a common reaction for locating, or for holding one's place in the visual analysis of sequential material.

There are other reasons why pointing may assist the child. Recent research (Zaporozhets, 1965) has shown that young children of 3 to 4 years often depend upon body or hand movement to help them learn the features of new objects, while the older child of 6 to 7 years can explore new objects with his eyes alone and without the support of his hand. What is first a visual and manual exploration of objects becomes a visual exploration only. When we introduce 5-year-olds to reading we can expect half of them at least to benefit greatly from body and hand participation in the knowing of new objects, shapes or forms. Some children will have a persisting need for this kinaesthetic source of information. The teacher's demand for no pointing, no tracing, only looking, is a demand which only the most able of young school entrants can meet.

The value of kinaesthetic exploration to supplement visual information at an early stage of reading instruction has been recognized by authorities like Grace Fernald (1943) who designed a remedial programme for backward readers around this particular concept. The organization of sequential actions needed in reading seems to be particularly assisted by this kinaesthetic analysis. However, it is a means to an end, the goal being to bring the child to the point where he can carry out such analyses at the visual level only without the need to trace or feel the spatial relationships.

Reading experts have criticized the use of pointing in reading because it has been associated with the persistence in older children of slow word by word reading and a bad habit is said to have developed. Observational records of the first year of reading showed all children passing through a stage of locating words one by one, as if the identification of written with oral symbols were better emphasized by finger pointing than by 'finger-flow' along the whole sentence. Once one-to-one correspondence was established good readers gave up using their hands as their speed of reading increased. In the author's researches most children passed through a word-locating stage but some children remained fixated at this level of behaviour.

# Theory About Serial Order

It is not wise in Developmental Psychology to describe what happens at one stage of development by analogy from behaviour of an earlier stage. For one thing the child becomes more complex as he gains experience. However, Jerome Bruner's explanation of the development of skilled actions (1974) is remarkably informative for understanding the sequential acts in beginning reading, even though he is describing how the *infant* learns to put separate acts into a controlled sequenced movement.

There are six stages to the development of sequenced movement.

**Stage 1**   The child attends to the task and performs some anticipatory actions.

**Stage 2**   This is the clumsy stage. A loosely-ordered series of actions occur, only roughly approximate, variable, and requiring much effort.

**Stage 3**   This changes to success with a short series of acts in proper serial order, allowing for some false moves, repetitions and self-corrections. There is a sharp noticeable alteration in the acts as if they had acquired a new structure.

**Stage 4**   Reinforcement or success modifies the action pattern so that it becomes less variable.

**Stage 5**   With practice the child does not need to attend to all sections of the sequence. Sub-routines are formed which the child executes with little attention. The child is freed to attend to new aspects of the task. The sub-routines can become part of a new series of acts in a higher-order structure.

**Stage 6**   With more practice the skilled performance becomes less variable, anticipation becomes more accurate, and speed and fluency increase because an economy of attention and effort has been made.

Learning directional behaviours and visual scanning patterns can be understood in these terms. And early reading behaviours may be thought of as sub-routines of the complex sequenced problem-solving acts of reading texts with understanding.

Bruner discusses the role of feedback and intention in the learning of sequences of skilled action.

● Within the nervous system before we act there are signals of our intended action. Our limbs would not respond to our intentions if this were not so. Because these occur before the action takes place they are sometimes called feed-forward (rather than feedback). These signals anticipate the shape of the act yet to occur.

● Learning is also helped by feedback signals that come as the action is being carried out. This might involve hearing what one is saying, as in reading aloud, or pointing with a finger to guide the eye movements needed. Feedback acts as a control system informing us when an error or mismatch of signals has occured.

● Knowledge of results occurs after the action is completed. Did you grasp the glass you reached for? Observing the results of an action leads us to anticipate the outcome on another occasion.

In performing a sequence of acts the child is helped by feed-forward, feedback and knowledge of results. At first he attends to some of these signals. But as the sub-routines are formed and linked the movements become more automatic and require less effort and less attention.

Reading as a skilled action sequence presents a further problem to the child. Directional strategies and visual scanning strategies become sets of smooth sub-routines, but reading remains a problem-solving task in which the reader must get the precise message of the author. So the young reader must be 'set for diversity'. There is no one skill sequence that will cope with the task. Reading is an active process of calling up sub-routines in ever-changing sequences to suit the task in hand. And when the reader encounters a difficulty with some higher order sequences he must be able to go back to the sub-sub-routines in the sequence for more detailed analysis. Only the learner can construct these action sequences. He can learn by using observed behaviours as a model. He can construct his complex behaviour from many experiences with models. He can be supported and encouraged to try and be rewarded for trying. But he must construct and coordinate the sequences. As Smith (1978) says, we give the child the problem; he must work out how to solve it.

Bruner's description of the learning of skilled sequences of action tells us that children have been controlling sequential behaviour from infancy. They have been practising putting constituent acts together in play, and in day to day activities to achieve their intentions. In play they have had the opportunity to use the signals of the feed-forward, feedback and knowledge of results processes, the trio of processes that control sequential actions.

From this theory of skilled action we may conclude that it will help the young reader to construct these action sequences if *he is encouraged to initiate the behaviour himself.*

Although the novice may know only very few words, as long as he controls the movement pattern of one-to-one correspondence, he has created for himself new opportunities to learn. Each word he says is matched to each pattern of black marks (separated by a white space) and every now and then his eye can check that what is said coincides with a remembered word — that limited sight vocabulary of ten or so words. The word by word technique enables him to check that his voice is saying the right word at those points where he *knows* a particular word pattern. In the following example he may know *Father* and *car* and may be content to render it thus,

Child:  | *Father goes to his car*
Text:   | Father is in the car

The child is aware that the visual and vocal experiences match (within the limits of his knowledge).

Hard on the heels of such controlled, serially-ordered achievement something happens. Bruner writes

'Here we come to a puzzle. Once the act is successfully executed and repeated with success, and the constituents are put stably into proper serial order, there often appears a sharp alteration in the structure of the act used for achieving an intended outcome . . . There appears to be a reorganization of components.'

(Bruner, 1974)

The new act that has been mastered soon becomes merely a sub-routine of a higher-order action. The mastering of sub-routines reduces the attention needed to regulate them so that they can be incorporated into a higher-order, longer-sequence act.

'Skilled action, then, may be conceived of as the construction of serially ordered constitutional acts, whose performance is modified towards less variability, more anticipation, and greater economy by benefit of feed-forward, feedback and knowledge of results.'

(Bruner, 1974)

The child succeeds in this serially-ordered task if he:

- is encouraged to venture, to try
- is rewarded for trying to act on his own
- is sustained through the formative and less than accurate stages of early learning
- comes to select more useful rather than less useful behaviours with the help of the teacher who gives feedback and knowledge of results when he is unable to gain these for himself.

# In Summary

To read English it is necessary to move from left to right along a line and to return down left for the beginning of the following line. It is also necessary to read a left page before a right page and to proceed left to right along a word if the sound sequence is to match something one has heard before. This seems self-evident.

Such learning takes some children only a short time. It takes the average child nearly six months to establish consistency in this behaviour. Observation suggests that when the method of teaching reading stresses fluency and reading for meaning, little progress can be made until the child has established constancy in 'left to right, return down left' movements and in left to right survey of words.

The child's movements have hitherto been unconstrained with respect to direction, and on entry to school he has to learn to relate himself (his whole body), two eyes (together), two hands (separately), to a page of print which has directional constraints. He must learn that it is made up of lines (which have direction), made up of words (which have direction), made up of letters (which have fixed orientation); these consist of particular strokes, circles and angles.

The child who learns to read with a language-experience approach to natural language texts, works down through that hierarchy (analytically) as he learns to read his books, and up through the hierarchy (synthetically) as he learns to write stories.

After a fairly consistent habit is established the young learner is still very easily thrown by new problems, new format, and other factors that can enter into the reading situation. A teacher may emphasize something the child does not understand. Because his directional habits are new they are easily thrown and lapses in his directional behaviour will be noticed from time to time. It is not easy to maintain consistency in the hierarchical behaviour of looking at letters within words, within lines, down a page. And so the child has, for the first year or two of learning, to read continually to control a tendency to go in other directions. The teacher will have made a significant contribution to the minimizing of problems in the shortest time possible if she can be sure that directional behaviour is established with some consistency at this early reading stage.

Any child who has been in instruction for six months and is still confused about direction needs special attention, otherwise he may continue to confuse himself by responding with an inappropriate directional pattern as often as he does with a correct one. By practising inappropriate directional behaviour he is learning a habit that will be difficult to overcome.

At 6 years from 4 percent to 16 percent of children still show directional errors when asked to 'Read with your finger'. They require immediate, special and individual attention to this problem without further delay.

If one is a young child, the learning of an arbitrary directional convention for approaching written language may be a matter of movement or placement of one's body relative to the visual field. There is a motor component to the learning. If the approach is made by eye scanning movements only, it is still a motor activity though less easy to observe. Eventually it becomes a brain scan, so that during a fixation of the eyes sequential attentional scanning without apparent movement gives little sign of the motor activity which was probably necessary during the acquisition stage.

As the child addresses the open book his first orientation is that of placing himself (or his body) in the right position to get the messages from the text. He must locate a starting position and move in a left-to-right direction. If the text has more than one line he must learn about the return-sweep action. These adaptations involve the movements of turning the head and pointing with the hand. Later this movement sequence becomes a sequence of eye movements or eye scanning, a motor activity of a controlled kind. Eventually it becomes an efficient habit as the brain directs attention, giving little indication of the movements that were needed to acquire it in the first place. This development will be discussed in more detail in Chapter 13.

## PRIORITIES FOR TEACHING DIRECTIONAL SKILLS

|  | Teachers' Rank | Author's Preference |
|---|---|---|
| **High priority** | | |
| Locate beginnings of words | 1 | 9 |
| Enlarge vocabulary | 2 = | 2 =(spoken) |
| Use context cues | 2 = | 10= |
| | | |
| **Next priority** | | |
| Picture interpretation | 5 = | 2 = |
| Left to right finger sweep | 5 = | 5 = |
| Locate letters as cues to words | 5 = | 12 |
| Recount story | 7 = | 2 = |
| Left to right eye sweep | 7 = | 5 = |
| | | |
| **Lowest priority** | | |
| Locate words to form a word concept | 9 = | 7 |
| Left to right word pointing | 9 = | 10= |
| Match line and sentence response | 11 | 5 = |
| Left to right letter attack | 12 | 13 |
| Locate words as cues to a sentence | 13 | 8 |

# References and Further Reading

Benton, A.L., *Right-Left Discrimination and Finger Localization*, Paul B. Hoeber, New York, 1959.

Bruner, J.S., Organization of early skilled action, *Child Development*, 44, 1973, 1-11.

Clay, Marie, M., Orientation to the spatial characteristics of the open book. *Visible Language*, 8, 1974, 275-282.

Clay, Marie, M., *The Early Detection of Reading Difficulties: A Diagnostic Survey with Recovery Procedures*, Heinemann Educational Books, Auckland, 1979.

Clay, Marie, M., *What Did I Write*, Heinemann Educational Books, Auckland, 1975.

Clay, Marie, M., Exploring with a pencil, *Theory Into Practice*, 16, 5, (December) 1977.

Day, Karen, C. and Day, H.D., Developmental observations of kindergarten children's understanding in regard to concepts about print and language development, Paper presented.

Downing, J. and Oliver, P., The child's conception of 'a word'. *Reading Research Quarterly*, 9, 1974, 568-582.

Elkind, D. and Weiss, J., 'Studies in perceptual development, III: perceptual exploration', *Child Development*, 38, 1967, pp. 553-561.

Fernald, Grace, M., *Remedial Techniques In Basic School Subjects*, McGraw-Hill, New York, 1943.

McDonell, G.M. and Osburn, E.B., New thoughts about reading readiness. *Language Arts*, 55, 1, 1978.

Moore, O.K., 'Orthographic symbols and the preschool child — a new approach'. In E.O. Torrance (ed.), *New Educational Ideas: Third Minnesota Conference on Gifted Children*, Minnesota Center for Continuation Study, University of Minnesota, 1961, pp.91-101.

Richards, I.A., Review of 'Learning To Read: The Great Debate.' *Harvard Educ. Review*, 38, (2), 1968, pp. 357-364.

Smith, F., *Reading*, Cambridge University Press, London, 1978.

Zaporozhets, A.V., The Development of perception in the preschool child. In Mussen, P.H. (Ed.) European Research in Cognitive Development. *Monographs Society Research Child Development*, 30, 1965, 82-101.

Zaporozhets, A.V. and Elkonin, D.B. (Eds.), *The Psychology of Preschool Children*, MIT press, Cambridge Massachusetts, 1971.

# Exploring Further

**Sensitively and slowly, help one child to increase his control over the directional learning needed to read and/or write.**

# 8  An Early
# Integration of Skills

Four sets of behaviour significant for reading progress have been described — attention to print, direction rules about position and movement, talking like a book, and hearing the sounds in words. As the child 'reads' his first books the teacher may observe his development in these four separate areas. She can use a check-list over a period of three to four weeks, noticing evidence of skills as they appear, or she can test the child for concepts about print when she considers him almost ready for transfer to the basic reading books.

To read a child has to make a time-space transformation. Sound patterns which follow one another in time have to be matched to letter symbol patterns spread out into space. The integration of skills cannot occur as long as the child is happily inventing the text which he is supposed to be reading.

One child, faced with the text 'so she took it to her nest to make it soft and warm' 'read' confidently 'so she took it to her hidey-hole to save it for the winter'. She had a great imagination and a feel for the skills required in reading, but several important changes needed to occur before she could read.

When Jerome Bruner (1974) wrote that 'the study of skill acquisition must take into account the serial structure of acts' he was referring to the behaviour of infants, but he could have been referring to this stage of learning to read. In the discussion of directional responses I referred to the learning of order and sequence and in the chapter on language the serial structure of sounds in words was explored. Early steps in visual scanning require the child's attention to the serial order. Controlling complex behaviours sequentially so that they can be executed slowly and smoothly at first, and automatically at a later stage, is just as much a feature of learning to read as it is of learning to hit a golf ball, or play a violin. The difficulties that some children encounter arise in this sequencing of actions, and in the coordinating of the four kinds of sequences.

## Skills

Observe the ways in which the child relates each of these four sets of behaviour, one to the other. This can be called integrating the references and the sounds of language with directional and visual cues. For success in reading all four types of behaviour must be related and focussed in a way that allows for smooth sequential progression through the continuous message of the text.

When the teacher works with a group of children who are ready to discuss a new book together, this relating of one kind of cue to another kind can be encouraged.

Any one child may have very few cues to use, but as a group and with the teacher's help, they can discover the precise message of the text. The teacher, by what she says, by her directional movements, and by directing attention to visual cues, language and to sounds, ensures that the group integrates the four sets of behaviour correctly. This is easier for the individual child because the teacher is directing the process. It will be some time before the individual child can control this relating of cues entirely by himself.

The peculiar patterns of children's attempts to match what is said with what is pointed to can be recorded. Records should be kept for several weeks because they will:

- provide a record of progress over that time
- help in evaluation of the child's readiness for book reading
- allow the observation that sequenced movement across print is smoothly and easily integrated with language responses.

The keeping of such records will help the teacher to become a more sensitive observer of the child's behaviour at this time.

## Page-matching

At first a child produces a stretch of speech as he turns a page. This is very noticeable if the book is a rather difficult one, for example a nursery rhyme, and a mismatch will occur where the pagination breaks a sentence into two parts.

**All the king's horses**            **Couldn't put Humpty**
**And all the king's men**           **Together again.**

Learning from books with such complex texts is difficult even for the intelligent child. There is too much room for error in trying to link what is said to what is written.

## Line-matching

In the following examples the child is achieving some measure of coordination of language and sequenced movement. The ability to match a line of text left to right with the correct language, locating the beginning and end of the line is a valuable achievement. The child realizes that he must match the beginning and end of what he says even if what happens in the middle is a mystery. One observer noted 'He cannot yet match one word in print to one spoken word but he likes to arrive at the last word on time and is confused if he doesn't.'

| Text: | Mother is knitting |
|---|---|
| *Child:* | *Mother is  knitting* |
| Finger: | x x       x x |

There are many ways of dealing with the mystery and children try most of them.

Text:   | My baby brother
Child:  | *My ba - by*
Finger: | x    x      x

Text:   | My baby brother
Child:  | *My little ba-by*
Finger: | x    x    x    x

The next example seems to be based on attention to letters yet achieves an appropriate sequencing of responses.

Text:   | Father is smiling
Child:  | *Father is smiling*
Finger: | x      x  x

The child is not clear what his problem is and his record may show many of these difficulties at the same time. For example:

*Letter-word confusion and syllable breaks*
Text:   | My big brother
Child:  | *My brother —*
Finger: | x    x    x

*Two responses per word and two words per response*
Text:   | My big sister
Child:  | *My big sis ter*
Finger: | x    x    x    x

*Correct word reading and syllabic breaks*
Text:   | The children are here
Child:  | √ *child-ren* √ √
Finger: | x    x    x    x x

*Talking without pointing and then matching*
Text:   |         My big sister
Child:  | *This is* √ √ √
Finger: |         x    x    x

*Word by word*
Text:   | Here is the dog
Child:  | *This* √ *a* √
Finger: | x    x x    x

Matching a spoken sentence to a single line of print is relatively easy. The beginning of the line is located and a left to right sweep accounts for the rest. Rhythm helps and the repetitive language structures in some caption books facilitate this learning.

One-line captions which began towards the top left corner of a left page, would create a correct 'position habit' for the directional movements required in reading.

The child of 4 to 6 years adopts position habits very easily and a consistent top-left starting point is therefore preferable to flexibility of layout until the child is able to use correct directional habits consistently.

## Examples of layout

When there are several rows of print on a page this is a much more difficult task. In addition to locating the top left starting point and making a left to right movement there is a return sweep to the next line to be mastered, a further step towards complete mastery of directional learning.

If the author slips a two or three-line text into the child's experience when all he has read previously has been one-line texts he has new problems. A child may fail to respond. More often he will try to solve the mystery of the new situation. The text

**Father is reading**
**the paper**

is intended to report a situation with which the child is familiar. What is strange to him is the problem of two lines of print. He may respond only to the first line.

| Text: | Father is reading |
| Child: | *Father is reading the paper* |
| Finger: | x     x x x x |

| Text: | the paper |
| *No response* | |

The second line may be treated in several different ways. He may —

- ignore it
- point to it in silence
- point to the first and speak to the second
- match one or two words and rush the rest
- draw out the last words until his finger reaches the end.

| Text: | Father is reading. |
| Child: | *Father is reading the pa* |
| Finger: | x     x x x    x   x |

| Text: | the paper |
| Child: | — —*per.* |
| Finger: | x |

Sometimes the child discovers a match of text and syllables that surprises us.

| Text: | Mother          is     talking |
| Child: | *Mother is talking on the the* |
| Finger: | x   x x        x   x |

| Text: | on the telephone |
| Child: | *tel   e   phone* |
| Finger: | x    x    x |

This example shows that the child is working on the problem — searching for possible solutions.

Published material lacks such consistency but a teacher can make sure that her own practice in class-made books is consistent. If there is a choice of readers then an order of preference might be —

- a top left start on a left page.
- top left to right one-line captions
- top left to right two-line captions
- slow introduction of further variability.

# Word and Letter Concepts

Early readers must attend to print, scan it, respond, move to another focus point, scan and respond and so on. What visual features do children use and how do they come to match oral language responses to those features.

The experiments of the Russian psychologist Luria linking the coordination of motor responding with oral language provide some guide. The motor task he used was simple: the child squeezed a rubber bulb. Luria showed a developmental progression from inability to coordinate squeezing and speaking, to coordination when the pulse of the message matched the rhythm of the squeezing. By the age of five years a child's motor responding could even be controlled by an instruction which did not have the same pulse as the squeezing action to be made.

The beginning reading task resembles Luria's task where the pulse of language matches the pulse of squeezing — Go, go, or Press, press, — except that the child must point and visually scan with the added constraint of left to right directional movement.

He must —

- break up the speech into word units
- locate the visual patterns
- move in the correct direction
- coordinate the timing of his pointing and looking with his uttering.

Young children are trying to discover how the flow of speech can be cut into word segments and matched to the flow of print.

It is false to assume that the child knows that his oral sentences are composed of word units. He has to discover what the word units of his speech are. He has to break down 'gimmethe' or 'apastate' into 'give me the' or 'half past eight' before he can match what he says to the printed text. He learns to break his speech into words separated by pauses, and tries to match units in speech to patterns in print. Sometimes he fails to find the word units.

| Child: | I see the | aeroplane / go / down |
| Text: | I see the | aeroplane |

At other times, he over-analyses:

| Child: | I see the | aer - o - plane |
| Text: | I see the | aeroplane go down |

Syllables sometimes confuse him as he matches speech to print. Some children get stranded for a time on the erroneous concept that a letter is a word, and this example shows how confusing this might be:

| Child: | This is a boy |
| Text: | A   b   o   y |

This can teach wrong associations to a child who misreads his favourite book for many weeks and establishes the erroneous habit rather firmly.

If some unusual behaviour of this kind is observed a teacher must try to decide whether it is just a temporary fluctuation or whether the child has been practising it for some weeks.

If a child is having difficulty with speech-to-print matching the teacher can increase the size of print and exaggerate the spacing. Exaggerating the spaces between words and between lines helps the child to locate himself. At the early reading stage the arrangement of words on the page should force the eye to group letters within words together and detract from the possibility of grouping across a space. Thus, the above confusion is less likely to occur with

This     is     a     boy

than it is with

This is a boy.

## Locating specific words

At this stage the teaching emphasis is on the whole sentence rather than words. Nevertheless the child soon shows that he is recognizing certain words in different contexts. When the child knows that a word is a pattern of marks he begins to locate the patterns that he knows. He finds first, last and repeated words easiest to locate. They are easier for him to 'perceive'.

| | |
|---|---|
| *Child locates first or last words:* | |
| Text: | Here        house |
| | Here is a big house |
| *Child locates repeated words:* | *is* |
| Text: | Here is my mother. |
| | Here is my sister. |
| | Here is my father. |

He also locates readily those few words he has learned to write without a copy. If a word like 'this' or 'here', 'is' or 'a' is used correctly when an alternative word would have been just as grammatical, one begins to sense that the child 'knows' that word. Here is a sample of reading behaviour from a girl aged 5:2 who had been at school for two months. An observer reported that she seemed to be using cues in the following order and from the following sources.

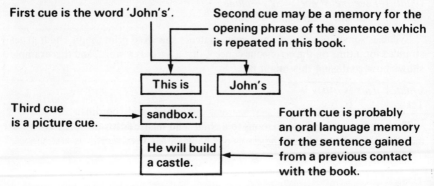

**First cue is the word 'John's'.**

**Second cue may be a memory for the opening phrase of the sentence which is repeated in this book.**

This is     John's

**Third cue is a picture cue.**     sandbox.

**Fourth cue is probably an oral language memory for the sentence gained from a previous contact with the book.**

He will build a castle.

Marlene 'read' the caption book correctly but the recorder felt that only one word, 'John's', was actually read. The probable sources of other cues are shown.

Notice that the child is using both language and visual cues and is relating these to past experience in order to select probable responses. She is entirely successful in repeating the precise message. This is good caption book behaviour. At 6:0 she was in the top 25 percent for reading progress.

# Reading the Spaces: A Sign of Progress

When the child can point one/after/the/other, and can find the words in his speech, he still has the problem of coordinating the two activities, that is, making the motor pattern of his hand coincide with the word-finding activities of his ears and eyes. Would the task be simplified by eliminating the pointing? Probably not. The location of the appropriate visual pattern to be attended to is perhaps a more difficult task than pointing.

One further difficulty has to be overcome. The activities that are integrated must be maintained for a period of time. Some children can keep at the activity once it is mastered. Others begin well, tire quickly, and their coordination, their locating, and even one-to-one correspondence slips away as fatigue takes over. Sometimes the fall-off of appropriate behaviour depends not on less effort but on distracted attention.

At first, children respond to caption books with the speed and fluency that is typical of their oral speech. As they develop skill in matching spoken words with print, fingers are used to point to those parts of the text that they suspect correspond to what they are saying. Fluency gives way to word by word reading. At that point the child over-emphasizes the breaks between words and points with his finger. He has taken a major step in integration of this early learning when his reading slows down and even becomes staccato. He may be thought of as 'reading the spaces'. He is demonstrating clearly to the observer the integration of the three sets of behaviour that have been described.

| The Eye Sees Word-space-word | The Voice Says Word-space-word | The Finger Points Word-space-word |
|---|---|---|
| Visual attention to print. | Talking like a book, composing sentences word by word. | Directional rules of position and movement. |

Rhythm can help the child to segment his speech and coordinate his speaking, pointing and looking. Here is an example of a child whose letter and word knowledge is very limited but whose awareness of 'the space between words' is emerging:

A wall
goe u

Translation: A ball goes up.

This synchronizing of skills is a high point of achievement in the early reading stage and is not behaviour to be hurriedly trained out.

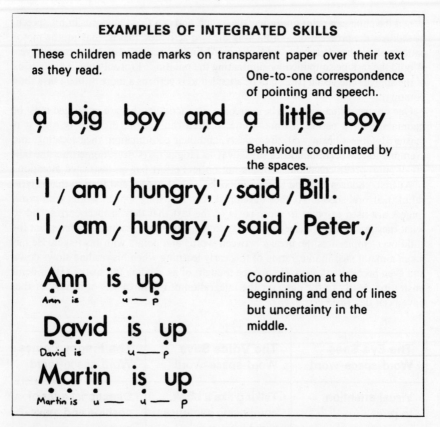

## EXAMPLES OF INTEGRATED SKILLS

These children made marks on transparent paper over their text as they read.

One-to-one correspondence of pointing and speech.

a big boy and a little boy

Behaviour coordinated by the spaces.

'I / am / hungry,' / said / Bill.

'I / am / hungry,' / said / Peter. /

Ann is up
Ann is        u — p

David is up
David is       u — p

Martin is up
Martin is   u —   u — p

Coordination at the beginning and end of lines but uncertainty in the middle.

'Reading the spaces' has been called voice-pointing. Single words are stressed and the spaces are 'heard' as distinct breaks between each word. Then when the child no longer needs to help his eyes by pointing with his finger he will, for a period, continue the voice pointing.

Voice-pointing can be used as a signal that things are coming together. It should not be taught because it would then have no value as a sign of progress. A child could be taught to read with exaggerated breaks between words merely by listening to and copying a model who did this. We would not know whether the child was using his eyes for locating cues in an appropriate manner.

Developmentally there is usually a gradual transition in good readers from finger-pointing, to staccato reading, to light stress of word breaks, and finally, to phrasing. The fast learners make this transition so rapidly that it may hardly be noticed. Slow learners may take several weeks to coordinate voice and movement, a further extended period for this to retreat to staccato reading and a slow, gradual change to dependence on eyes alone. But if the child has passed through this sequence of behaviour we can be reasonably confident that his visual scanning patterns have become systematically organized for the reading task. On the other hand, children who appear to 'read' fluently may not be visually responding to features in the print in any systematic or precise way.

A search of observation records in one research sample showed that three weeks prior to promotion to the basic reading series 40 percent of the children had begun to exaggerate the breaks between words, and a further 9 percent were children who had already passed through the stage of finger- and voice-pointing and were dependent on visual analysis alone. Thus, for 49 percent of the sample this learning took place in the early reading period.

One group of children had particular difficulty with the integration learning. Those children who typically reacted quickly and spoke quickly were sometimes unable to slow their movement across print to a pace which permitted the very necessary matching of speech to visual patterns. After 7 months at school, one boy's observation record read:

> *Began the first page slowly matching correctly, but then speeded up, dropped pointing and invented the text with only approximate line-matching. Asked to point to what he reads he can for a brief period slow down but then races ahead and drops the movement and matching component out of the reading task.*

The aurally oriented child whose visual attention is hard to control has difficulty in discovering the 'match' between his language and the printed text. Sometimes the coordination is difficult because of motor inadequacies. One record carried the observation 'Pointing seems to be the stumbling block'. But as long as a child cannot locate the word he is saying in the line of print, he will remain a non-reader. One week a boy's record carried the comment 'speech is far too fast for locating words'. The following week the boy complained, 'I can't keep up with the words with my hands. They're too fast' (i.e. his own speech).

In contrast, the observer's comments on a child who was succeeding with this early integration of skills was: 'Word controlled; voice-pointing; perfect matching.'

# Word by Word Reading and Pointing

When are these behaviours appropriate and when do they indicate a problem? In the records of children who *succeeded* in learning to read these behaviours were present. Both pointing and word by word reading were useful for the beginning reader who was taught by a language experience approach. Part of the learner's task under these instruction conditions is to isolate word units in his speech, and in the printed text, and match the two.

However, research studies of children who fail in learning to read suggest that the children read word by word, that they point with their fingers and that these behaviours should be eliminated at the outset and avoided. The implication is that they cause the reading failure.

Careful observation of children who are learning to read has shown that as the child makes the transfer from pre-reading books to reading books and for some variable time thereafter, it is appropriate for the child to strengthen his locating behaviour by pointing with his hand or his voice. Once he has established accurate locating responses with his eyes alone there is reason to discard the finger pointing and to step up the demand for fluency. Word by word reading is not to be hurriedly trained out unless the teacher is certain that the child is visually locating the words he is saying. Some slower children were deprived of the very props they had spontaneously discovered when teachers forbade them to use their fingers or insisted that they use only a card as a guide to the line being read.

Questionable procedures like pointing and word by word reading, memorizing the text or depending on picture cues are techniques to be approved as long as they facilitate the development of new insights. By implication, since they are props rather than techniques to be retained in the mature behaviour system, they must at some point give way to better responses. Pointing gives way to accurate visual locating, auditory memory for text gives way to visual memory for form, word by word reading gives way to phrasing and anticipation of sentence structure, picture cues give way to semantic and linguistic cues and letter-sound relationships. It is the direction that development is taking that is vital, not the questionable procedure itself.

The reappearance of behaviour like this long after the developmental transitions should have been made, may be regarded as diagnostic signs that the task is in some new sense difficult.

# Search, Check and Error Correction

In research records of book-reading behaviour when a child was trying to read he sometimes rejected an error response and tried again. Such spontaneous self-correction was very important for reading progress.

Earlier we saw that a child not yet matching his speech and visual behaviour might be content to read 'aeroplane-go-down' for 'aeroplane' and not know he has made an error. But a child may be vaguely aware that an error has occurred. When he can 'read the spaces' and match what he says accurately with the word patterns of his text he has several new means of detecting errors.

## The finger signals an error

The child sometimes finds he has more speech patterns than word patterns; 'There's no more words.'

Child: | *I like my Father*  (**Self-correction**)
Text: | My Father

If he over-analyses his speech he is then one visual pattern short in the line.

Child: | *I am a pi- lot*  (**Self-correction**)
Text: | I am a pilot.

If he hesitates and tries again, if he reconstitutes his speech response to make it fit, a self-correction strategy is beginning to form. The child who learns to take self-correcting action because of such mis-matching has made another big advance.

## The eye signals an error

A child may utter a sentence which is semantically and syntactically possible but which is incongruous with the picture. This leads him to rephrase his sentence. Visual cues enter into the self-correction process.

Child: | *Country school*  *What's the bus doing there?*
Text: | School bus

Where the child knows only a few words such as 'Father' or 'car' he may give a response which only checks these words.

Child: | *Father goes*  *to his car*
Text: | Father is  *in the car*

The visual cues and the speech responses are matched within the limits of the child's knowledge of two words. But even this knowledge can produce an awareness of error when a known word is uttered but does not appear in the text.

Child: | *This is a farm*  *Why does it say 'Here?'*
Text: | Here is a farm

Discovering errors in this way makes the child conscious of the important fact that print carries one particular message which he must reconstruct from all possible messages. It forces him to choose between alternatives, to make decisions on the basis of cues, from print, from language, and from direction and position.

At this point, when the new entrant begins to construct his sentences word by word to coincide with the precise message of the text, he tries to correct his own mistakes. This usually coincides with his teacher's promoting him to a basic reading book. For the 'average' child it has taken six months to learn the early reading skills. These transitions must be observed by teachers sensitively and must not be hurried unduly. They should be fostered deliberately when appropriate behaviour fails to develop in a reasonable time, usually by 5:6 years.

Some children do not notice their errors. They invent the text fluently and confidently. The reader will need a kind of inventiveness when he anticipates a passage incorrectly and has to rephrase it to match exactly with the text. Although it can lead to error, inventing is behaviour one can do something with, unlike stalling and no response. A shy child who is too hesitant to respond to his books is hard to help, but the child who continues to regard reading time as an invitation to construct creatively his own story has completely missed the point — that reading is a matter of extracting, relating and processing cues to decode a precise message.

# What is Progress?

Should the teacher be pleased with this reading?

Child: | Mummy cooks
Text: | Mother is baking

One cannot tell without an indication of the direction and pace of this particular child's learning. The response is semantically correct and it matches with the picture. Perhaps the letter 'M' provided a cue, or possibly some memory of the story. In a child who had not previously used picture cues, letter cues or memory for the story, such a response could indicate progress. But if this type of paraphrase has been typical of the child's responding for some weeks or months then rather than a step forward this response may represent a stamping-in or rehearsal of inappropriate behaviour.

In the early reading stage important reading behaviour is being learned. Children seem to progress in four sets of behaviour

- visual attention to print
- directional rules about movement and position
- talking like a book
- hearing sound sequences.

## What are the signs of progress?

One signal that the child has reached the hurdle of integrating several skills is that his reading no longer sounds like fluent natural speech. One may observe:

- *Very slow and/or more deliberate reading.* For example one little girl read me 'We have three goldfish' very slowly and then added quietly, 'I know what that says.'
- *Word-by-word reading that is correct.* The reading is controlled at the level of individual words. One child gave evidence of this. She was struggling with the recurrence of the word *be* for the third time. She said, 'I get (forget) that word all the time.'

- *Increased use of pointing.* The coordination of several skills is made easier by pointing behaviour.
- *Unusual pauses.* It is as if the child were checking or sorting out something.
- *A more serious attitude is adopted by the child to the reading task.*
- *Searching and checking are further signs of progress.* The child's response becomes controlled by the text in preference to the picture. One little boy showed an early tendency for careful checking. He expected the texts to begin a sentence with *Father.* He sounded an initial *f* sound as if expecting the text to begin with *Father* but the word was *Mother.* He knew the word *Mother* so he stopped, looked at the picture, found Father in the picture but not Mother, looked back at the text and said *Mother.* Obviously his reading response was controlled by the printed form of the word, not by the picture.

Then, when the initial signs of several behaviours being controlled at the same time are present we can begin to notice examples of children trying to relate two sets of information, one to the other.

The following example demonstrates *integration of present experience with a previous encounter displaced in space and time.* The text was,

**I can ride**
**I can ride my bicycle**

Betty was unable to read *I.* She went spontaneously back three pages without prompting looking for a remembered instance of *I.* She re-read *Here I* . . . stopped, went forward three pages and read *I come* . . . 'No!' She studied the picture and said, *I ride.* Her mother coming to the rescue said 'That's *ride* but you have to read this,' pointing to *can.* Betty read two lines, *I - can - ride, I can ride* . . . but she was now stuck on the word *my.* She turned back one page, asked her mother to read *See my bicycle,* repeated softly *my* as if detaching it from that text and storing it in her memory, turned back to the page she was working on, and completed the text.

Relating a word to a previous encounter, searching for more cues, attempting to relate form to sound, and succeeding, this processing of cues helps the child to categorize sound-letter relationships in ways that are probably more effective than traditional 'phonics'.

Even knowing for certain that you don't know the answer can be an indication that information held in memory is being checked.

The word he wants to read is *were.*

He pauses.
He shakes his head (meaning, perhaps, he doesn't know it).
He tries *went.*
He says 'I don't know that word.'

This can be contrasted with the following example.

Child: | *You must see Scot home*
Text: | You must send Scot home

The context, sentence form and some letter-sound relationships are undisturbed by the error. This causes the child no disturbance he does not work on it, and he does not correct himself or learn from the incident.

When a text becomes word-controlled in the sense that some of the words are known to have a precise identity, there is further awareness of error when a known word pattern does not match with what is said.

Child: | I    *it doesn't even say 'I' there.*
Text:  | Wake

The achievement of matching techniques provides opportunities to relate cues from several sources to the task of decoding the precise message. The integration of several simultaneously available behaviours is achieved — saying, moving, matching and usually checking.

Another type of comparison occurs in the process of self-correction as the child directs his attention to a *discrimination between two words*.

Child: *ride* | SC    *come* | SC    *horse* | SC    *This* | SC    *little* | SC
Text:   run     can      here     The      like

# Controlling Sequences of Responses

The complex, integrated sequences of behaviour in reading are controlled by particular features in the text that are recognized. At first amid varying degrees of uncertainty the child locates islands of certainty.

At the Instant Reader stage the child may respond to the dot of the i or the capital M in Mother. This is the hitching-post to which he ties the rest of his response, hoping that he is correct.

In the familiar story the child locates a word he knows and builds a response around it.

Then the child's reading of the text comes to be controlled by particular words even though he can only recognize one or two. This might be called word-controlled inventing. For example in the text

**I am sweeping,**
**I am running,**
**I am jumping,**
**I am hopping,**

the child's behaviour may be controlled by his recognition of the word 'I' or the word 'am'. However ineptly he matches what he says with the text, at the point where he utters the word 'I' all his behaviours are coordinated. The child may not even know that this is happening. The first word that the child learns to control is usually his name but the next is one of the frequently occurring words in the text. One example would be 'is' which has a distinctive and relatively simple form. Or it might be a word which is fostered by the teaching programme such as 'Here'.

*When is the stage of integrating these early skills past?* The early quick responses based on memory for oral language are displaced by slower-acting cognitive modes of functioning as the child tries to use cues, and cross-check his information. When the child starts to think about the reading task, to structure it cognitively, his reading becomes slower but he has much greater ability to verify his responses as a result. He checks a response against other things he knows.

As he becomes more skilled at extracting the message while seeing, saying, moving and checking, the child's reading then increases in pace. The child's phrasing improves so that the word by word reading tends to disappear although breaks between words are still heard. As the child reads one notices the grouping and phrasing that the child is doing, rather than word by word reading. A comment indicating such a transition to more fluent reading was 'an interesting voice, soft and with expression'. In one sense the first major struggle with reading is over.

# An Easier Way to Reduce Reading Failures?

Waiting for 'readiness' will not organize early reading behaviour in a way that provides a good foundation for later progress.

Having a 'good programme' for a large group and not watching individuals learn will result in the survival of the fittest. Those who can, will learn; those who cannot, will become confused or develop false concepts and handicapping strategies.

There is nothing in my research results to suggest that contact with printed language should be withheld from a 5-year-old child on the grounds that he is immature. (The intelligence quotients of the group studied ranged from 85 to 156.)

There is much research to show that training perceptual skills on pictures and geometric forms does not readily carry over to reading progress. This is probably because the child is not able to make the translation to the reading task. There is a strong case for training the immature child on the task of printed language and for giving him supplementary tuition of a more controlled, detailed and structured kind in his area of weakness.

However, if a child shows immaturity in some or all of the four sets of behaviour, the directional learning, visual scanning, hearing the sounds, or the language aspects of the task, it is consistent with current research on normal children of this age that his new task (reading) be approached through as many channels as possible, so that strong skills can support the strengthening of the weak ones. Rather than leave the child who is poor in language playing in the developmental group, he needs an introduction to the early reading stage like other children and, in addition, he needs more attention and enriched experience in the area of his weakness.

The sets of learning observed during the early reading stage are fostered by contacts with written language. The visual perception of print, the directional learning, the special types of language used in books, and the synchronized matching of spoken word units with written word units will only be learned in contact with printed language. Individual differences will emerge as the fast learners master these tasks in a few weeks while the average and slow learners take much longer.

However, it should be noted that when a child takes six months to establish a consistent left to right approach to lines of print, he will already have had many opportunities to practise wrong responses. The fast learner who mastered the habit early is saved from such error practice. Slow learners cannot be pushed with undue haste into learning new skills, which they need to build slowly, but there are dangers in leaving them practising poor procedures for prolonged periods. One might even suggest that six months of muddlement is more than than enough to create poor readers out of school entrants with average or superior intelligence. Certainly, some planned action to speed up the learning of the early reading stage should be initiated after the child has been at school six months.

To avoid making wrong decisions about children, since both undue haste or prolonged delay can be detrimental to the child's progress in reading, careful records of the tentative beginnings of reading behaviour are needed (see Chapter 9 of this book and Clay, 1979) and smaller classes will be required so that teachers may become more sensitive observers of this early behaviour, and are able to reinforce individual efforts.

# References and Further Reading

Bruner, J.S. Organization of early skilled action *Child Development*, 44, 1973, 1-11.
Clay, Marie M., *The Early Detection of Reading Difficulties: A Diagnostic Survey with Recovery Procedures*, Heinemann Educational Books, Auckland, 1979.

# Exploring Further

**Observe and record the ways in which a child relates four sets of behaviour, one to another — attention to print, sound segments in words, directional rules about position and movement, and talking like a book.**

# Part 3

# First Reading Books

# 9 Learning to Read with Natural Language Texts

The construction of texts for reading acquisition has benefitted little from research efforts in recent years. Publishers have responded to new enthusiasms of theorists and teachers and new texts graded according to 'new' principles come onto the market from time to time. However, there is little basis for deciding why one text is more difficult than another. Many factors have been shown to be related to text difficulty — vocabulary, sentence structure, meaning or concept-load, conventions of printing (such as justified print versus a sentence per line), or changes in language style, such as an increase in embedded clauses — yet the well-established formulas for readability cannot take many of these into account at one time. It is in beginning reading that the greatest liberties have been taken with language in well-intentioned attempts to simplify the task for the young learner and grade texts with a gentle increase in difficulty.

The Alexander Turnbull Library collection of early infant readers dating from 1880 is described by Price (1975) in an article called "Lo' I am an ox". That title is taken from the first page of the reader published in the 1890's where the young child is introduced to reading by using only two letter words and producing texts like

**Is my ox to go in as we go by?**

To illustrate the liberties we take in writing beginning reader texts, some are included here with comments. A comparison of the sentence patterns in the examples shows that the written language can be simplified in many different ways.

| | |
|---|---|
| Fries, C. C., *Linguistics and Reading*, Holt, Rinehart and Winston, Inc., London, 1963. | Gray, W. S., Artley, A. S. & Arbuthnot, M. H., *Guess Who?* Exeter, Wheaton, 1951. |
| PAT<br>RAT<br>BAT<br>    A RAT<br>    A BAT<br>PAT A RAT<br>BAT A RAT<br>PAT A FAT CAT<br>PAT A FAT RAT | Oh, oh, oh !<br>See Puff jump down.<br>See Puff jump and go.<br>Jump down, funny Puff.<br>Jump down.<br>Jump down.<br>Go, go, go. |
| In this text the visual form and letter-sound associations are controlled on the just-noticeable-difference principle. | This is a controlled vocabulary text for emphasis on repetition of sight vocabulary in 'meaningful' stories. |

Gibson, C. M. & Richards, I. A., *First Steps in Reading*, Pocket Books, New York, 1957.

This is a hat.
It is this man's hat.
It is his hat.
This hat is his hat.
That is a hat.
It is that man's hat.
It is a hat.
That hat is his hat.

In this text the letters, letter-sound association, and the function of words in sentences are controlled.

Daniels, S. C. & Diack, H., *The Royal Road Readers*, Chatto & Windus, 1954.

I am Frank Dodd. My job was to go into the forests to get animal skins. I had just slept in my tent but now the sun was up, so I put my pack on my back and went on.

The phonic-word approach of these texts stresses letter-sound associations in regular words but meaning and interest are also important.

---

*Ready to Read* texts, Department of Education, Wellington, 1963.

BOOK 1
Bill is asleep.
'Wake up, Bill,'
said Peter.
Sally is asleep.
'Wake up, Sally,'
said Mother.

BOOK 4
'Where is Timothy?
I am looking for Timothy,'
said Susan.
'He is not in the sandpit.
He went away,' said Tai.

BOOK 15
'I know I am only a little
mouse and you are the king of
all the animals,' he said.
'But, if only you will let me
go the day will come when I can
do something to help you.'

This text is relatively uncontrolled except in the gradual introduction and repetition of basic vocabulary, i.e. function words. Speech forms are intended to be close to what is natural for children aged 5:0 - 6:0.

Rasmussen, D. E. & Goldberg, L., *S.R.A.*, Chicago, 1964.

Wag bit the net.
'I can rip the net,' said Wag.
Wag bit and bit,
and the net began to rip.
'I did it! I did it!' said Wag.
Wag the dog ran to dig.
But Peg the pig did a jig.

In this text letter-sound associations are important but it is claimed that they are presented in 'natural' sentences as 'interesting' stories.

---

Hart, N.W.M. and Walker, R.F. *Mount Gravatt Reading Series* Addison-Wesley, Sydney, 1977.

Soon I saw another leaf on my plant.
And then I saw another one.
So I had three leaves, and
I saw more leaves coming.

The text is compiled from lists of two and three word sequences from oral language samples of children of school entry age.

In the 1970's there has been a call to use texts that reflect the child's natural language and to avoid the sterile qualities and uncompromising imperatives of the controlled vocabulary texts; like

**Run, Janet, run.**
**See John.**
**Come here, John.**

*What is a natural language text?* It tries to retain all the qualities and cues of a child's natural language, so that the language processes he has operated for three or more years can guide not only his spoken language but also his reading. Wherever possible all the cues a child is used to responding to in speech should be present in the text. *The difficulties to be avoided are those that arise from the complex aspects of the language which he does not yet use in his speech.* Language experience approaches to beginning reading have used the child's language as a starting point but have been unable to exercise control over vocabulary, sentence structure and concepts in order, to achieve a sequencing of learning opportunities.

Another recent emphasis by some authors of texts is attention to messages which carry meaning for the young reader. Instead of texts like

**Pale ale**   or
**BAT A FAT CAT**

it is assumed that alert school entrants understand a great deal about life around them. They come to school knowing many things about the world they live in. Good teaching uses that knowledge and that alertness, and encourages the child to respond to the meaningfulness of the stories read to or by them. In some reading programmes the understanding of the messages in books is given top priority.

To the child the message is more important than letters, sounds or words which are, of course, only the means to the message. Many published reading schemes concentrate on the more mechanical aspects of reading — knowing the letters and sounds.

Reading is made up of patterns of complex behaviour. Given the infinite variety of texts an adult has to be flexible to be a reader. You have to have a brain full of alternative strategies. It is more complex than finding the fault in a car engine or understanding why this week's cake collapsed. Any author who claims to have described an easy route to reading deserves very critical appraisal. Proceed with extreme caution. It is possible that 90 percent of the important and necessary learning has been left out of any 'easy' programme — left to the child to pick up, or the teacher to catch up with in her supplementary programme.

## Examples of natural language texts

There is a dilemma in this topic too. Spoken language is not the same as written language. We do not speak as we write. They can be described as different dialects because they use a different vocabulary, different conventions (for example, cannot, can't) and different structures for sentences. The author has to choose language that is more explicit, and express it in more formal ways to make up for not having his listener in an actual situation; with facial expressions, gestures, information, stress and the chance to rephrase to overcome his listener's failure to understand.

There have been two approaches to this mismatch between spoken and written language.

Firstly authors have recorded actual language and constructed early reading books with the structures and vocabulary that children use (Hart, Walker, Gray, 1977). The Queensland scheme was built upon an analysis of the two and three word sequences only, which would not be considered by any linguist as a valid approach to the English language structure. But, accepting for the moment the texts as good replicas of children's spoken language, what are we doing by presenting them as reading acquisition texts? The pupils will acquire expectancies for that kind of language. They will in all probability, find actual book language difficult. Perhaps it is not necessary to create false expectancies.

A second approach is to prepare the child for book language early by urging parents and preschools to enrich the child's language and experience by many shared experiences with books. This builds many appropriate expectancies — about stories about what to see in books, about the language of books. If the child lacks this experience on entry to school, teachers can provide many shared experiences with books as a preparation for reading. In this approach the assumption of rich experiences with books leads to a call for using actual story books in place of graded readers. (I will return to some further problems with this later.) This approach is sometimes described as developing a literacy set in preschool children.

I have no quarrel with that as an ideal, but I have sympathy for the many children who ought to have had the experiences such a programme assumes and who have been neglected. I suspect that every child must learn to link his preschool language skills to his school reading activities, and the child who has not been read to from appropriate books for preschoolers must learn to enrich his spoken language dialect by the addition of written language alternatives.

## Little Books

All teachers of reading acquisition classes have seen the problems of children who make progress slowly and who know they are being held on one book because they are unable to read. A major gain in the publication of readers has been the Little Book approach. Each small book contains one story of 100 to 200 words. There are several books at one level of difficulty. These allow for flexible movement of individual children vertically up through the difficulty sequence or horizontally to parallel supplementary material of the same level of difficulty. Although the move to 'little books' was initiated in the interest of children's morale and motivation, they have achieved another important change. They are aligned with a change in theory about the reading process.

Horizontal shifts would, according to older theory, allow the child to practise the vocabulary many more times. In more modern explanations of reading progress, horizontal shifts provide the child with *more opportunities to practise reading strategies and to put complex activities into smoothly operating sequences*, before an increase of text difficulty presents new challenges.

In the research studies which provided the background to this book the children were using the *Ready to Read* series, first published in 1963 by the New Zealand Department of Education. In several respects this series differs from other beginning reader series. They begin with twelve little books, each containing one story. These are grouped in ascending order of difficulty as Red 1, 2, 3; Yellow 1, 2, 3; Blue 1, 2, 3; and Green 1, 2, 3. They are followed by six longer books each of about 2,000 words and containing 4 to 6 stories. At each level there are many commercially published supplementary readers (see References page 169 for some supporting texts for teachers).

On the whole pupils who make progress slowly, do not feel they are being held on one book which they cannot master. A new and perhaps an easier book presents fresh opportunities to leave old failures behind. Children do recognize signs of their success and failure in reading, even at 5 years, as these comments from parents' diaries indicate. (They refer to a different series of reading books.)

---

*He tells me how he would love to be on Book 5 and everyone else is on Book 5. He is straining to finish Book 4.*

---

*A great achievement now Book 1 is finished. He is very pleased and talks continually about being on Book 2... This has been a great boost to him. A new lease of life in printing and reading is at last taking place.*

---

When 'Little Books' are used for beginning reading this joy in accomplishment comes to the child more often.

# A Gradient of Difficulty

An advantage of a field-tested basic reading series is that it exposes the children to new challenges, at a pace that fosters an increasing control over richer and more varied texts. This provides an essential core to a reading programme.

Critics say that graded series of reading books simplify texts in various ways that make them boring, trivial with awkward language and over-controlled at the letter, word or sentence level. Children's story books on the other hand are meant to be enjoyed by children. Some teachers have used a judicious selection of story books to provide a gradient of difficulty to replace a graded reading series. But it is doubtful whether *all teachers* or *all children* can free themselves from the advantages of a graded series. It provides a set of marker buoys to indicate the progress being made. If the texts in that series have, heuristically, a gradient of difficulty, then until we are better able to characterize the difficulty level of story texts we probably need a core series to provide us with benchmarks to progress.

There are good reasons for much imaginative teaching and many interesting excursions away from that basic series and into judiciously chosen material of high interest and better literary quality when this is possible, and there are teaching techniques as simple as familiarizing children with the plot, the language and the characters that will increase children's control temporarily over a story they really enjoy.

In New Zealand schools story books chosen for their memorable quality, high interest and special satisfactions in language, are 'enlarged' or 'blown up' into a 'big' version with big print that allows every child in a reading group to see the detail of letters and words. Enlarged text makes it possible for a large group of children to participate and share in the pleasures of the story being read to them and at the same time enjoy a clear view of print detail.

The text of the enlarged book is an exact copy of the original. As far as possible the original line layout is preserved. This helps the children transfer back to the original small book, when reading it to themselves.

The texts are illustrated but are not necessarily elaborate, exact versions of the original book.

Teachers select from a range of papers — brown, white or coloured — to make the books. Usually the paper is doubled to add lasting quality and light cardboard covers back and front help to protect the pages. The layout of the original trade book guides the format — square, rectangular etc. They are always assembled so that they can be used as a conventional book is used, that is, pages turned and text read with left page before a right-hand page.

The book is stapled together down the spine with heavy duty staples and this is usually bound with book cloth for extra strength.

An easel (designed to hold a small chalkboard) is used to display the book for working from. A strong cardboard backing sheet and bulldog clips hold it in place.

The children sit in an informal group on the carpet in front of the easel with the teacher seated on a small chair to one side of the enlarged book. In this way all obtain a clear view.

The materials used for shared book experience are continuously and readily available for long periods in classrooms so the children are able to return frequently to re-read a wide variety of familiar material in this enlarged form.

I recently used *Green Eggs and Ham* (Seuss, 1960) in a reading recovery programme with a 6-year-old problem reader who could not hope to read it, given his very small reading vocabulary. But his spoken language was very good and he adored the story. It was too complex and the text was too varied for him to memorize it completely but his expectancy for the repetitive lines was quickly built up with shared reading. (I read a page and he read a page.) To get it right he had to keep a strict control over the visual cues. This was what he had been unable to do — pay visual attention. *Green Eggs and Ham* did what the graded series had failed to do; it used his strengths (language and memory for language patterns he heard), kept him interested and active on the task, and forced him to work on his weakness (visual attention to cues to check on his language expectations). For another child the constant play on words and rhymes would have been a frustrating fiasco. For this child it was the right book at the right moment.

## Vocabulary

In a graded series of readers control is exercised over which words are introduced, how frequently they are repeated, and the rate at which new words appear. This controls the gradient of difficulty in these dimensions and brings with these controls the problems of unnatural language, belonging neither to the spoken nor the written dialect and sometimes referred to as *primerese*.

The *Ready to Read* books broke with these traditions in an interesting way.

Two types of vocabulary are used in these stories. There are basic vocabulary words, 63 of the small, difficult and frequently-occurring words of English. These words are introduced gradually and repeated frequently. Children need not be kept on one book until they know every word in it. They meet these basic words again in subsequent books in other contexts. As the child encounters the basic vocabulary again and again he will tend to build up fast recognition responses.

The second type of vocabulary is introduced for the interest it carries, and is, in a sense, expendable. The child reads 'escalator', 'Viscount' (an aeroplane), or 'shouted' in one book but does not need that word again. The writer of the books believed that, stimulated by the 117 interest words, the child found the harder basic words falling into place. Basic words are introduced at the rate of about 6 per book and interest word loads vary from 5 to 16 per book. It is also recommended that from the early stages the children should be encouraged to use various reading skills to work out unknown words. This is in direct contrast to the practice adopted for sight vocabulary reading books when words were taught ahead of the reading.

Despite early scepticism this has proved a workable set of assumptions. Children can learn to read well by this approach. And as a result, we can experiment with stories and poetry a little more because, in written language the same principles hold. The heavy-duty vocabulary accounts for a large percentage of any text so, in well-chosen literature stories, the basic words are the heavy duty words and the special vocabularies can be treated as interest words, expendable rather than having to be learned for all time.

As far as possible new words are introduced in 'significant contexts'. The illustration might suggest a meaning for an unknown word, or the climax of the story, or the humour expressed might highlight the new word. A word like 'after' was considered to be colloquially familiar to the child in the phrase 'Look after Timothy', and only later would it be used in the less significant context of 'after lunch . . . . ' If a child does not recall the word quickly in an unfamiliar context he can be reminded of the earlier story containing the word. He is asked to recall stories and incidents which give these words context and meaning, rather than to engage in isolated word study. This practice is supported by the principle that young children tend to learn things first in relation to a specific context and such learning gradually gains independence from its initial context.

A deliberate attempt was made to avoid introducing close together words which children confuse. Therefore 'was' and 'saw' were kept apart, and so were 'house' and 'home'. This is supported by a general teaching principle, that gross differences are easier to learn than fine ones and should precede them.

## Punctuation

Punctuation was used without fuss from the beginning as it provides cues which help to organize reading behaviour. A quarter of the children at 5 years, half at 6 years and almost all at 7 years say that a full-stop 'tells you when you've said enough'. It is a very important signal and its function is probably learned during creative writing lessons. One study of 7-year-olds showed that pausing and falling pitch at full-stops were important features of good fluent reading and were absent from the records of poor readers. The good oral reader hesitates at the end of a sentence so that his voice may express one thought clearly before he starts the next sentence with a new thought. Poor oral readers tend to neglect proper phrasing and consequently pay less attention to meanings and punctuation. Children's writing also illustrates their attention to punctuation. Notice the approximation to quotation marks in this example.

The man seid 'Go!"

## Active problem-solving

The changing content and contexts of such Little Books and good supplementary readers discourage repetitive responses to the same type of text and force the children to think as they read, recognizing familiar words in new contexts. They encourage an active and constructive approach to reading rather than a passive recalling of 'sight' words. This active searching and checking is a valuable foundation for progressive gains in reading skill.

With this kind of text the young reader develops the expectation that all reading will make sense and that he can use a variety of cues — the pictures, his understanding of the story, the context in which the word appears, and its letter-sound features.

One approach to instruction for this type of text is that teaching does not need to precede the reading of the text. Teaching can take place effectively when the problem arises during a group lesson as a small group of children read the book with the teacher. The teacher helps the children to look at words (using a small blackboard), make comparisons, look at beginning letters, use the context, predict from the story, or even use the picture. When the trouble-shooting has been done, and ways of solving difficulties explored, the teacher can decide whether further opportunities for practice of particular skills on that type of problem should be provided for the group or for individual children.

A child does not need to recognize a word in isolation before he can read it in text. Because he reads the word using meaning and context on several occasions he can come gradually to attribute a particular identity to that word standing alone. After an accumulation of experiences with the word in context the child can add it to his reading vocabulary. There are particular advantages in this learning sequence.

When the word is encountered in a new context, the visual memory will tend to revive memories of the grammatical and meaning contexts that have commonly occurred with that word in the past. This should increase fluency in reading and help with the decoding.

If these procedures work, and I believe they do, then the method encourages the pupils to depend on their own solving abilities, and to think flexibly. English presents so many exceptions to any rule that such a flexible problem-solving approach to reading should be necessary, as this example demonstrates:

**A little boy came running out of the woods.**
**He had tears in his coat and tears in his eyes.**

Some experiments point to an advantage in training children to read texts with variable rather than constant letter-sounds correspondence because a mental set for diversity' helps the transfer of learning to other new words. Natural language texts, compared with phonetically controlled texts, have variable letter-sound relationships. The main emphases are

● reading for meaning
● teaching at points of difficulty
● knowing words in grammatical and meaning contexts before they are learned in isolation
● dealing flexibly with problems.

All these relate to another major tenet of the writer of the reading scheme and the reading books — that separate reading skills such as using picture and context clues, phonic analysis, structural analysis, and so on, create artificial divisions in reading. Children who read confidently and intelligently must use all these aids together and interchangeably. This coordination of strategies is the most difficult and critical task in learning to read.

## Letter-sound correspondence

There are several reasons why this text has very little to say about the use of phonic cues in reading. The children observed in several longitudinal studies in New Zealand were being taught to read in a programme where historical tradition, the new texts, and the instructional procedures together minimized an emphasis on phonics.

The vocabulary of the Little Books includes words beginning with most of the consonants and some of the consonant blends. The child can be taught to work out a new word for himself, using context and the way a word begins. Attention to different endings will distinguish words like 'look, looked and looking.' A beginning is made with help in attending to the root word and to the variations. For any child with articulation difficulties or immature language this is enough emphasis on the isolation of sounds and sound clusters between 5 and 6 years. Analysis of sounds and blending, and structural analysis and blending can be taught in addition to the use of context, comprehension and initial letter skills but the books are not constructed to emphasize an analytic sounding approach to word attack.

What units of language do New Zealand teachers of first year classes stress? Here are the combined answers of 11 teachers:

| TEACHERS RANK THE IMPORTANCE OF UNITS STUDIED | |
| --- | --- |
| Sentences | 1 |
| Words | 2 |
| Phrases | 3= |
| Initial Sounds | 3= |
| Labels or Names | 5 |
| Letters, alphabet names | 6= |
| Medial or final clusters of sounds | 6= |

By using simple sentences as reading texts, teachers permit children to practise integrating their responding to letters, to words, and to phrases. Within the sentences the child can attend to words. Within the context of meaning he can visually explore first letters. He can read for meaning but examine detail if need be. He can 'drive in top gear and change down to a lower gear' at new or difficult parts of the text. The child is being asked to use all his skills on the run to extract sense from a printed text however simple.

One criticism of this approach to reading instruction is that it does not state boldly that the teaching of phonic cues is an important part of the programme.

The i.t.a. research, and more recent research, suggest that a forthright approach to teaching, and reinforcing, letter-sound relationships is one important aspect of teaching reading that has been too much neglected in the past. Specific ways of organizing phonic cue training and insight should be given more attention wrote Hemming (1971).

Yet the child of 5:0 to 6:0 has almost no prior experience in segmenting the sounds within words so he has to learn to hear those sounds, (see page 63). This is difficult learning for the slow learning child.

From a study of fifth grade readers Borganz (1974) suggests that to prepare students for the changes needed in word perception as older readers, we should train them to search for *the most economical stimulus* held by the orthography. Reading should be seen as a problem-solving activity involving search and testing at any level of language rather than a mere focus upon sound sequences.

The success of the children studied and recent developments in the theory of the reading process (Smith, 1978) makes it doubtful that teaching a set of simple letter-sound-associations bears much relationship to the very complex psychological analysis of sound cues that successful readers carry out. When well-designed research records how children use sound-symbol relationships in reading continuous texts rather than how quickly children can be taught to sound out single words by single letters we will be better able to make bold statements about 'phonic cue training'. For too long teachers have assumed they know what 'phonics' were and what 'phonics' did. Linguists and psychologists have been less certain.

Letter-sound associations are very useful because —

● as first letter cues they narrow uncertainty and limit the possible responses.

● they are the smallest discriminating units (bit/pit, bin/bit, bit/bet) which are at times the critical cues, especially for many three letter words.

● close to the beginning of instruction the child associates letter clusters with sound groups and uses these larger units, (ed, thr, ing) in reading new words. This happens for many letter clusters that are not specifically taught.

● the mature reader only rarely uses letter-sound associations in their simplest form.

● dependence on letter-sound associations is a low-level strategy which retards later reading progress around the level of the third year of instruction, i.e. the child does not overcome it and re-organize his knowledge of single letter-sound associations into a strategy for searching for meaning. If he is to recognize the regularities of the spelling patterns and meanings in words that change their sound patterns, like rise/risen, baron/baronial, this shift is critical.

When we do wish to pay instructional attention to letter clusters Venezky (1974) provides guidance about the difficulties. He says

'The problems in defining "regular" and "irregular" are solved by simply throwing out these terms and adopting the more precise labels "predictable" and "unpredictable", along with their various subclasses. For the educator, the task then becomes one of deciding at any level of reading or spelling instruction which words contain patterns that can be transferred to other words, which contain frequently occurring but nontransferable patterns, and which words should be taught as isolated whole units.'

There is another important reason why this text has little to say about 'phonic cue' use. The behaviour described was recorded objectively as children read. Neither the records of 5-year-olds nor the 7-year-olds showed evidence of letter-sound associations being used in more than 5 percent of error processing. In tests of letter identification children gave phonic associations for 2 percent of their correct replies. The error analyses show that 43 percent of the errors made by children in the first year of instruction had letter-sound correspondence with the text, while in the third year, 80 percent of the errors constrained to match some (but not all) letter-sound relationships. Obviously letter-sound relationships, singly or in chunks are usable cues in reading and the New Zealand child, despite the fact that his programme does not emphasise this kind of relationship, increases his efficiency in use of these cues in the early years of instruction.

# Using Little Books

In a teacher's manual for the *Ready to Read* books, Simpson (1962) detailed the progression of skills which she imagined emerged from the reading series at each stage. It is only necessary to summarize it here:

Red 1, 2, 3:     Little trouble with interest words.
Reading confidently some basic words — 'is', 'are'.
Frequent lapses.
Supported by reading in groups.

Yellow 1, 2, 3:  Using picture and context clues.
Discriminating between words like 'said' and 'shouted'.
Recognizing a number of words in isolation.
Depending on context.

Blue 1, 2, 3:    Using word beginnings more frequently.
Working out unfamiliar words.
Emphasizing the initial sound.
Encouraged to read silently for short stretches.
Supported by the sound of his own voice.

Green 1, 2, 3:   Children using many cue sources.
Some basic words like 'who' and 'where' still difficult.

# Using Supplementary Readers

To maintain a child's confidence in a problem-solving approach, the reading must be easy enough for him to get an unfamiliar word from the context. As he focusses his attention on that new word he notices some details — how it begins, what it resembles — and these cues help him decide whether his attempted response is correct or not. A quantity of reading at an easy level is important for confidence in this problem-solving approach. When it is available, children do not say, 'We can't read that. We haven't learnt the words.'

A definite progression is built into the Little Books, and teachers must beware of accelerating a child too rapidly through this graded sequence of experience. Designed as a first-year learning task, they are often part of the second year's work, depending upon the rate of a child's progress. Supplementary readers by private publishers have been graded to fit the progressive stages of the twelve introductory books. They may be selected for various purposes:

● preparatory to a basic reader.
● provide practice and application for new knowledge following a basic reader.
● used to encourage independent reading of a text simpler than the instructional level for a particular child.
● used to revise teaching points.

Children who learn quickly may read a basic and a supplementary book each week. As their control increases they can attempt simple story books, and write stories for their particular group.

For the less able child a longer period may be spent introducing a particular book, working with that book, and several parallel supplementary books may precede the next book in the *Ready to Read* series. Charts which recast the text in slightly altered ways will force the child to look closely, think, and consider his responses. In the extra time taken, a consolidation of previous skills may be made and extra word study and problem-solving practice may be introduced.

# Text Characteristics Influence the Child's Expectations

In beginning reading books texts are often arranged on a one-sentence one-line basis:

**A pig comes to school.**
**A calf comes to school.**
**Mary comes with the calf.**
**Penny comes with the pig.**

When a two-line sentence is used the second line usually begins at a distinct break in the spoken sentence:

**William the goat**
**will not come.**
**Get up, William,**
**said Michael.**

When an analysis of the sentences in the Little Books was made, 48 percent of the lines began with direct speech and 21 percent with a narrative sentence, so that 69 percent of all line beginnings were also sentence beginnings. In 6 percent of the lines the narrative was continued from the previous line, direct speech was continued in 8 percent of the lines, and the source of direct speech (e.g. 'said Mother') occurred at the beginning of 17 percent of the lines.

| LINE BEGINNINGS OF 'READY TO READ' LITTLE BOOKS | | | |
|---|---|---|---|
| | Narrative | Direct Speech | Source of Direct Speech |
| Beginning Sentence | A pig comes 21% | 'Get up, William' 48% | Mother said 2% |
| Continuing Sentence | . . . will not come 6% | . . . and go home 8% | said Michael 15% |

Thus a new sentence invariably begins on a new line in these books and the beginning of a line is frequently a new sentence. The child learns to anticipate that the end of the line will be the end of a sentence. In the following example the child shows that he has learned this expectation, which will often increase his fluency on these particular texts, although in this instance he has made an error.

| | |
|---|---|
| Child: | *The children are playing* |
| Text: | The children are playing |
| Child: | *Where is Timothy?* |
| Text: | with trucks and bulldozers. |

Direct speech is a major part of the texts. The sequences 'Mother said' and 'said Mother' (or equivalent constructions such as 'The Teacher said', 'shouted Harry', 'said the Headmaster') occur in these four positions, with different frequency.

| | |
|---|---|
| A.  '——,!?'   *said Mother.* | 83% |
| B. *Mother said,*   '——?!' | 8% |
| C.  '——,!?'   *he said.* | 4% |
| D.  '——,!'   *said Mother,*   '———.?' | 4% |

It would be consistent with the characteristics of the texts if the young reader assumed that

| | |
|---|---|
| ● a new line begins a new sentence | 69% |
| ● a new line probably requires a direct speech construction | 73% |
| ● direct speech probably calls for the use of 'said Mother' (or an equivalent construction). | 54% |

Developmental psychologists have shown that young children aged 4:0 to 6:0 can develop such expectations in learning experiments and it is reasonable to assume that children could adapt their responding to the characteristics of their reading texts, not only for the features illustrated above but for many other features. When the reading book series is changed these features change dramatically. A high-progress reader may be stimulated by the change. A low-progress reader may lose confidence because what he expects to be true of the text no longer works.

This brief discussion of textual characteristics leads to the conclusion that reading behaviour will be the result of an interaction between the child's oral language habits and certain linguistic characteristics of the particular texts used. Whether the vocabulary of the texts is familiar to the child is one factor to be considered, but there are many other features of texts, to which the child must adapt if he is to decode the message fluently and rapidly. Frequent, repetitive contacts with texts of specific characteristics are likely to establish high expectancies for certain constructions. If the slow learner adapts his responding to the characteristics of a particular type of text this may help him to make decisions about words.

# What Skills Are Fostered?

Any method of instruction must selectively stress some aspects of the mature reading process to the neglect of others. What aspects are being taught in the schools used in my research?
There is a high dependence on oral language skills

● as a source of responses
● to support fluency by creating appropriate expectations of what comes next
● for developing checking strategies; rather than traditional word-attack techniques.

Five-year-olds begin reading sentences. The use of detailed visual cues tends to be learned very slowly over the first year of instruction. The children develop considerable facility in error detection and correction as a result of checking strategies but analytic methods of word attack for new vocabulary were not found to be well developed even in the high progress group studied. This lack may become particularly noticeable when children are transferred to the larger books of the *Ready to Read* series.

In sum, the aspects of reading behaviour being fostered at a high level of competence in the best readers, are fluency, meaning and error-detection at the level of words within sentences, rather than visual discrimination, letter-sound associations or word-attack. The foundation of these latter skills is being laid slowly over a period of time. To critics who claim that reading *is* using the letter-sound relationships and word-solving skills this seems a poor start. For those who believe that fluency, meaning and knowing when one has made an error are important, this pattern of skills looks like a good beginning. A foundation of flexible word-solving techniques keeps children reading quantities of material and as a result of success they get more opportunities to learn more about reading. The priorities would be right, as long as the analytic skills receive more attention when the first skills have been woven into an integrated on-going activity.

At its best, the behaviour fostered is very similar to that of the mature reader except that the child has a very limited number of specific responses to a few sources of cues. Development should be in the direction of more responses, finer discriminations and greater flexibility.

One can argue that this approach is appropriate for young children who come to the school with relatively mature and stable language skills which can provide a good anchorage for new learning. In contrast, the visual discrimination that must be acquired is new learning and will probably be learned slowly. Similarly, the sound segments of words are something the child has paid little attention to in the past and this learning may also be acquired slowly.

It is logically possible to design a programme limited in vocabulary, in the letters used, in the regularity of letter-sound relationships, or in regularized alphabets, so that the learning is fed systematically into the child's experience. But children differ in general intelligence and in the specific abilities required for reading. They arrive as new entrants, having had varying degrees of opportunity to use that potential to the full, as a result of very individual sets of experiences. They may be under-developed or highly fostered by their preschool encounters. They have formed interests and have learned to be selective in the stimuli that catch their attention. And if the most interesting word a child can first learn is his name (or that of a family member) children start from very different knowledge of the alphabet and print. The preparation programme that allows any child to pick up a particular fragment of knowledge about print which he can recognize; and extends his response from there, utilizes the prior knowledge of all children to best advantage in classroom instruction. Any procedures such as the Little Books, which emphasize individualizing instruction, should be valued.

Strategies of searching, checking and error-correcting expose the child to quantities of perceptual experience, so that he may notice new things about print despite his visual and phonological innocence. Active search keeps the child responding and 'sensorially open', as Bruner (1957) described this. The child's active interest in books provides the means of extending his visual discrimination of print, his letter-sound association, his reading vocabulary and his expectancies of linguistic occurrence. A low score in tests of visual perception and letter-sound associations is not serious if the strategies for obtaining these by self-correcting procedures are clearly present at the end of the first year.

In the following examples one child has a dependence on sight-word memory and does nothing about his errors. The other child has an 'ear' for error and sets himself the task of finding out what is wrong. As this child searches for the reasons for the misfit he is most likely to discover something new about written language. He should have access to the teacher at this point to supplement his earnest but inefficient sorting of cues.

| ✓  ✓  ✓  The teacher said | ✓  ✓  ✓  The teacher said |
|---|---|
| to \| SC   ✓  Hullo \|      Timothy | -     ✓  Hullo   Timothy |
| ✓ ✓ ✓   ✓  I am Miss Davis | ✓ ✓   -   -  I am   Miss Davis |
| ✓      with me \| and see  Come    and meet \| | ✓  ✓  ✓  Come and meet |
| ✓ people\|Asks   ✓  ✓  the boys \|Told  and girls | ✓   -   ✓   ✓  the  boys  and  girls |
| Came \| SC  ✓  ✓  Come  \|     and  meet | ✓  ✓  ✓  Come and meet |
| -     ✓   Roy  Tai  and  Rangi | -     ✓   -  Tai  and  Rangi |
| . 14 words correct<br>. 2 self-corrections(SC)<br>. Every error syntactically and semantically possible with some use of visual cues also. | . 16 words correct<br>. No self-corrections<br>. No attempt at any error or new word. |

In any learning which is complex there are opportunities for missing links, weak links, devious routes where more direct ones could be taken, and contrasts between high skill on which the child leans and the weaknesses that he avoids. Even among high progress children there are those who are over-dependent on their oral language strengths and who neglect to add other important skills. There is plenty of scope for error learning in beginning reading, against which the best defence must be strong error correcting strategies.

The approach recommended for introducing the *Ready to Read* books provides a suitable starting point. It will prove to be a good method if the child goes on to learn

- the discrimination of letters
- the concepts about print
- the probabilities of combining the words and structures in English (primarily by using 'natural' rather than regularized texts)
- an awareness of sounds and clusters of sounds within words linked to their representation in print.

If each of these aspects of reading is established in a limited way in the first year of instruction, they can be extended and applied with increasing flexibility in subsequent years.    However good the tuition, chance occurrences in individual life histories may bring about blocks to skill learning at any time. In writing her scheme, Simpson (1962) recognized that 'Children progress slowly, individually and irregularly.'

There is in the last paragraph a warning for the proponents of any particular reading method. It will be a good method if the reading behaviours which it fosters are known, if the risk areas which it creates are also known, and if later instruction eliminates the risks and in time develops *all aspects of the reading process* towards increasing flexibility of reading skills.

# Texts For Slow Progress Groups

While creative, varied or flexible approaches to writing and reading seem appropriate for high progress readers, slow progress readers probably have great difficulty discovering the regularities in such a rich reading environment. For them there is reason to make the regularities so obvious that they trip over them in the same place on several occasions. Regular contact with familiar material in familiar settings will suit the slow progress reader better than trying to force on him a flexibility of which he is not yet capable with texts whose characteristics vary widely.

A caution must be stated, however, in connection with the selection of simple material and regular or controlled materials for these slow progress children. While complex and varied material may defeat their efforts to read, materials of a limited or controlled type will only develop habitual responding for that type of material. This learning will not transfer readily to more complex texts. For a slow child, if the regularity of the texts is increased at any time to facilitate correct responding, a variety of language structures should be reintroduced as soon as the new skill is established.

The ability of the young child to deal with complex language is grossly underrated by programmes designed in small steps with phonemes as the minimal teaching units of language. It is an acknowledgement of this when reading specialists urge teachers to supplement and vary the prescribed programme as they see the need. There is room for more scientific study of this problem of controlling textual material and classroom activities for the slower 50 percent of school entrants to reduce their confusion and bewilderment, and the problem seems to be one of finding a way to order the material on more than one dimension although multi-dimensional sorting of language material is a formidable task.

Why not change all children to regularized texts? This would slow up the progress of the top 50 percent of beginning readers, although regular texts have a special role at particular times for these children. For example, changing a high progress child to a strictly phonetic text will force him to attend more to letter-sound relationships. Not only does this make the child's reading more flexible but, according to Bruner, such changes should stimulate the child to formulate more generic rules about the nature of written language.

Very careful attention should be paid to any difficulty order in the series of reading books. When a graded sequence of reading is available children must not be given a book that calls for too great a step forward. A graded reading series may be constructed for flexibility in progression but the options are more often how many extra books the child will need at each level, rather than how many books he can skip. Careful record keeping and a good observation record of a child's accuracy on a previous reader should be the basis for accelerated promotion of a child through the reading series (see Chapter 10). If the child is promoted, careful checks should be made on his progress in the ensuing weeks. Some children never recover their balance after well-intentioned but unwarranted acceleration.

# References and Further Reading

Bruce, D.J., 'The analysis of word sounds by young children', *Brit. Journal Educ. Psychol.*, 34, 1964, pp. 158-170.

Bruner, J.S., 'On perceptual readiness', *Psychological Review*, 64, 1957, pp. 123-152.

Hart, N.W.M., Walker, R.F., Gray, B., *The Language of Children: A Key To Literacy*, Addison-Wesley, Sydney, 1977.

Hemming, James, personal communication, 1971.

Horton, J., *On The Way To Reading.*, Department of Education, Wellington, 1978.

McCullough, Constance M., 'The language of basal readers', in R.C. Staiger and O. Andresen, (eds.), *Reading: A Human Right and A Human Problem*, International Reading Association, Newark, Delaware, 1968, pp. 67-72.

N.Z. Educational Institute. *Reading Units For Junior School* (Rev. Ed.), NZEI, Wellington, 1978. p. 93.

Price, H., Lo I am an ox!, *Education*, 3. 1975.

*Ready To Read*, School Publications, Department of Education, Wellington, 1963 (18 titles), (Also published by Methuen, London, 1966).

Reid, Jessie F., 'Sentence structure in reading primers,' *Research in Education*, 3, May, 1970, pp. 23-37.

Samuels, S.J., 'Effects of pictures on learning to read, comprehension and attitudes', *Review of Educ. Research*, 40, 1970, pp. 397-407.

Simpson, M.M., *Suggestions For Teaching Reading In Infant Classes*, Department of Education, Wellington, 1962. (Also published by Methuen, London, 1966.)

Strickland, Ruth G., *The Language Of Elementary School Children*, Indiana Bulletin of School of Education, Indiana University, 1962.

Suess, Dr, *Green Eggs and Ham*, Collins, New York, 1960.

Venezky, R.L. Regularity in reading and spelling. In Levin, H. and Williams, J.P. *Basic Studies On Reading*, Basic Books, New York, 1970.

# Exploring Further

**Learn to take running records of a child reading a book. What did you notice about that child's reading behaviour? Refer to** *The Early Detection of Reading Difficulties: A Diagnostic Survey with Recovery Procedures* **to explain what you found. What do you think reading is?**

# 10 Progress on the First Reading Books

If we were to plot the heights and weights of 5-year-old children on a graph we would find that they scatter around an average in a bell-shaped curve.

For beginning reading, the curves of attainment are different. At some point in the child's history a decision is made that he begin to read the written language. Usually it is society that decides, and in New Zealand the time of beginning is determined by a long-standing practice that the child enters school on his fifth birthday.

Only very few children can read on entry to school so the great majority are clustered around a score of nil on tests of aspects of the reading process such as word knowledge, letter knowledge, writing vocabulary. Children move away from this no-score of zero position at different rates. These children do not come to reading instruction on an equal basis. They turn to a new area of learning and bring their past experiences to bear on this. But the actual acts of reading are novel behaviours acquired at this time.

Some curves of reading attainment at several ages illustrate what has been found in several careful observation studies.

● A normal distribution of scores emerges only after many months of instruction, where the learning is open-ended and continues for years, as in the learning of reading vocabulary.

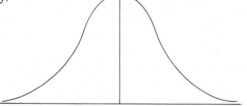

Standard Normal Curve

● If the learning is a closed set of learning, as in letter naming, letter identification, or letter-sound correspondence, the curves move through three phases like this.

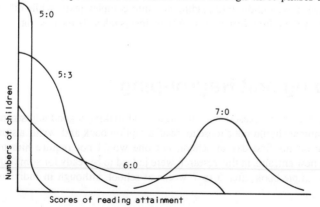

• If the learning is a skill which moves from awkward discovery in the early stages to smooth automated execution, as in directional behaviours or the visual analysis of the symbols of print the learning curves are difficult to plot.

The length of the early reading period for different groups of children can be illustrated from three research studies completed in Auckland. Clay (1967) reported on a 1963 to 1964 sample of 5- to 6-year-olds at the time the new reading series was introduced into the schools. Robinson (1973) used two samples of 6-year-olds, and Ng (1979) provided records for 242 children tested within 2 weeks of their sixth birthday and for 52 competent readers (randomly sampled from the top 50 percent of the 242 6-year-olds) who were tested at 6:0, 6:6 and 7:0. The book levels reached by the later samples (Ng and Robinson) were comparable, and they were higher than those reported by Clay. In the first two years of a new reading scheme the hundred children who were studied in 1963 to 1964 in five different schools could not read any book or caption book on entry to school. Within 2 weeks some 10 to 15 percent read their own names. One year later, at 6:0 the children were reading from the first to the fifteenth book of the *Ready to Read* series. Three children were still on Early Reading material, 8 were reading the first Red Book inaccurately, and 11 had read Red 1 at the 90 percent level of accuracy but had gone no further. This made a total of 28 percent from a representative sample of children from English-speaking homes unable to read beyond the first Little Book of the basic series after 12 months at school. This does not, in my opinion, report failure. It underlines the importance of the Early Reading period in which there is so much to learn that the slower children take the best part of one year to reach mastery of the basic skills. Of the remainder of the group 50 percent had progressed successfully to or beyond Yellow 5, the fifth book. Of the high progress children 14 had completed the first 12 books and were reading the larger books (13, 14 and 15) in the series.

In the second study in 1973 two further groups of children were studied. At 6 years they had made faster progress into reading than children in the earlier study. Perhaps this was because the teachers were more familiar with the reading programme at this stage. But one can expect that much variation from school to school, and from one research group to another any way.

It is the similarities in the three graphs that tell the most interesting story, that some children move rapidly into reading and into complex texts, while others move very slowly in their first year at school, into independent book reading.

# Grouping and Regrouping

There appears to be no reason why an eager child making a good adjustment to his new environment should not choose to 'read' a caption book and 'write' a story about his drawing on his first day at school, but one would not require him to do so. Usually the new entrants in this research were judged to be ready for some direct contact with a simple book after 5 to 7 weeks at school, although in individual cases children waited much longer than this for promotion to a caption book or home reader, sometimes as long as six months.

| WEEKS FROM SCHOOL ENTRY TO BOOK READING | | | | | |
|---|---|---|---|---|---|
| Reading Progress Middle Child of 25 | Promoted to | | | | |
| | Caption Book | Sup-plemen-tary Reader | Ready to Read Red 1 | Ready to Read Red 2 | Ready to Read Red 3 |
| High Group (H) | 5 | 14 | 16 | 21 | 26 |
| High Middle (HM) | 7 | 18 | 21 | 24 | 27 |
| Low Middle (LM) | 7 | 21 | 31 | 35 | 36 |
| Low Group (L) | 7 | 28 | 36 | 45 | 51 |

| NUMBER OF WEEKS BETWEEN PROMOTIONS | | | | | |
|---|---|---|---|---|---|
| Reading Progress Middle Child of 25 | Entry to Caption | Caption to Sup-plemen-tary | Sup-plemen-tary to Red 1 | Book Reading | |
| | | | | Red 1 to Red 2 | Red 2 to Red 3 |
| H | 5 | (9) 11 | (2) | 5 | 5 |
| HM | 7 | (11) 14 | (3) | 3 | 3 |
| LM | 7 | (14) 24 | (10) | 4 | 1 |
| L | 7 | (21) 29 | (8) | 9 | 6 |

The uniformity with which teachers introduced children to early reading books is interesting. It suggests an awareness that early reading skills have to be learned on printed texts and are not acquired in play with blocks and puzzles. However, if the uniformity means that the same expectations were being held for all these children, the poorly prepared and the well-prepared, then there has been far too little observation of what each individual child is capable of doing. All may be introduced to early reading books but the teaching goals should already be differentiated according to the teacher's observations of the child's current performance.

Contrast the uniformity with which teachers introduced children to caption books with the differential timing of their transfer to a supplementary basic series and then to the basic readers. Most children spent between 9 and 21 weeks on early reading activities before they received a first reading book which was simpler than the basic series. At first glance the tables seem to reflect the time it takes children of different abilities to master the early reading skills, but when one looks at the number of weeks between promotions some important questions arise. Is the high middle group being hurried unduly through their books as the end of the year approaches? The high progress group were given more time. Has the low group been adequately prepared when they stay 9 weeks on their first basic reader?

These results suggest that teachers judge children's readiness for book reading not from behaviour prior to contact with books but rather from children's attempts to respond to print and to books. Teachers are aware that the preparation for book reading is a matter of learning certain skills from interesting encounters with print.

There is only one good reason for promoting children to the next stage of a programme. That is because their behaviour has been observed closely and they are now ready to acquire a new set of skills, fostered by the next stage of the programme. It is not in the interests of successful reading to promote children to a more difficult stage of the programme

- because of the pressure of new entrants entering the class
- because set times (six weeks or a term) have been allotted to each stage
- because the school year is running out
- because the child has been in a group 'long enough'.

## Questions of classroom grouping

A questionaire completed by 11 teachers in the research schools in 1964 is a source of ideas about methods which they favoured. These have been grouped together below to answer the questions, 'What is a reading group? How is it taught? What does the teacher try to teach the group?' These are the teachers' comments:

*What are the characteristics of a reading group in your class?* They will be of mixed age and of widely varied general ability but they will have in common similar reading attainment at that particular point of time.

Groups will change as children find their own pace and level. Fast-moving groups are no problem. They may be larger than groups of slower children. There is a tendency for children to accumulate in the 'slow' group.

*When and how does group membership change?* As children become ready to read books they are promoted into reading groups. Otherwise the organization is extremely flexible, and children move according to individual progress. A fast learner goes forward to a high group. Children who are unhappy, slower or disinterested change groups in a 'reshuffle'.

'A second opinion' is often given to the class teacher by the Supervisor of Junior Classes who tests knowledge of basic words at regular intervals for all children.

*Why do you change a child to a new basic reader?* Because he is ready to progress. Because he can proceed to the next basic reader without having a suffocating number of unknown words.

*Why do you give a child a new supplementary reader?*
- To stimulate interest.
- To revise and consolidate basic words.
- To avoid reading the same book again.
- For a slow child a change of book may mean a change to a new book of parallel level, not one he has previously struggled with.

*How do you teach in groups?* A class is grouped for reading into four attainment groups of 6 to 10 children. More than 10 is unworkable. Activities from current books are set for the class while the teacher works with each group in turn.

At first the teacher will use one large book or a wall story and a small blackboard. All children will read together but not in unison. Later, children will read aloud from their own small books, and more advanced groups will read silently.

The teacher aims to increase motivation and effort by initial discussion of pictures, characters in the story, unfamiliar concepts.

All children help to read the story aloud. The teacher uses question and answer methods to get the precise wording of the text, but this discussion for elucidation during the story is kept to a minimum. A whole story is completed on the first day, and re-read on subsequent days.

For word study, attention is given to initial sounds and other teaching points follow at the end of the text.

Meaning is emphasized throughout.

Finally the text is re-read.

*What do you teach in group reading?*
- I teach understanding related to the story.
- I use a small blackboard and give special examples as errors arise.
- I encourage children to find and correct errors.
- I group initial letter words in a list:
    shaving
    shouted
    shop
- I invite discovery of a new word by analogy:
    went
    sent
    lent
    **bent**
- I use words again the next day or next week.
- I observe closely what children are saying and doing.
- I try new tactics, a new approach.
- I work with a particular word, emphasizing it.
- Word study of new, difficult or forgotten words.

*In what order of importance do you rank early reading skills?*
1 Children maintain interest in reading books.
2 Children know that reading should make sense.
3 Children learn and accumulate reading vocabulary.
4 Children use picture clues to help interpret the text.
5 Children use picture clues to trigger the memory for the exact text.
6 Children accumulate basic vocabulary.
7 Children use following sentence structure to provide clues.
8 Children learn sound-to-letter correspondence for initial consonants and clusters.
9 Children accumulate interest vocabulary.
10 Children learn sound-to-cluster correspondences for structural analysis.
11 Children practice independent problem-solving techniques on print.

The author's choice: 1, 2, 11, 8, 10, 6 and the use of preceding sentence structure which was not listed by the teachers.

# The Progress of a Successful Reader

The reading behaviour of a child who was well prepared by her preschool experiences and who made very good reading progress at school will be described, using as an example the scores for the middle child of the top 25 percent of a research sample (Clay, 1966). She will be called Helen.

● Helen entered school at 5 years.
● Her adjustment was good and she settled quickly.
● She had a high intelligence, being at the lower limit of the superior group (I.Q. 118 to 128).
● She mastered left to right directional control within 3 weeks.
● She was given a caption reader after 5 weeks.
● At 9 weeks she was given a pre-primer of an American Basal series and read it well, with some word knowledge, some detection of errors, and the use of several cues to achieve a precise response.
● At 11 weeks she was promoted to the basic series, Red 1.
● She was placed in a new class.

● Promotion through 3 Red books took 10 weeks because she read many supplementary readers during this period.
● After 6 months at school Helen read a basic reader and a supplementary reader every 2 weeks. Each week the quantity of reading increased.
● Helen read fast, at the rate of 1 word per second. Her accuracy on a book, 2 to 5 days after it was introduced, was about 95 percent. Her responses were fast and accurate.
● On easy or familiar material Helen produced errors which she did not notice because she read so fast that her voice was outrunning her visual check skills. But usually she was quick to detect an error because it was very obvious in her accurate reading.

● New vocabulary was absorbed readily.

● Helen was accurate with her first responses, making 1 error in 37 words, and with her self-corrections, for she successfully corrected 1 error in 3. She was satisfied only if her response was highly probable.

● To achieve self-correction Helen's major strategy was returning to the beginning of a line or sentence (55 percent of the self-corrections).

● Helen did not read ahead to gather context; she returned, took a fresh run.

● Helen's knowledge of syntax in English guided her responding. She substituted words that could have occurred in English in that position 76 percent of the time.

● She repeated lines to confirm correct responses (32 percent of repetitions).

● Helen's main strategy for decoding new words was not a sounding one. After rapid search she decided 'I cannot read this' and asked to be told. After one prompt she solved the word subsequently.

● Her error responses did not show letter-sound associations, 50 percent of the time.

● Helen had completed the twelve Little Books at 6:0.

● She had fast efficient techniques for extracting a sequence of cues from a text.

● She expected her sentences to be meaningful and highly probable.

● Letter-sound awareness was paid less attention than syntax.

● Sound associations were not used (overtly) very often.

The top 25 percent of children in these Auckland studies could not be expected to make better progress under any reading scheme. They enjoyed reading and writing, they were proud of their attainment, they made the transfer to larger books effortlessly, and they read fluently for meaning, if their efficient self-correction behaviour can be used as one criterion of comprehension. These children needed a short time on a book, absorbed new vocabulary readily, quickly detected errors, corrected themselves effectively. They used meaning and grammatical cues with some accuracy but they could, with profit, have paid more attention to the visual analysis of words and to letter-sound associations. This could be done, as it is possible to define them as high progress readers, some time after the first 3 to 6 months of instruction. By the time they are promoted to the large books of the *Ready to Read* series, they should be able to approach the increased vocabulary load with more word-solving skill than merely remembering a word from one appeal to the teacher because good readers appear to do their own analysis of the relationships between print and sound, even when the instructional programme does not stress these.

# How Did Less Successful Readers Respond?

The reading behaviour of a child who made average progress in this research group differed in many respects. The child whose I.Q. was on the high side of average (I.Q. 107) took 16 weeks to master left to right directional control across print. He was given a caption reader after seven weeks at school and a supplementary reader after the directional control was achieved, at 19 to 20 weeks. After 6 more weeks he was promoted to Red 1, the first basic reader, at which time he was already attempting to correct his own errors. He completed the Yellow books by the end·of the year. After one year he was where the high progress reader was at 5:6. He read about as much printed material in one year as she read in six months. He made errors once in every 10 running words and normally read with about 90 percent accuracy. He corrected 1 error in 6, and read at the rate of 1 word every 1.5 seconds. Thus, as well as taking twice as long as the high progress reader to cover the same ground, the average child had made more errors, read less accurately, engaged in less self-correction and habitually read half as slowly. This pattern of behaviour suggests a learning experience that differs markedly from that of the high progress reader. It is not merely proceeding at a different pace.

Children who made moderately good progress seemed to have the right approach to reading but had not constructed reliable bases for sampling cues and making decisions. They need to pay more attention to visual form (bearing in mind that initial letters probably are the ones which help to classify words in a maximally useful way at this level). They need to use sentence structure to anticipate what might follow and to learn better use of cues for checking their guesses. More time could be spent building up auditory expectations for the words that occur. As a group this moderate progress group was hurried through the reading books at a pace which the children could not sustain and one improvement to their instruction might have been to hold them a little longer at each stage to consolidate efficient responding. Also teachers must be prepared to accept a temporary drop in fluency as legitimate when a child is trying to use new kinds of cues or information in the on-going activity.

## The low progress group

The middle child of the slowest group was also given a caption reader at 7 weeks and also took 15 to 16 weeks to master directional behaviour. By the end of a year he had moved through to Red 3 but he had had unsuccessful experiences with books. He made 1 error in every 3 words, usually read with 60 percent accuracy and corrected 1 error in 20. Yet he was trying to read at the same pace as the average child, one word in 1.5 seconds. Over the vacation, he forgot a great deal more of the limited skills he had learned than children in the higher groups. His foundation for future progress in reading was basically unsound. Some children in the slow group had pronounced directional difficulties which had to be overcome before they could begin to respond appropriately to texts. The lower half of the first year entrants did not do much reading in their first year and perhaps two reading periods a day could be organized for them. High progress children will create their own sparetime practice at home. Slow learners will not. Probably this is just as well because low progress children need close supervision to reinforce their few correct responses. As they try to read they destroy the semantic and syntactic context with their error behaviour and they need help and encouragement to put the fractured utterance together again. Rhyme, rhythm and memory for the text are legitimate props for these children. Special attention to the predictability of their texts and reading environment is also important.

# The Amount of Reading Done

Observation records of book reading were taken at weekly intervals for the 100 children in the Auckland research study and the amount read varied with the progress a child made because the better readers spent a higher proportion of the year in the book reading stage while the poorer readers spent much more of the year in the preparation stage.

Each observation record tallied the number of words read. The reading usually consisted of one of the Little Books, or a supplementary reader or 6-10 pages of some other book. This was estimated to represent roughly one-sixth of the child's reading experience per week.

Using this estimate we may say that the child making superior progress read something in excess of 20 000 words in his first year of instruction, the HM child 15 000 words, the LM child 10 000 words and the L progress child probably less than 5 000.

## NUMBER OF WORDS READ IN WEEKLY OBSERVATIONS
(First Year at School — medium case of each quartile group.)

| Progress Group | Words Read | Estimate of Words Read per Year |
|---|---|---|
| H | 3 570 | 20 000 |
| HM | 2 601 | 15 000 |
| LM | 1 680 | 10 000 |
| L | 757 | 5 000 |

The H and HM children were known to be reading and printing at home to a greater extent than LM and L children, which would tend to increase the differences. Such differences in the quantity of reading might have been expected but their size is interesting. Although the children were being given equal educational opportunity these figures probably reflect the amount of teaching time spent with each group. Teachers may protest at this claim but it takes longer for a child to read the larger texts to begin with. What would happen if twice as much time was devoted to the L and LM group? One suspects that when a child fails to respond to the initial efforts of a teacher to get him started on reading and she begins to think of him as a slow developer, there is a likelihood that the amount of urging she gives him will tend to decrease. There is a natural tendency to devote time to those who are responding and an excuse in the maturation concept for 'letting the others come in their own time'. Slower children may well benefit from a break with traditional timetabling, and the opportunity for brief reading periods twice or even three times each day.

Slow progress children also need many more opportunities for independent reading than they usually get. In our concern to move them into more advanced texts we often reduce the opportunity to practise their skill on easier material. High progress children have such opportunities. A wide selection of materials suited to their lower level of skills should be available.

# Recording Reading Behaviour

The teacher of new entrants needs less prescription of what to teach and more opportunity for sensitive observation of precisely what her children are doing, so that she can acknowledge a small-step learning gain with enthusiasm. The teacher has to know what direction the learning or development of individual children is taking. She must reinforce accuracy until the search and check procedure becomes self-reinforcing. She must foster a delicately balanced integration of early skills.

How does a teacher know when a child is failing to progress to a better quality response if much of the behaviour is implicit rather than expressed in some overt form? A teacher knows the developmental progress of a child

- if she knows the child well
- if she has some records which catch current behaviour in such a way that it can be referred to some weeks later
- if she sets aside time for observation periods when she pays close attention to precisely what individual children are doing.

The teacher, like the child, will become more articulate about the behaviour observed as a result of doing this.

Knowing what to look for, remembering to arrange to observe it, and making some record of the behaviour noted, are the means to improved observation by teachers. The unlined exercise books which children use in some schools for their drawing and printing activities provide an excellent record of the child's development in creative writing. Each day's activities need to be dated because a child may not move left to right through his book. Blackboard examples of a child's work do not provide a record. Caption books or daily drawing and writing activities provide much opportunity to observe what a child is doing, but only cumulative records allow an accurate assessment of the direction of progress.

Once the child is reading a book a running record can be used as an observation technique. (See Clay, 1979.) It can be employed when a critical decision about promotion from a book or class has to be made, or when reasons for slow progress or error behaviour are being sought. Explicit standards can be recommended. The child is ready for promotion from a book if he reads it with 1 error in 20 words (or 95 percent accuracy). This standard is too demanding for children who learn slowly and if these children read with 1 error in 10 words (or 90 percent accuracy) a teacher may consider this satisfactory. But the child is also ready for a change of book when he reads it from memory and cannot be helped to observe more detail in the text, as these diary records indicate.

> *Just rushed in from school and said he could read 'The Fire Engine' and recited it off by heart.*

> *Terence said tonight that he has read the same book at school all the time. It is called 'Early in the Morning' and he is very put out because he doesn't get a new one. I told him it must be because he doesn't know it all properly.*

Some tolerance in the time a teacher is prepared to spend to bring a child from a 90 percent to 95 percent accuracy level must be allowed, from 1 week for the best readers to 3 or even 4 weeks for the poorest. The real gain in skill lies not in the books, or the accuracy with which the child reads, but in the new insights about print that he learned during the reading of the book, plus the practice gained in operating in print in suitable ways. A running record of reading behaviour will show the teacher whether the child is actively sorting and relating cues.

A child should read to an observer those pages of his reading book for which his teacher has prepared him. At this level of achievement new, unseen material will not give good observation records. It is possible for the child to read a whole book of about 12 pages (with alternating text and pictures) at one session. The most strategic observations to make are oral responses to the written text, including true report, error, attack, repetition, self-correction, and comment on words or letters — all carry top priority for recording. Responses having to do with direction, such as pointing, pausing between words and syllables, and tracking errors are next in priority after the oral responses. If desired a reading rate can also be observed: after warm-up on three pages, the child's reading of a page is timed with a stop-watch. Take three time records per day per child and the total number of seconds is divided by the number of running words in the written text. (Records are often spoiled when a child omits or invents large sections of the text.)

To achieve objectivity in such observations it is necessary for the tester to be a recorder of behaviour and not a stimulus of behaviour. All comment, teaching points, helpful replies, leading questions, and pointing guides have to be dispensed with entirely, during a reading observation. A guiding maxim would be 'Record now; teach later.'

# A Cumulative Record

The graphs which follow record weekly observations of reading behaviour. Along the vertical axis is a scale indicating the level of reading book the child is attempting. Across the horizontal axis is the time in weeks. Lines of progress tending to be horizontal show poor progress; lines rising vertically indicate good progress. If teachers kept such records for individual children, passing the records from class to class, and from school to school, the child's new teacher would know immediately the level of book the child was currently reading.

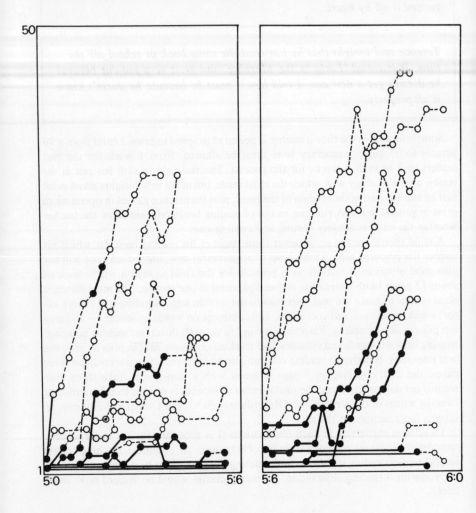

The graph of the children who were 5:0 to 5:6 illustrates that

- some children did not move from the early reading behaviour level
- some children moved to books and back to early reading skills
- some children established accurate reading very early
- some young children moved very rapidly through the reading book series.

The graph of 5:6 to 6:0 illustrates that

● some children in their second half year of instruction continued to have horizontal non-progressive records

● some children who had not left the baseline before 5:6 made rapid progress in this period.

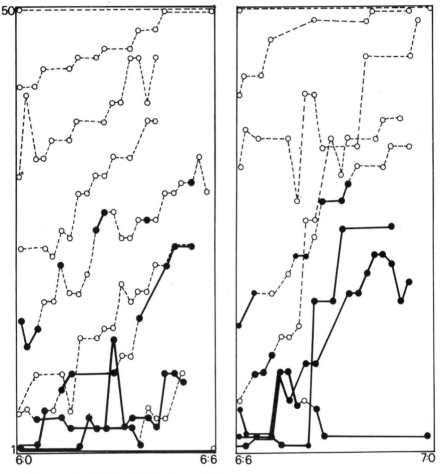

The graph of 6:0 to 6:6 illustrates that

● some children continued to have horizontal non-progressive records
● some children began at this late stage to read with accuracy
● some children had already finished the whole basic readers series.

The graph of 6:6 to 7:0 illustrates that some children had still not left the early reading level. They had been at school two years.

Graphs of reading book level plotted against time at school will locate

● children who have been unable to move from the early reading skill level
● children who are making excellent progress
● children who have moved out of early reading skills into book reading and back to the preparation period again.

## A cumulative record including accuracy

If the class teacher were careful enough to take a running record of the child's reading, and to work out the accuracy level with which the child is reading, important additional information would then be available. In these graphs the weekly observations of reading behaviour were recorded and checked for accuracy. If this is too time-consuming for a class teacher then by taking one reading group per week she could cover her class each month, once in two months, or at least once a term. She could plot on a graph the reading book level with an accuracy check. What would this add to the information we already have? The graphs plot the below 90 percent accuracy records with a solid line and black dots. The above 90 percent accuracy records are plotted with a dotted line and open circles.

The graph of 5:0 to 5:6 illustrates that

● some children established accurate reading very early and showed no change from this
● some records show fluctuations between accurate and inaccurate reading
● some records show a sudden switch from inaccurate to accurate reading without any subsequent relapse.

The graph of 5:6 to 6:0 illustrates that

● some children were promoted progressively on books without reading accurately
● some children with inaccurate but rising records began to read accurately towards the end of the period, but others did not.

The graph of 6:6 to 7:0 illustrates that

● some children who could not read accurately were being moved rapidly through books of increasing difficulty
● mixed records with solid and dotted lines persisted.

Overall the graphs illustrate that a check on accuracy makes it possible to locate children with consistent dotted records whose needs are being met by the teacher and the programme even when they are promoted three or four steps in the reading books series. It also permits us to locate children who are reading with uncertain accuracy, that is, children whose behaviour system is running roughly. Presumably they have needs which are not being·met. They are basing their decisions on inefficient cues. They may be being moved too fast, prepared inadequately, have insecure strategies, or poorly organized behaviour, or they may have faulty concepts of what is required.

Most serious of all, children with black vertical records are being forced daily to practise errors, to use inefficient strategies, and to build habits on this foundation.

| STYLE OF PROGRESS | | | | | |
|---|---|---|---|---|---|
| Accuracy Above the 90% Level | Reading Groups | | | | |
| | L | LM | HM | H | Total |
| All records | 0 | 3 | 4 | 23 | 30 |
| The Last 7 Records | 2 | 12 | 20 | 6 | 40 |
| A Majority above 90% | 0 | 2 | 7 | 3 | 12 |
| 50/50 | 3 | 4 | 0 | 0 | 7 |
| A Minority above 90% | 8 | 7 | 1 | 0 | 16 |
| No Records above 90% | 19 | 4 | 0 | 0 | 23 |

The weekly reading histories of the 128 children in this study could be readily divided into 6 styles of progress (see table above).

*Style 1.* All records were above the 90 percent accuracy level. This accounted for 30 children.

*Style 2.* At least the last 7 records were consistently accurate above the 90 percent level. This accounted for 40 children.

*Style 3.* A majority of records were above the 90 percent level. This accounted for 12 children.

*Style 4.* Approximately half the records were accurate above the 90 percent level. This accounted for 7 children.

*Style 5.* A minority of records were above the 90 percent level. This accounted for 16 children.

*Style 6.* No records were above the 90 percent accuracy level. This accounted for 23 children.

In summary of this section then, either a record of reading books completed or of accuracy records, but preferably both, will locate those children who need extra help in the first year of instruction.

### Sudden change

In the style of progress analysis (see table above) the largest category of children are those whose records ran from inaccurate or mixed records to a sudden emergence of accurate records which was maintained consistently over at least the last seven. It was as if something had clicked into place. Notice on the graphs the number that changed suddenly and without relapse from solid black lines to dotted lines and open circles. This is strong evidence to support the idea of a behaviour system (see Chapter 14).

The behaviour system for reading was, quite suddenly, in working order. This transition is worthy of closer attention, with a careful analysis by research of the periods before and after the changeover. But the evidence points strongly again to the critical importance of the first year instruction.

# The Quality of Teacher Judgement

The judgement that a child is ready for promotion to a particular book is a highly skilled one and the graphs and tables are evidence that those judgements are often correct. A teacher who thinks that a child is able to skip three or four steps in a book series is proven correct when the child masters the book easily in one or two weeks at a level of 95 percent accuracy. By the same token, her judgement is sometimes wrong; and the child who fails to gain the required skill must be moved back to easier material. Such flexible movement up and down is desirable when it is the result of sensitive observation of the child's behaviour and what that behaviour implies. Fluctuations, large leaps forward, movements backward in the series to consolidate or recapitulate, are movements to be expected under satisfactory conditions of instruction. The characteristics of a satisfactory record would be predominantly forward or upward with consistently accurate reading, but fluctuations will occur.

On the other hand, the promotion or demotion in book level may not stem from sensitive observation of the child's reading behaviour, but arise

- for administrative reasons
- because the end of the year is approaching
- because there has been a change of class and the child is fitted into an existing group
- for casual or rigid attention to the sequential steps in a reading programme
- even to interest the child, without having regard to his achievements.

In none of these cases are the teacher's decisions determined by what the child is currently able to do. Without accurate observation of reading behaviour teachers' judgements of appropriate promotion are liable to be unsuitable.

One further point should be made about promotions through the series. Teachers' decisions become more appropriate the further a child moves up the scale of difficulty. At the early reading stage fluctuations are greater, the ups and downs more pronounced. The drops in accuracy are less readily predicted and sudden gains are surprising. Two different explanations can be offered, and both are thought to be operating concurrently. The child's behaviour is difficult for the teacher to observe in the early reading stage, and she may have difficulty knowing what his current skill is. But, in addition, there is evidence to suggest that the child's behaviour is being organized at this point in time into an efficiently functioning system, and it is possible for him to make big gains as he discovers new ways of relating some aspects of behaviour. The behaviour system can suddenly improve in efficiency. Even at this early stage the failing child, if not detected, may practise bad habits daily until they are firmly established in an inefficient system for processing cues.

The conclusion from this is that more time and more care will be needed closer to the beginning of reading than will be necessary once a satisfactory system of processing information has been established.

# Organizing For Observation

Records of reading book promotions kept by infant room teachers will show the horizontal/vertical tendencies of children's progress. The direction of change over time between any two points at which checks are made is important.

More informative records would be provided if accuracy counts were made for those children who sound like poor readers and/or those who have horizontal records.

Administrative and staff commitment to a concept for prevention revolves around provisions of appropriate organization for the keeping of such records.

● First year reading progress should be carefully monitored by sensitive observation accompanying each stage of teaching, (Clay, 1979). Classes must be small; or we are going to generate inefficient behaviour systems. Time for observation must be available. Although the techniques are simple, teachers will have to be taught to use them, and encouraged to develop them.

● A second stage in a prevention programme is a check as each child reaches his sixth birthday. A staggered age of entry would mean that this survey would be carried out at any point during the school year for individual children. If it is obvious that the child is making satisfactory progress this survey need not be detailed.

● A flexible and experienced teacher, well versed in individualized teaching techniques, and especially qualified in a wide variety of approaches to reading instruction, must be available for intensive and sustained re-teaching of low progress children in their second year at school on the basis of the results of this diagnostic survey.

● Considering the importance of the first year of instruction for shaping an effective versus an ineffective behaviour system the staffing of these early classes must be very carefully selected.

# In the Second Year of Instruction

A study of competent readers, the top 50 percent of a random sample of the age group, is of particular interest (Ng, 1979). The graphs below show the progress of these children on the *Ready to Read* texts which they were reading at 90 percent to 94 percent accuracy. At 6:0 the group was spread widely across the graded reading series (from *Yellow 3* to *Stars in the Sky* or Book Level 6 to Book Level 17). The distribution narrowed at 6:6 and again at 7:0 at which time all children were reading above the *Sweet Porridge* (Book Level 16) level. Identical progressions were found at

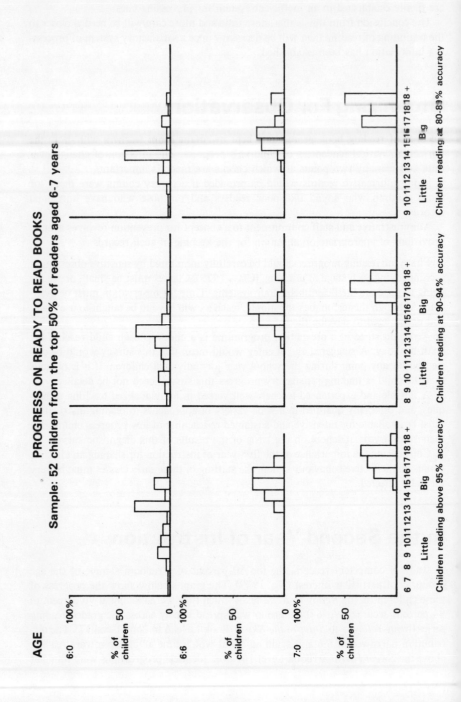

**PROGRESS ON READY TO READ BOOKS**

Sample: 52 children from the top 50% of readers aged 6-7 years

two other levels of difficulty, above 95 percent, and between 80 percent and 90 percent. The more competent children were reading beyond the last books of the graded series. Ng says

'By testing the children on material at the three levels of accuracy one can get a clearer description of not only what the child can read in class with a certain degree of accuracy but also what children can do with unseen material and how far ahead of their class group they are.'

Another study was made of children's progress in relation to promotion policies (Wade, 1978). For this study a set of graded paragraphs replaced the most advanced books used by Ng's children, and extended beyond the basic reading series into more difficult paragraphs, giving 25 levels of difficulty from first books to the end of the third year of instruction (Junior 1 to Junior 3).

| READING BOOK LEVEL AT OR ABOVE 90 PERCENT ACCURACY | | | | | | | | | | |
|---|---|---|---|---|---|---|---|---|---|---|
| *Ready to Read series* | | | | **Little Books** | | **Big Books** | | **Journals** | | |
| | | 0 | 1-3 | 4-6 | 7-9 | 10-12 | 13-15 | 16-18 | 19-21 | 22 + |
| **European** | J1 | 1 | | | | | | | | |
| | J2 | 2 | 4 | 3 | 2 | 4 | 24 | 50 | 32 | |
| | J3 | | 3 | 3 | 4 | 8 | 35 | 235 | 328 | 83 |
| | S2 | | | | | | | | 4 | 22 |
| **Other Ethnic** | J1 | | 2 | 1 | | | | | | |
| | J2 | 5 | 10 | 1 | 9 | 5 | 20 | 22 | 7 | |
| | J3 | | 17 | 4 | 7 | 6 | 52 | 88 | 86 | 2 |
| | | | | | | | | 1 | 3 | |
| **Total** | | 8 | 36 | 12 | 22 | 23 | 131 | 396 | 460 | 107 |

Random sample of 29 schools in Auckland (Wade, 1978)
1195 children aged 7:2-8:2, tested July-September 1978.

There are several important points to notice in this table for 1195 children between 7:2 and 8:2 when tested.

● After two years in school children were spread from non-reading to advanced levels of reading. This is a situation to be faced by any educational provision and any panacea offered.

● There are 2 'Other Ethnic' children for every 1 European in the low progress children.

● There is 1 'Other Ethnic' child for every 2 Europeans in the high progress group.

As the Standards in Education report (1978) claims that the reading attainment of average and better children is continuing to increase there would be profit in finding ways to raise the effectiveness of the 129 children who have very low progress for their age. The payoff would be considerable in terms of educational effort, economic investment, and, most of all, personal satisfaction and long-term insurance for feelings of self-worth (Clay, 1979).

A third area of interest in the 6 to 7 year age group is reported in Ng's study (1979). She asked children at 6:0, 6:6 and 7:0 to read two strictly phonic texts, taken from the Daniel's and Diack (1958) Royal Road Readers. One was easy and one was difficult. The question was: *Are children who are taught on natural language texts with a minimum of letter-sound training able to read texts which are constructed on 'phonic' principles?* At 6:0 the answer was that they found the task difficult. By the age of 6:6 they were improving and by 7:0 they had little difficulty in reading such texts with the same accuracy that they achieved on natural language texts, but not without critical comment. Some seemed to find the texts quaint or odd.

# Follow-up

Children studied intensively during their first year at school between 5:0 and 6:0 were retested at 7:0 and 8:0 and the relationship between their early progress and later outcomes in reading skill were reported as correlations (see table below). If we consider that a correlation of 0.70 or above indicates a high relationship between two kinds of behaviour which are changing rapidly and are two years apart in time, then this follow-up study which used tests of word knowledge as a criterion of reading progress has some very consistent results.

● Word Tests at 6:0 ranked the 83 children in the same order, more or less, as tests at 7:0 and 8:0.

● Book Rank at 6:0 based on running records of the graded reading books was also highly related to later reading status.

● Letter Identification at 6:0 was also a clear predictor of later status.

● Concepts about Print scores at 6:0 had a stronger relationship with later progress than might have been expected since, once mastered, these would have little further contribution to make to progress.

● Individually administered tests of general intelligence had only that degree of relationship with later reading that is found between the intelligence of brothers and sisters.

● Reading readiness scores at 5:0 had lower relationships with later progress than any other variables.

| RELATIONSHIPS OF READING PROGRESS AT 6:0 WITH LATER STATUS AT 7:0 AND 8:0 | | | | | |
|---|---|---|---|---|---|
| | 6:0 Word Test | 7:0 Schonell R1 | 8:0 | 7:0 Fieldhouse NZCER | 8:0 |
| Word Test at 6:0 with — | — | .90 | .80 | .88 | .83 |
| Book Accuracy and Rank at 6:0 with — | .93 | .80 | .69 | .77 | .72 |
| Letter Identification at 6:0 with — | .84 | .86 | .81 | .80 | .83 |
| Concepts About Print at 6:0 with — | .79 | .73 | .64 | .69 | .70 |
| General Intelligence (S.B. 1960) | .55 | .54 | .48 | .50 | .55 |
| Metropolitan Reading Readiness at 5:0 with — | .55 | .49 | .45 | .43 | .48 |
| Self-correction rates averaged 5:0 — 6:0 | .67 | .61 | .60 | — | — |
| Error rate averaged 5:0 — 6:0 | .85 | .78 | .77 | — | — |

All correlations are significant ones but those above 0.70 can be considered high in a longitudinal study across time.

The sample was 83 from 100 children who could be traced two years after completion of the original study (Clay, 1967).

One interpretation of the Readiness Test results is that children are changed by the programmes of their schools from their entry status. However, a pessimistic note is struck by the consistency in rankings after 6:0 years. In relation to their classmates children were in the same ranked positions at 7:0 and again at 8:0 as they were at 6:0. Schools programmes had served to confirm rather than alter the 6:0-year-old status.

The range of reading ability had widened but few if any children had made marked changes in their reading status.

A reading recovery programme (Clay, 1979) was the outcome of analysis of these correlations. The purpose of the programme was to alter the progress patterns of the slower progress children between 6:0 and 7:0 in such a way that such correlations would be reduced.

# References and Further Reading

Clay, Marie M., 'The reading behaviour of five year old children: a research report,' *N.Z. Journal of Educational Studies*, 2, (1), 1967, pp 11-31.

Clay, Marie M., 'Language skills: a comparison of Maori, Samoan and Pakeha children aged 5 to 7 years,' Part I, 1970.

Clay, Marie M., *The Early Detection of Reading Difficulties: A Diagnostic Survey with Recovery Procedures*, Heinemann Educational Books, Auckland, 1979.

Daniels and Diack, *The Standard Reading Tests*, Chatto and Windus, London 1958.

Ng Seok, Error and Self-correction Behaviour in Speech and Writing. Unpubl. Ph.D. thesis, University of Auckland Library, 1979.

Wade, T., Promotion Patterns in the Junior School. Unpubl. Dip. Ed. thesis, University of Auckland Library, 1978.

# Exploring Further

**Record the progress of a class or a group of children now, or over a term. Graph or tabulate your findings.**

# 11　Error Behaviour: What Does It Tell Us?

## What Is Done With Unknown Words?

When sufficient observations have been carried out of what children actually do when they encounter new words some long-standing beliefs may turn out to be myths. For example, teachers insist that children miss out a difficult word and go to the end of the sentence in order to complete the meaning. There is some strong, (though incomplete) evidence that despite this training, children return to the beginning of the sentence! One can guess the reason — the syntax or grammar which establishes the relationships between words is often destroyed or changed if words are omitted. Part of the 'context' which supports early reading behaviour is grammatical context which is probably more important than meaning. The question 'Does it make sense?' applies equally well to grammatical sense as to semantic sense. Could teachers be wrong about training children, at this level, to read ahead?

An analysis of the teacher's manual for the *Ready to Read* books (Simpson, 1962) suggested independence in reading depended upon the following skills. (The author rearranged them in a preferred order of importance.)

- Anticipating the sentence pattern.
- Using context.
- Recognizing the salient features of a sufficient number of words to provide the basis of a reading vocabulary.
- Using structural analysis.
- Using phonetic analysis.
- Using picture clues.

None of these skills was to be used in isolation. The use of context is considered to be most important and the other skills are to be used in association with this. The most important test for the child to make is 'Does it make sense?' A steady growth in the ability to use reading skills is essential to meet the challenge of each new book.

Two small independent surveys carried out in 1968-1969 by New Zealand Department of Education advisors, checked what children said they did at a difficulty and what, in fact, they did. The children who were in their second and third year of instruction read two test stories matched to two levels of the large books in the *Ready to Read* series. At the first difficulty they were asked 'What do you do when you come to a word you don't know?' Some may have thought up an answer to oblige the questioner, and it does not follow that what they said was what they did in practice.

The main categories of what they said were:

| Response | 7 years (100 children) | 8 years (50 children) |
|---|---|---|
| I don't know | 29% | — |
| Say the word in parts | 23 | 65% |
| Miss it out and go to the end | 15 | 4 |
| Look at the beginning | 7 | 10 |
| Look for little words in big words | 3 | 6 |
| Spell it | 5 | 8 |
| Work it out, think it up | 8 | — |
| Write it down | 4 | — |
| Ask the teacher | 3 | — |
| Look at the picture | 2 | — |

The surveys reported on the success of teaching in the following manner:

*At 7 years* — children were having little success when they tried to blend known parts in order to work out a word.

*At 8 years* — 88 percent of the children did not use more than one method of attack and 12 percent used two methods. Few children use the main methods of attack emphasized in the source book.

It was also reported that when children came to a word they did not know they went back to the beginning of a sentence! Even those who said they would read to the end of the sentence were seldom observed to do this!

Research has some contribution to make to understanding this problem (although not all the answers are to hand). Reading skills applied to unknown words are learnt in one setting and must be transferred to new words. Learning by linking or association is not sufficient. The child must learn with such transfer in mind. From a set of experiences with particular words a child must derive some intuitive rules which account for the relationships of letters and sounds and which can be applied to new words.

*Will the discovery of rules be automatic with sufficient experience?* In one experiment of learning to read Arabic words, some English-speaking adult subjects, taught by a whole-word method, analysed the component letter-sound relationships of Arabic for themselves, but some did not (Gibson, 1965). Individuals may vary markedly in the degree to which letter-sound relationships, simple or complex, are induced without specific instruction as they learn to read.

High progress readers operate as if they know the rules of letter-sound correspondence although they may not be able to verbalize these. When we start with whole words only some children will deduce the letter-sound correspondences. Some specific transfer of training experience is required by other children.

*What units of the spoken and written language should we start to teach?* Hirini was about 6 years old, and proved to be very clear about her word-solving behaviour when her teacher questioned her.

| Teacher | *'What do you do when you come to a word you don't know?'* |
|---|---|
| Hirini | *'I think what it is and if I can't guess it I just read on.'* |
| T | *'You read on?'* |
| H | *'Yes.'* |
| T | *'And how do you try and work out what it was?'* |
| H | *'I'd look at it if it had a word at the front and then I'd think the noise.'* |
| T | *'And try and make the noise?'* |
| H | *'Yes.'* |
| T | *'Where else would you look?'* |
| H | *'At the back too . . And I'd look at a word that was up on the wall and I'd think that is the same word and I have seen that word before.'* |
| T | *'Does it worry you when you come to a word you don't know?'* |
| H | *'Not very much'* |
| T | *'A little bit?'* |
| H | *'Just a bit.'* |

Eleanor Gibson (1965) reported research which shows that children in their first year of teaching instruction make use of clusters of letters in a given position in a word which has an invariant pronunciation. (For example, not many older children have difficulty with '—*tion*', irregular though it is.) The functional units they use can be one letter but may be three or four. Such patterns of letters which regularly give the same sound, function as units which organize perception. They are perceived more easily than strings of letters which are unfamiliar and so they lead to rapid responding. By comparison, single letter analysis is slower, requires more learning, allows for more error and is more difficult to re-instate as a word. The larger the pronounceable units a child can discover and use the less learning effort will be required.

When children in the two surveys reported earlier claimed that they 'say' a difficult word in parts (23 percent of second year children and 65 percent in their third year of school), this seems to be their way of reporting this approach to pronounceable clusters of letters. A natural language text may provide a good basis for the child to discover clusters of letters of invariant pronunciation and yet retain a set for diversity which will facilitate the learning of exceptions.

Teachers were asked what they did with errors in individual reading and what they said when a child hesitated or stopped. Their replies have been listed. Consider each statement and decide towards what specific reading skill the comment was directed (the author's choices are indicated by a single asterisk and her preferences by a double asterisk).

*What do you do when a child hestitates or stops?*
- Help him to read back a little for context.*
- Miss it out — now go back.

- Read on for the meaning.

- Give another word starting that way.*
- Emphasize the beginning sound.*
- Say, 'Get your mouth ready for it.'*
- Say, 'Look at the beginning.'
- Say, 'Try the first sound.'
- Say, 'What does it start with?'
- Say, 'What is another word that starts like that?'

- Say, 'Look for something in the picture that starts like this.'*
- Say, 'Look at the picture.'
- Say, 'What would make sense?'
- Say, 'What do you think it might be?'

- Use questions to direct his thinking.*
- Wait, giving the child time to process cues.*
- Tell him*

*What do you do with errors in individual reading?*
- Say, 'Nearly right but not quite,' (i.e. reward effort).**
- See if the child can correct it.**
- Tell and revise in another context.**

- Ignore until confidence is well-established.*
- Point out a cue that will help.*
- Look again, using a cue that will help, (from meaning, word study or pictures.).*

- Give individual attention.
- Flash cards.
- Homework.
- Let it pass.
- Go over it until correct.

Children who need help may develop strategies for getting the teacher to intervene. They look up at her, look away, wriggle, ask for help. One child said w-w-w for any word, and told her remedial teacher that it usually got her the help she needed.

# Errors

It would be consistent with much that is written about reading to argue that the rate at which errors are made causes success or failure and that merely selecting appropriate material will enable the child to perform above a level of 90 percent accuracy.

In spite of the fact that the teachers in the Auckland research study were carefully extending or supplementing children's experience as seemed appropriate, in actual practice large differences in the rates of making errors appeared in the observation records. Low progress children made 1 error in every 3 words and Low Middle children made 1 in 8. The High Middle group made 1 in 15 and High Group 1 in 37. The very best readers made less than 1 error in every 100 words.

A correct reading response fits neatly into a matrix of relationships. It fits at all levels of language organization and with all the associations of visual perception which the school entrant has learned. An error response may fit a number of these relationships but may be incongruent with one or more. Thus, in the common 5-year-old reading error 'I are sleeping', the part of speech, word order, verbal meaning and first letter correspondence are retained, but word agreement and letter-sound relationships could produce in the reader an awareness of something wrong. When something seems to the child to be a bad fit he frequently searches for more evidence against which to check his response. If he is successful in his search he corrects it, but often he cannot solve the problem, although he knows that it exists.

It is commonly asserted in books about teaching reading that 'the context' provides the child with cues and that he must learn to 'read for meaning'. These terms are not precise, for context may be semantic or grammatical context. Faced with a meaningless set of printed symbols the child does not lack ingenuity in making his guesses but, as the following examples show, the sources of information are wide.

There is clear evidence from several research studies that the errors young children make are more often guided by the grammatical structure of the sentences read rather than by the letter-sound relationships in the words. Errors can be of many different kinds.

(a)   The picture is misunderstood (no semantic correspondence).
      *Father is ringing up on the phone.*
      Father is shaving.

      *I am tired.*
      I am waking up.
(b)   The meaning is retained.
      *I will wash the car today.*
      I will hose the car today.

      *Father is razor blading.*
      Father is shaving.
(c)   The word is of the same grammatical category.
      *They all chuckeded him out of bed.*
      They all pulled      him out of bed.
(d)   The word sequences are grammatically equivalent.
      *I will go and get lunch.*
      I will get          lunch.
(e)   One word is altered to agree with another error.
      *We go      for the bread. Mother's looking.*
      He goes     for the bread. Mother     looked.

(f)   Some letters and sounds are matched.
      *Paint    How remembered let   Went too fast.*
      Picture  Now recited          Tell Want to   fly

These examples suggest that it is not sufficient to complain that a child is 'guessing' instead of 'reading'. Obviously some guesses are responses to more of the complete matrix of cues than others. One can conceive of some errors being 'better' than others, depending on which relationships one prefers to stress. Some writers about reading have stressed the importance of semantic context, others have stressed the letter-sound associations, and these two viewpoints have been the source of much chicken-and-egg debate over teaching method. Currently reading experts advocate that both aspects be prominent in any reading programme.

An analysis of the 10 525 errors substituted for text by the research group of 100 children produced these important facts.

- Five-year-olds anticipated the class of word which should occur next in a sentence with 79 percent accuracy. That is, they frequently replaced a noun with a noun, or a verb with a verb, as the previous examples show. These children used an acceptable substitution for a sequence of words 58 percent of the time [see above (a), (c), (e), (f)]. Taken together single word and sequence substitutions were linguistically equivalent to the text in 72 percent of all substitution errors.
- By comparison letter-sound correspondence between text and response played a much slighter role at this stage. It occurred in only 41 percent of errors.

| ERROR ANALYSIS | | |
|---|---|---|
| Substituted a word of the same grammatical class. | 5 035 examples | 79% |
| Substituted several words in a phrase of the same grammatical structure. | 2 639 examples | 58% |
| All grammatical substitutions. | 7 674 examples | 72% |
| All letter-sound correspondences in single word substitutions. | 2 388 examples | 41% |

The summary table shows that the grammatical context was a significant source of cues to the young reader taught by this particular method on these particular books. It follows that the child's control of sentence structure will be most important in determining his attempts to read. It should be remembered that such dependence on grammatical structure occurred on natural language texts. If the texts were regularized in various ways this would almost certainly reduce the value of grammatical cues.

Although only 41 percent of the substitutions showed any letter-sound correspondence by 6:0, other studies have reported visual cues used as often as language cues by the third year of instruction showing that learning was proceeding in an appropriate direction.

# Sources of Errors

*Errors may result because the child needs to learn some better categories for sorting the environment.* It could result from immature oral language habits

I *are* running
  am

from immature visual perception habits
  *at the*
  after

from slow absorption of new word forms and concepts

  *Viscounted*
  Viscount

or from failure to anticipate the probabilities of the written language of the book.

  *Here's*
  Here is

*Error may result from interference when strongly competing ideas rise to the 'tip of the tongue' first, and obscure the correct response.* Competing responses may be thought of as words of similar semantic meaning (quick, fast : look, see) and words of similar syntactic relationship (run, jump, look) or words which represent opposites (right, left; up, down). The competing pair, 'was' and 'saw', frequently fit the grammar of the sentence, fit the meaning, and have identical letter components:

  Martin was the boy . . .
  Martin saw the boy.

These two words are distinguished by the directional cues and by letter-sound relationships, but the child may not have learned to use these cues.

*Error may result from frequently practised responses masking, or preventing the use of, other responses.* The beginner who accepts 'M' as equivalent for 'Mother' will produce mistakes, for example with the word 'Martin'. The common speech error of using the plural 'are' for the singular 'am' in the 'I am' construction at first blocks the use of the correct response in reading. This type of error often stems from oral language habits and tends to be eliminated as behaviour comes more and more under visual control, and letter-sound relationships begin to be established.

*Errors may be learned by systematic practice of wrong responses.* For most children systematic error tends to be short-lived, and is corrected in a few weeks if new material is presented. But, when a child is held on a book which he repeatedly renders wrongly this situation allows him to practise the errors. Reading mostly to oneself, or to another child, if either child is weak on error-correction techniques, is inviting this systematic practice of error.

An example of the systematic error is given below. A boy, who has been at school seven months, reads from a preprimer of a basal reader:

| Child: | Oh Tim |
|--------|--------|
| Text:  | No Tim |
|        | Oh jump |
|        | Go up |
|        | Oh jump Tim |
|        | Go up    Tim |
|        | Oh jump jump jump |
|        | Go up   up   up |

This is very likely to train the response 'Oh' for 'Go' and 'jump' for 'up'.

If the child regards this responding as successful and nothing occurs to create a suspicion of misfit then systematic error responses are being learned.

*Error may reflect ignorance of the cues that could be used.* Until he has mastered the reading process the beginning reader is, by definition, ignorant of many sources of cues which cannot all be introduced to him at once. The child who cannot distinguish 'fire' and 'fire engine' is ready for a further advance in word and letter discrimination.

*Error behaviour may result where a child does not search effectively* even though he may have learned the appropriate cues. He is too precipitate in saying 'I don't know'. Children who fail to search also fail to learn how to use cues effectively and do not develop error-correction techniques.

*Error may result from an increase in speed of reading* to a point where it is beyond the subject's capacity to process all the information or apply all the error checks, so that errors are overlooked during otherwise fluent reading. Errors occur if the type of text changes markedly from what the child has come to expect so that he predicts wrongly. Too rapid promotion on books can produce this kind of error. A change to a different series of readers in which the language has different regularities (look-and-say to phonic regularity; natural language texts to strictly controlled vocabulary texts) may increase the occurrence of errors. Such a change may be used intentionally to force the child to attend to some new feature. But for poor readers drastic changes in style of text are not suggested.

# Self-correction

Unprompted, children often correct their own errors (see Chapters 7 and 8). They stop, return to the beginning of a line, and try again. Sometimes they comment aloud on their problems. When you hear a child read do you notice those errors which a child makes but corrects through his own efforts? When I set myself the task of recording all the reading behaviour a child produced, it became noticeable that some children were working very hard at correcting their own mistakes. Self-correction appears early when only a very elementary knowledge of reading has been achieved. If we give the new entrant interesting caption books which encourage him to construct stories out of his oral language habits, and if we observe carefully, we soon find the child searching for information in the book which will confirm that what he invented was in fact on that page. Pictures, the general shape or pattern of the print, a letter he recognizes, any of these may provide some measure of confirmation that he is on the right track. In fact, self-correction behaviour appeared in the records of 90 percent of a research group three weeks before their promotion to book reading.

When the child recognizes that he must choose a particular word to fit all the available cues he develops search and check procedures which have been described by many writers about perception and thinking. High progress children used cues from several sources — meaning, grammatical structure, letter-forms, and letter-sound relationships, and if the children sensed disagreement between their first response and some of the cues, they searched for a different response which would resolve the problem.

- A child alert to meaning reads: *Dad, let me paint you,* and exclaims, 'Hey! You can't paint you!'
- A child who observes visual pattern reads, *said* for *shouted* and protests, 'It hasn't got the same letters as *said.*'
- A child with a 'near-enough' attitude reads *Here is* for *Here are* and ponders '*Is* is not there. Oh well! Too bad!'

Usually the children who thought errors had been made went back to the beginning of a line, wiping the slate clean as it were, and tried again. They were often successful on the second or third trial. The courage to make mistakes, the 'ear' to recognize that an error had occurred, the patience to search for confirmation — these were the characteristics of children who made good progress in their first year of reading. Although the child's detailed knowledge of cues may be rather limited and poorly learned, confirmation is obtained when cues from several sources are checked one against the other. If such a process is successful the child is likely to become aware of new ways in which he can discriminate between words. He learns at those very points where he makes an error that he recognizes.

Some very intricate self-correction behaviour occurred in the research records. The observations showed that a child who was aware that 'something was wrong' went back over the line or tried several responses until the error was corrected. Signs of children's dissatisfaction with their own responses were frequently noted. They stopped, looked puzzled, complained, repeated the line, or ran a finger along a word. An unsuccessful attempt at self-correction can be quoted as an example.

A high progress reader aged 5:6 came to the text 'Look after Timothy' and worked at the *after* in this way:

- 'It wouldn't be *at,* it's too long.'
- 'It wouldn't be *hats.*' (This was semantically appropriate but linguistically awkward.)
- 'It wouldn't be *are,* look, it's too long.'

- The problem was not resolved and the child left it.

Three pages further on the word was read correctly without effort. It is exceptional for the school entrant to be able to state what he is doing in this way, and the verbalized reasons for his decisions may not be the significant ones. In the above example the expressed reasons for dissatisfaction are size and meaning but it should be noted that two of the three trials correctly categorize 'after' as a word beginning with 'a' and all three have at least two letters in common.

Of 10 525 errors in the Auckland research (Clay, 1969), self-correction occurred spontaneously in 26 percent. The top 50 percent of children corrected 1 in every 3 or 4 errors while for the low groups the self-correction rates were 1 in 8 and 1 in 20. All groups used self-correction, but the better readers used it more effectively. Half the self-correction (52 percent) was achieved by returning to the beginning of a line, and most of the remainder by repeating a phrase or a word. Self-correction rate was more closely related to reading progress scores in the first three years of instruction than either intelligence or reading readiness scores. But even so, self-correction is a useful sign only for a short period. It emerges towards the end of the early reading period and later it disappears as good readers change from solving their errors aloud (after they have been pronounced), to working out the problem silently (before the error has been vocalized). This change to pre-processing is illustrated by a child's comment.

*Child:* | *Bill*
Text: | Bill

Then *Child: I nearly said Peter there!*

Errors and self-correction are considered together in the following figure.

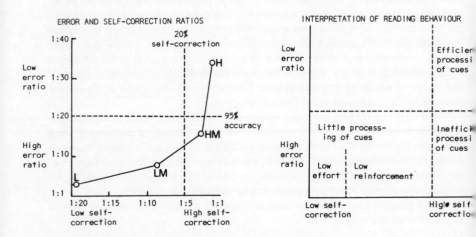

- The H group seemed to be using cues efficiently.
- The HM group tried to use cues and resolve inconsistencies but they did not operate in an efficient manner.

● The LM group attempted to use cues but they made so many errors that it was difficult for them to recognize when they had made a correct response. They showed low effort and bewilderment before complex stimuli.

● The L group seemed to make little effort to relate anything to anything. They seemed to be 'waiting for the light to dawn'. And it never did! They never seemed to know when their behaviour had been appropriate. Both these low groups need their reading individually supervised with frequent praise for correct responding.

One error proved particularly sensitive and may be a useful sign for teachers to observe. Watch the construction 'said Mother' and 'Mother said' (and similar sequences of the same construction). The two top groups tend to correct themselves on this segment of language and the two bottom groups fail to notice the word order. The high groups may predict the construction at the level of words or letters and search for confirmation that 'said' and 'Mother' occurred in that order. The low progress groups may use the construction as a whole, fitting it loosely into the sentence without checking on word or letter units, or word or letter order.

The child is able to respond to dissonance or consonance in both the grammatical and meaning aspects of language. A reader may become conscious of a difference between what he has said and one of the several messages from the text when:

● The response does not make sense — in the sentence, in the story, or with the pictures.

● The response makes sense but some visual feature of the print is incongruous with the response given.

● The number of locating movements of hand and/or eyes does not match with the number of words spoken.

Each of these incongruities forces the child to consider alternative ways of expressing his ideas. This establishes a need to choose between alternatives and the child develops an awareness that there is a precise identity for the word in the text which allows for no difference between what is said and what makes sense. In time, a smooth predict-and-check procedure is established, using phrases and sentences as the units of meaning. The competent reader is, however, able to check his response in a more detailed way to resolve a conflict, down to the visual discrimination of individual letters, if need be.

The child who can cross-check cues from movement, from visual and from language sources has an awareness that identity consists of agreement in all details. He has developed a way of learning from his errors. As he searches and checks, more and more detail in the print attracts his attention. He is sensitized to more of the interrelationships in language which can provide cues and checks. High progress readers made many errors which gave them opportunities to develop effective search and check procedures. Long stretches of correct reading with a full measure of grammatical meaning and story cues provide a rich backdrop to error when it occurs. Children then become progressively better at self-correction. For a long time we have recognized that the proportion of error in reading is important, and authorities recommend that the child read with 95 percent accuracy. A higher error rate blurs the matrix of cues. The child becomes confused and instead of a progressive gain in skill, the activity becomes non-progressive. There is scope in the very complex activity of reading for much error behaviour, and a good defence against this is strong error correcting strategies. These strategies can be developed by the young child who is still in a stage of intuitive rather than logical thinking. As children respond they gradually become aware of what they are doing and become able to employ analysis at a conscious level. None of the error detection and correction devices were very accurate at the Little Book stage but working in concert they were useful.

# Teacher Attention to Errors

What happens when teachers attend to the errors that their pupils make? McNaughton's analysis (1978b) shows that teachers provide two types of information for children.

● They ask questions or give instructions about how to respond correctly.
● They give a correct response.

If a teacher delays prompting or helping until the child has read to the end of the sentence readers become more efficient than if she attends immediately. Immediate attention —

● restricts the child's opportunity to self-correct
● deprives him of the post-error content
● restricts the kind of help she can give.

McNaughton suggests that most errors which are not self-corrected should be attended to but, if more than one error in ten is occurring it may be important not to attend to those errors which hardly change the meaning at all.

It is most important that the teacher's statements should be brief so that the pupil can keep his attention on the contextual cues.

# The Seven-Year-Olds

Some children from 6 Auckland schools were studied in their third year of instruction. Their average age was 7:10 (mean I.Q. 102). They read 3 to 5 short passages of prose graded in difficulty from the teachers' supplement to the 6 to 12-year levels of the Ginn readers (Russell, 1966). A detailed analysis of their errors showed some interesting facts about the cues the children must have been using (Williams, 1968).

All were guided by the sentence structure and word order to some extent, like the younger children. A strong trend was still noted for the substituted words to be of the same grammatical function as the text word indicating that many children are influenced in their choice of word by the grammatical structure of the sentence. Readers were deeply entrenched in the sentence pattern leading up to the error. Results varied with the quality of reading. The best readers had 80 percent grammatically acceptable substitutions, the average readers 70 percent and the low progress readers only 62 percent.

Meaning was also involved in error behaviour. Of all errors 80 percent were acceptable within the meaning of the story for the high progress group, 65 percent for the average group and 54 percent for the low group. The good reader matched his attempts to both sentence structure and meaning in 80 percent of his trials. For the average and low progress groups their responses were more often matched for structure of the sentence than for the meaning.

Do the child's guesses indicate that he is using letter-sound correspondence to guide his attempts? Overall there was almost no observable word analysis or word attack. Audible analysis of words into syllables or sounds was noted in only $5^1/_2$ percent of the errors or attempts. In a further 6 percent of responses there was a delay of such a degree that the recorder was able to assume private solving taking place before a successful response was given. Thus only $11^1/_2$ percent of word study was 'phonic' or 'syllabic'. Teachers should watch and listen. They will probably also notice that such word solving is rare in book reading.

Four kinds of word analysis behaviour were tallied — syllabic attack as in *sur-faced*; compound words as in *can-not*; letter sound combinations as in *sl-a-sh-ed*; mixed letter and syllable attack as in *w-ait-ing*. Of the four types syllabic attack was the most common, even at this young age. And the group most likely to use a letter-sounding approach was the high progress group. But they also used larger clusters of letters than the low progress groups. These findings are consistent with research findings on pronounceable units (Gibson, 1965).

Nevertheless, perhaps the child responds unconsciously to letter-sound correspondence as he makes his guesses. An analysis of all single word errors for letter-sound correspondence showed that 87 percent of the children's attempts involved some letter-sound correspondence with no marked differences between progress groups. These figures are high compared with 41 percent quoted earlier for 5- to 6-year-olds. Beginning letter or clusters were the same in 80 percent of the errors indicating a high degree of matching choices to initial letters. Last letters or clusters matched in 53 percent showing fairly well-developed attention to inflections and suffixes. Minimal attention was being paid at this stage to medial letter groups. The focus of attention appeared to be initial concentration on the left end of the word, then a quick visual sweep through the central section with sustained attention on the final element.

Errors of position or order (reversals) accounted for only $2^1/_2$ percent of all substitutions. Left to right sequencing behaviour appeared to be firmly fixed as a major convention in reading. But first letter groups or first and last letter groups provided cues with medial sections of words receiving less attention.

A high progress reader at this level makes few errors. When he does fail to solve a word and match it exactly to the text there are 4 chances in 5 that it will fit the sentence grammatically, and that it will be meaningful in the context, and 9 chances in 10 that it will match some of the letter-sound features of the word. (The attempt will probably correspond with beginning and ending sounds but not with those in the middle.)

High progress readers at this level read faster than the high progress primer readers but the low progress readers of both groups read at the same slow rate. The high progress reader gathers his cues and selects his responses at a fast rate, but he also adapts his speed at a difficulty and after an error. The slow reader has less flexibility and reads slowly word by word.

The skills of the average and low progress readers in these three aspects of cue gathering — grammatical, semantic and letter-sound correspondence — should be developed and strengthened, in that order, and emphasis on sounding out or syllabic attack limited to a breakdown technique and not the sole approach to words.

At the third year of instruction half of all the successful attacks on words involved self-correction behaviour — that is, it arose out of an error which was noticed by the child so that he searched for more cues and solved it. Most of the self-corrections involved going back to repeat a single preceding word or returning to the beginning of a line. Rates of self-correction varied with reading progress, being 1 in 3 errors for the high progress group, 1 in 4 for the average group and 1 in 8 for the low progress group. When the language pattern of the errors was an acceptable one, syntactically and semantically, the likelihood of self-correction was greatly reduced.

Repetition of correct text which had occurred in the records of first year reading appeared again as a kind of confirming check of the correct response. Repetition occurred when the reader had an expectation for a second response which conflicted with the letters he was about to read and when the words were not a language pattern that sounded natural or acceptable to him. But the teacher can look upon repetition as an indication of efforts to search for, check, and confirm responses.

These findings seem to indicate that high progress readers are gathering cues from meaning, grammar, letter-sound relationships and cross-relating these in an active process of search and check. The average and low progress readers use fewer types of cues, make less effort to relate these, and do this processing less accurately and more slowly.

One of the first things a remedial teacher may do is to encourage her pupil to 'read the punctuation'. Nothing destroys sense more rapidly than to drone through phrases and punctuation marks, pausing at points which are syntactically in the middle of a meaningful segment. A second study of children in their third year of instruction looked at these features of reading behaviour and found that good readers paused after phrases and whole sentences at punctuation points, but poor readers stopped and stressed a word at a time, and often a syllable at a time. Even when the words were familiar they punched them out with even pitch and heavy stress as if grouping had no significance. Good readers appeared to gain in speed and understanding from anticipating whole stretches of text and checking to see, visually, if their predictions were correct. Good readers were operating at the sentence and phrase level. They could move to the word level when necessary, and could use letter-sound correspondence to distinguish between similar words or to analyse new words. The low progress groups seemed unable to use cues beyond the syllable and word level. They were over-committed to the idea that reading was word recognition and sounding out.

# In Summary

Any correct response in reading fits a matrix of relationships in a sentence like the pieces in a jig-saw puzzle. A mis-match along one or more dimensions of this matrix produces errors. A child may use cues from more than one source in selecting a response, and when he is conscious of some disagreement in the cues he begins to search for an alternative response.

A word's identity is checked at the level of sounds or letters, and in this limited sense those authors who stress the learning of letter-sound associations and sounding-out operations as the essence of reading are correct. The rules which relate the sounds of the language to the letters, however unsystematic, are the ultimate reference for the precise pronunciation and discrimination of most written words. But 95 percent of the reading activity of the good readers does not involve this analytic behaviour.

Efficient reading can be described in terms of Bruner's (1957) definition of perception. Some primitive identification of print is made and some expectations of what will follow are aroused in the reader in the form of probabilities arising from past experience with oral language and with reading. These expectations narrow the alternatives to a few which can be checked against a young child's limited knowledge of reading. This knowledge is initially based on a limited awareness of cues. But it is the nature of the language code that several sources of cues converge in the case of a correct response to produce consonance rather than dissonance.

The child gradually learns to respond to more of the rich sources of cues in the text, to search actively for the cues, to relate one to another with greater precision, and to increase the accuracy with which he makes his decisions about what to notice and what to ignore.

On familiar material anticipations can be made and checked on the basis of a few cues without undue risk of error. A detailed search is only made on unfamiliar material or when some error seems to have occurred. Bruner suggests the following behaviour outcomes may follow from such a detailed check.

● An increase in sensitivity if the choice is near to being correct, causing a closer look.

Child: | *hot*      *top*    *tap*   (Self-correction)
Text:  | tap

● A decrease of search in that direction if the choice is not close to that required.

Child: | *Look*    *and*    (Change of direction)
Text:  | A fire

● Stop searching if the input fits.

Child: | *tractors*   (This fits within the limits of the child's discriminatory criteria)
Text:  | trucks

● A gating or filtering system to stop further searching.

*Child:* | *here is*    ('Oh! *is* is not there! Oh well! Too bad!')
Text: | here are

Research suggests that the good reader manipulates a network of language, spatial and visual perception cues, and sorts these implicitly but efficiently, searching for dissonant relations and best-fit solutions. Many sources of cues allow for confirming checks and act as a stimulus to error correction. Habitual responses will be continuously emerging as the result of successful performance.

There are two major questions the observant teacher can ask about a child's reading responses.

1  On a text of this level of difficulty what evidence can I find that the child responds to cues at the

● letter level
● cluster level
● word level
● word group level
● sentence group level
● sentence level?

2  What evidence can I find that the child relates his other experiences to this reading task?

● life experience
● story experience
● familiarity with this story
● an earlier part of the story
● another word known in another context
● other experiences with letters of symbols.

# References and Further Reading

Bruner, J.S., 'On perceptual readiness', *Psychological Review,* 64, 1957, pp. 123-152.

Clay, Marie M., 'Emergent Reading Behaviour,' Unpubl. doctoral dissertation, University of Auckland Library, 1966.

Clay, Marie M., 'Reading errors and self-correction behaviour', *British Journal of Educational Psychology,* 39, 1969, pp. 47-56.

Clay, Marie M. and Williams, B., The reading behaviour of Standard One Children. *Education,* 1973.

Russell, D.H. et al., 'The Ginn Basic Readers', Ginn and Co., Boston, 1966.

Gibson, Eleanor J., 'Learning to Read', *Science,* 148, 1965 pp. 1066-1072.

Goodacre, Elizabeth, 'Hearing children read', *Child Education,* June 1971:

Goodman, K.S., 'Analysis of oral reading miscues: applied psycholinguistics', *Reading Research Quarterly*, 1, 1969, pp. 9-30.

Goodman, Yetta, 'Using children's reading miscues for new teaching strategies', *The Reading Teacher*, 23, 1970. pp. 455-459.

Meares, Olive, Some children talk about print. Belmont Reading Clinic, Auckland, 1972.

McNaughton, S.S., Instructor attention to oral reading errors: a functional analysis. Unpubl. Ph.D. Thesis, University of Auckland, 1978.

McNaughton, S.S., Learning in one-to-one reading instruction: outcomes of teacher attention to errors. Paper presented to IRA Conference, Dunedin, N.Z. , 1978.

Nurss, J., 'Oral reading errors and reading comprehension', *The Reading Teacher*, 22, 1969, p. 523.

Reid, Jessie, 'Learning to think about reading,' *Educational Research*, 9, (1), 1966, pp. 56-62.

Weber, Rose-Marie, 'The study of oral reading errors: a survey of the literature', *Reading Research Quarterly*, 4, 1968, pp. 96-119.

Weber, Rose-Marie, 'A linguistic analysis of first grade reading errors', *Reading Research Quarterly*, 5, 1970, pp. 427-451.

Williams, B., 'The oral reading behaviour of Standard One children', Unpubl. M.A. thesis, University of Auckland Library, 1968.

# Exploring Further

**Make a study of one reading group's errors on three texts of different levels of difficulty. Refer to** *The Early Detection of Reading Difficulties: A Diagnostic Survey with Recovery Procedures* **for more help.**

# 12 A Predictable Environment is Necessary

## Promotion Policies

How important is continuity for the school entrant? We are concerned when older children in higher classes have three teachers in one school year; but who are the more flexible beings — older children with greater security and experience, or little children in a strange new world? Although the school entrant has a great need for a consistent and predictable environment he is unlikely to get it. In good schools the admission and promotion policies which take account of individual progress rates among the entrants promote the better ones frequently to new and higher groups. This respects individual differences in rates of learning but it destroys the continuity of people and procedures in this strange new world of the school. One of the necessary conditions for learning for the young child is a predictable environment in which he can recognize consistency and regularity. An environment is most powerful when it is relatively constant over a period of time and when it also has a here-and-now consistency so that several activities are mutually reinforcing. Part of this contemporary environment for the young school child is the teacher, her personality and her teaching procedures. A young child must get used to a new teacher before the child can recognize the consistencies that the teacher is providing. The child must stay with this teacher for a significant period of time if the teacher is to influence the child's behaviour in any stable way.

Teachers are different. A little child must adjust to a day filled with the idiosyncratic expectations of a particular teacher. It makes a great demand on that child if his teacher is changed frequently. Several teachers in his first year of school will not provide the consistency and regularity in his learning environment that is necessary for a sound foundation to his education.

Schools with individualized programmes are often guilty of promoting children too frequently from teacher to teacher. Fast learners may even have as many as five teachers before the end of their first year. Schools which admit children at one time in the year, or at term beginnings are more likely to commit a second kind of error, keeping children whose needs are very different lock-stepped in a programme which has a surface homogeneity.

For the best progress, the young child needs a predictable environment and if the teacher and her peculiar demands change frequently, only those children who can adapt to change will make good progress. A six monthly move from new entrants class to the next teacher is probably the maximum movement that should be tolerated. At present, children are often moved merely for administrative reasons because the class reaches a capacity roll which forces the change. Some flexibility may be achieved by such organizational solutions as having two new entrant classes rising to maximum rolls of 20 to 25 children each. Another suggestion is the 'split-schedule' with slow learners coming to school at 9.00 am and leaving at 2.00 pm, and fast learners attending from 10.00 am to 3.00 pm. Reading activities for half the class could then be scheduled at the beginning and end of the day.

Even the promotion of the fast learners should be watched closely. They may do well under any circumstances but they may do even better if not required to make too many new adjustments in a year. The high progress group should not be held in their progress by rigid promotion policies but neither should they be accelerated through five teachers in a year if they are to reach their optimum performance.

The average child's repertoire of skills is very limited, and occurs in response to a limited range of materials. When a child is passed over to another teacher, that teacher should know exactly what the child can read successfully (at the 95 percent accuracy level). Some glaring mistakes in promotion were observed in individual cases in the research study when as many as 3 books in the graded basic series were skipped, not by a competent child making good progress, but by a poor reader. The complaint here is not that the child must proceed step by step through the basic series but that he must move forward from competence at the 95 percent accuracy level to an activity which he can master at a similar level in 3 or 4 weeks at the outside. Children in the lower groups cannot tolerate separation by over-promotion from the things they 'know'. The differences become too big to be challenging.

# Variety or Regularity?

Slow children who remain in early reading groups for long periods, even up to one year, are very vulnerable to stultifying practices. They are rarely learning nothing. They are responding in set ways and forming habits, probably bad habits, because of the very regularity of the activities they face — the same games, the same cards, the same early reading book. Repetitive activity which does not continually call for new kinds of learning from the child can produce faulty learning which becomes habitual at this time when it should be constantly changing. The entirely predictable environment does not lead to progressive gains in skill.

Children come to school with different strengths and weaknesses. No single sequence of learning tasks could be appropriate to children of diverse experiences. The teacher has the difficult task of arranging her programme so that consistency and regularity are evident to the individual child and yet stultifying reptition is avoided. She must provide for the diverse needs of individuals in the group and yet not be so flexible, varied or different that the slower children are unable to locate fragments of familiar knowledge in all the variety of activities in her programme.

The richer the child's preschool experiences (including language experience) and the more competent his performance at entry, the better he will learn from an environment where activities are varied. The poorer the child's background experience and current performance the more regularity he is likely to require in his learning environment.

# Consistent Reinforcement

When any child makes his first attempt at some new kinds of responses he needs to be praised. Psychological theories of reinforcement are clear on this point — behaviour will be repeated if it is positively reinforced by attention or praise. The teacher needs opportunities to engage in sensitive observation of precisely what her children are doing. Then she can acknowledge a small-step gain with enthusiasm. She can praise a tentative response which is good. She can prevent the consolidation of inappropriate responding into erroneous habits. The teacher's greatest fault at this stage would be 'not noticing' that poor quality responses were crowding out better ones. Good teachers know what to look for. They set time aside for observation of what individual children are doing. They know the direction in which a child has been moving, and they keep brief but continuing records of the changes that occur. They are sensitive observers of change in early reading behaviours. They know which new attempts are pointing in the right direction and they foster these with praise.

# Attendance

A school psychologist examining a child with reading problems will pay close attention to any reports of frequent absences in the first years of school. These occur often because the 5-year-old may run through a range of infectious diseases from measles to chicken-pox after contacts with a large group of children. Chest complaints, ear trouble, poor emotional adjustment to school — the reasons for non-attendance are numerous. This is unavoidable in many cases and has not been thought of as too serious because the learning of the first year has not been considered very important.

On the contrary, when the child's responses to books are haphazard, inconsistent, here today and gone tomorrow, one way to increase his general uncertainty and confusion is to expose him to teaching on an 'on-off' basis. He gets to know what is expected of him, then has a week at home, and when he arrives back in the classroom his group is learning things for which he has no foundation. The longer the absence the greater the gap he must bridge. Very seldom does the busy class teacher take the child aside and teach him the necessary bridging skills. For example, one little girl was absent on the average 3 days per fortnight through asthma in her first two years at school. She remained with the same reading group and was expected to keep up without extra help.

One form of adjustment occurs when the teacher notices a child's confusion and demotes him or her to a lower reading group, his plight undetected. Here is what some teachers do after a child has been absent for 1 to 3 weeks (note that none suggest individual tuition):

● I try to keep him in the same group by sending his books home and by having him read the material for the period he missed.
● Watch very carefully.
● A slower child may be placed back one group.
● A bright child may read with two groups or just continue and catch up.

The child from the better home with the higher intelligence has more resources to bridge any gaps in the teaching by himself. But, ironically, the poor attendance records are often found among children who have fewer home opportunities to learn, lower ability and parents who do not value education. These children need careful appraisal of their status and special tutoring if they have been away from school for more than a week.

# The Effects of the Long Summer Vacation

To gain some measure of the effect of a break in schooling on the research group, children were tested at the end of a school year. They were asked to read their books and a running record was taken of the accuracy with which they were read. After a summer vacation of 7 weeks, at the beginning of the school year they were asked to repeat that reading and a record was made for comparison. When the children were asked to read the book which they had read before the holidays at the 95 percent accuracy level, three quarters of first year entrants lost very little reading skill in the 7 weeks vacation. But the lowest 25 percent of the sample, who could ill-afford to forget the little they had learned, had dropped in accuracy. They performed poorly before the holidays and forgot a great deal during the 7-week break.

In practice, it is probably unusual for a new teacher to know what book the child had last completed with success. This is regrettable and a fault to be overcome. As early reading responses are very specific to the materials studied, some record of the books children have completed successfully in their previous class should always be available to their next teachers as a matter of routine.

At the beginning of a new school year teachers should expect their pupils' previous teacher to supply them with such information. And they should be cautious about moving pupils up or down just to conform to the new reading groups they are trying to form.

# Change of School

When a child changes school the teaching method and the basic reading series may also change. It is an insurance against confusion if the teacher of the school which the child is leaving sends the child to his next school with a note of

- the book he last read successfully
- the book he was attempting when he left the school.

A wise teacher in his next school would hasten his adjustment by asking him to read a book which is well within his capacity and familiar to him. A step backwards in the reading series while he gains his balance in the new environment would be appropriate. Or the enrolling Supervisor of Junior Classes who frequently tries the child out on a book before placing him in a class, could well take an observation record and an accuracy check to find a book which the child can read with 95 percent accuracy. Teachers who are used to a concept of appropriate levels of reading materials described as independent, instructional and frustration levels are really working in the same terms as the accuracy levels described in this book. Above 95 percent accuracy represents independent reading, from 90 to 95 percent accuracy represents instructional level at the completion of the learning task and below this represents frustration level.

Children who change schools during the first two years of reading instruction are an 'at risk' group and must be paid special attention if reading problems are to be reduced.

# Continuity of Personal Achievement

In promoting a young child through his books, classes, or schools, one must remember that his learning is specific to a limited range of materials and situations. He will recover from any change most rapidly if his prior learning is easily transferred to the new situation. In this case, the change can be stimulating and challenging and lead to seeking further change. The opposite effects can be imagined.

Continuity of personal achievement for the child is most important. At times of promotion, term vacations and changes of school, it is advisable to begin the child on familiar material before introducing new books. If this seems obvious it is necessary for me to assure readers that the most hopeless errors are made at times of change for some children. Drastic demotion or, worse still, unreasonable promotion to a level that was far too difficult, were recorded during research observations. Not frequently, to be sure, but damaging to individual children's reading progress.

# Exploring Further

**Study the procedures used when children are moved from one reading group, class or school to another. What do you think should happen?**

# Part 4

# The Reading Process

# 13 The Visual Perception of Print

Children have to learn to 'see' real objects, pictures and symbols. Their eyes move across a surface as they scan in some systematic way to see whether there is something they can recognize, something they have seen previously. If these symbols are letters they occur in words as complex sequences. At first the child can isolate only a few unconnected features. As he becomes familiar with a particular pattern which recurs he begins to survey it in some systematic way. In his preparation for reading the child must develop a scanning sequence that is appropriate to printed text, and then he must practise this scanning pattern until it becomes habitual.

However, it takes the child several years to explore all the details and all the combinations in words and letter patterns. Although the child is introduced to letters and writing close to his entry to school, his skill in seeing particular letters as distinct from any other letter probably undergoes changes for the first three years even for the best readers (Clay, 1970; Gibson, 1975).

To the literate adult, reading letters seems to be extraordinarily simple.

'This illusion arises from the fact that, at this higher level of development, the operation occurs by then as abbreviated, generalized, perfected and automatic mental behaviour which requires no effort and causes no problems . . . learning a new skill cannot and consequently must not start from its final form . . . but on the contrary proceeds by consistent changes of its first forms to its final mental form.'

(Elkonin, 1974, 559-560)

Children learning to read must discriminate the set of letters used in an alphabetic writing system. This does not mean that they must make all the discriminations without error *before* they can proceed with reading. On the contrary, if they have learnt a few letters and a procedure for learning letters they can learn the remainder while reading.

What visual units are used in reading? Experimenters are still exploring this vexed question and programme constructors are still jumping to conclusions. It seems to be consistent in work completed so far that a change occurs as children move from early to later reading levels.

As children read more there are changes in the amount of visual information they are able to ignore and still retain accuracy on more and more difficult texts. They scan for less visual information, their speed of reading increases *and* their error rates fall. Juola (1979) relates this to an explanation of how we form units which we use as we read. More detailed information, or smaller units, are not used unless the larger unit is not recognizable.

There is a danger that the child will learn wrong associations at any point in the learning sequence. Whatever method is adopted for teaching reading some children will stray off into strange procedures at some point. If a child is taught to detect and correct his errors he has a built-in safeguard against practising errors while his visual perception of print is still inaccurate. Similarly, if a child has several ways of solving a problem then when immature perception causes error, another approach to problem-solving is possible. In the physical sciences, when a process involves risk, safety factors and error detection devices are built into the controlling system. These are also required in a complex learning task like reading.

Children's experiences in their preschool years have led to a great variety of skills in visual perception. Research has shown that the 3-year-old explores objects and forms manually by touching, manipulating, tracing with fingers and turning things over. The 4- to 5-year-old uses both touch and visual exploration together to investigate shapes, supporting one with the other. By 6 years many children can systematically explore forms and objects with their eyes alone. These patterns of visual exploration are, in fact, motor skills (Zaporozhets, 1965; Zinchenko and Lomov, 1960; Lynn, 1966).

On entry to school the slowest children will still learn best by having their hands guided passively through a manual analysis of the forms and letters. Teachers who guide the hand of a hesitant new entrant know this. The average child at this stage will benefit from information about print coming to him from both hand and eye. He may be able to discriminate better the shapes which he can handle or make movements with, rather than the ones he can merely look at. When he tries to write, this directs his attention to letters in a particular order and forces him to work sequentially at the survey of print. But the writing he is copying should be in front of him where he can trace or 'feel' it — not across the room on the teacher's blackboard.

Only the most advanced 5- and 6-year-old children will be able to depend on their eyes alone when they enter school. This would seem to give them an advantage but it is not necessarily so. It is more difficult for the teacher to check the effectiveness of the child's survey of print when he is a fast, visual learner. While most will learn to organize their behaviour in an orderly manner some will speedily scramble the sequence of letters or words. And this will not be observable.

One approach to beginning reading that is currently stressed is multisensory and is known as VAKT. It emphasizes that the visual, auditory, kinaesthetic and tactile senses should be used simultaneously in beginning reading activity. Research results suggest that more effective learning takes place for an equivalent number of practice periods when the stimulus has both visual and auditory qualities than when it is presented to eyes or ears alone. Confirming incoming messages consolidates one meaning. Incoming messages which do not agree signal the possibility that an error has occurred. The total approach seems to suit the young learner and ensures that an efficient learning system is developed.

There is a body of research (Bryant, 1974) which shows that young children between 4 and 6 years can make judgements and inferences that surprise us. Careful experimentation shows that children who cannot pick out two squares of the same size with any accuracy can perform the task if the squares are framed by a sheet of paper or a small table top. While the absolute judgement is too difficult for them, they can make a relative judgement using external frameworks to organize their perception.

Not all children who can make such inferences do so in an actual situation. A gap exists between what can be done and what is actually done.

Children made judgements about orientation by using different features of the background. For example children could make judgements about two objects facing in similar orientations if both were present simultaneously, or if they were presented successively. In the latter case Bryant suggests the child must have been using different features of the background to distinguish between horizontal/vertical lines, and oblique lines.

Applied to early reading this may provide a simple explanation for some often-observed behaviours. Think of a child who

- starts to write in the top right hand corner of a page
- does not distinguish M W or b d.

If such a child has not established an internal coding of features that distinguish the directional schema, or the letters in question, and if instead the child has habituated an attention pattern which seeks to make a relative judgement from the framework created by the edges of the page, then the top-bottom frame for M W, or the left-right sides of the frame for b d, or the corner frames for the start of writing, may be difficult to distinguish.

Using a simple match/mismatch judgement which takes the framework into account as well as the point or letter, children might have difficulty in distinguishing the confusible features of this figure.

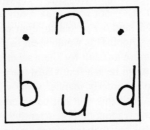

# Attention to Letters

Here are some diary entries made by the mothers of two boys just beginning school.

---

*12 Jan.*
*First attempt at drawing mainly stick figures. No interest in printing or reading.*
*29 Jan.*
*Holidays finished. No writing attempted, not interested in reading or words. Balls, and outside playing take up holiday time.*

---

*28 Jan.*
*Terence finds his left hand hard to cope with. Quite useless with right one.*
*Seems to want to write backwards and upside down. Sees his twin brother*
*print his name and gets very discouraged and won't try any more.*
*29 Feb.*
*Likes to go over my printing of his name. Will do this very slowly and*
*carefully.*

Whatever the method used to teach reading, at some point, not far from his first attempt to read a book, the child must pay attention to letters. This is not to say that he must learn some letters before he learns to read some words, but he probably will. At first, when he appears to be recognizing a few words he is probably noticing a particular letter or feature. Mothers' diaries of the home activities of a group of children over the first year at school suggest that much spare time was devoted to letter learning, when this was not an activity stressed by the methods used in the schools.

'Asked for name letters to be printed and started to copy them.'
'He copied over large print in the newspaper with a crayon, showed it to me and pointed out some similar letters.'
'He showed a little friend how he could write his name and copied her name after his.'
'Wrote his first name in sand very clearly without anything to copy.'
'After drawing he wrote his name. It seems as though he has that firmly in his mind.'
'Used a ball point pen to make up an "Office Game". Wrote out cards with real and made-up words in printed letters and figures.'
'Was given a toy model aeroplane and asked for *Christchurch* to be printed on the wing. Had apparently seen this on a visit to the aerodrome.'
'Read his book to mother. Then copied words from the book for about 30 minutes.'
'Copies stories from books but also writes lovely letters to her Daddy who is away at present.'
'Came in from school and said he could write *up*, and *to* and did so without any copy.'
'Told us he had been dreaming about printing last night. He remembered printing the letters *M A C* and wanted to know what the word was.'
'He is attempting to write his name but only letters on paper at first.'
'He is becoming interested in letters more than words, e.g. "Does '*S* start my name and start Bruce's?"''

The exploration of print is a serious business!

# The Identification of Letters

Letters are the components by which words are differentiated. How do children learn to distinguish all the letter forms used in our written code from one another?

Many of the difficulties children have in discovering the identities of letters are observable in their early attempts to copy words. The example below was written from right to left, and can be translated, 'A rocket goes up'. This child is currently discovering the shape and consistency of the letter 'e'.

**A rocket
goes up.**

In experiments where young preschoolers learn to read using the 'talking' typewriter the child strikes a key and the computer says the name of the letter. Soon the child is able to name the letter before the machine has to do it for him (Moore, 1961; Pines, 1968). Chalk and blackboard are provided for the child to draw letters and symbols he has seen in typewritten form. When the child knows the letters he reads and types out simple sentences. Reports suggest that the child refers to the symbols with alphabetic names.

Durrell (1958) found that 6-year-old children who learnt to read successfully in the first year of instruction had acquired a large amount of letter knowledge prior to entry to school, but there were wide individual differences. He found early skill in letter knowledge a good predictor of early progress in reading, during the first year of instruction. Knowledge of letter names and sounds does not, he claims, assure success in acquiring a sight vocabulary but lack of knowledge produces failure. It seems that letter discrimination is a necessary but not sufficient skill for reading progress.

The visual discrimination of each of these symbols one from another is a large learning task, and the accumulation of skill is slow and gradual over the first two years of instruction for children who begin school at 5 years. Karl writes his name as 'Kpnl', points to the 'n', says 'I got that wrong', but fails to see the 'p' is also wrong. Too little attention has been paid to the size, complexity and, particularly, the gradualness of this perceptual discrimination learning.

Letter identification deals with the number of letter forms which the child knows well enough to identify in some way and the rate at which he adds to this store of knowledge. Calling a letter something which distinguishes it from other letters is giving it an identity, even when that identification is of an unexpected kind. One child spelled 'big' as 'b — — i — — gigglygoo!' The 'g' had an identity distinctly reserved for that peculiar form.

At 6 years individual differences range from Grant who regards 'G' as his name, and who would presumably respond to all words beginning with 'G' similarly, to Jimmy who could tell you all the alphabet names, all their sounds, a set of words beginning with each letter and other interesting details if you had time to listen.

Children have to learn to perceive the symbols of the alphabet. Each letter must be contrasted with every other letter so that thousands of discriminations are involved. The discriminations are made initially on some basis that works for a particular child and they do not match any of the systems which adults think of. This is not, at the early stage, phonetic learning or alphabetic learning or even key word learning — it is something inarticulate and unsystematic that works for an individual child.

The child who discriminates adequately between all these symbols is free to build his sound associations for clusters of letters. He has directional behaviour and letter symbols under control. This is not an argument for more direct teaching of letter symbols. It is a call for the insight, on the part of teacher, that while new entrants are reading their little books, and writing their first stories, they are building up a vast amount of visual discrimination learning, which is vital to subsequent progress. What we have overlooked for too long is the fact that before a child can attach a sound to a letter symbol, he has first of all to be able to see the letter symbol, in the sense that he can see it as as an individual entity different from other similar symbols. Whether he makes the discrimination at first on the basis of alphabetic names, sound equivalents, or some rather personal association like 'the first letter in my big brother's name' is not important.

Gradually, the child who is making these discriminations more or less accurately, tidies up his systems and develops phonetic, alphabetic and visual systems for distinguishing between letters. He then has little residual 'trouble with symbols'! As with the directional learning, if there really is some organic basis for a child's failing to make such discriminations, waiting will do no good. Some aids must be devised to assist the child to establish each letter symbol as a recognizable entity, distinct from similar signs. For the child who has difficulty it would be wrong to attempt to hand him our basis for making the discrimination (which, incidentally, is probably one we acquired late in our development and is unlikely to be the one by which we first learned). Instead we should arrange for him to make successful discriminations, on whatever basis is viable for him, and through successful practice allow him gradually to systematize this knowledge.

# The Colour of Paper

For most children and for adult readers black print on a white ground is very satisfactory. Tinker (1966), an authority on legibility found this to be so for adults and he assumed that children from the age of 10 would react like adults. He did not study young children acquiring reading skills. Some beginning readers find a slightly reduced contrast of brightness easier to 'see' (for example, black print on unbleached paper, black on the brown paper of teacher-made 'large books').

Using a case study interview technique over several years Meares (1972, 1973) has described the reactions of a sub-group of her reading clinic cases to brightness contrasts of print on paper. Several colour contrasts, were reported by these children to be easier for them to see than black print on white paper. These were

- black on cream
- black on light grey
- white on grey.

A few children who seem confused by print may profit from an exploration of how easy or difficult they find the colour contrasts.

Meares is careful to say that only individual children probably 'see print' differently and her report implies that the variables which disturb children may lead them to be placed in different groups, some disturbed by one thing and others by something different. The problems occur because of

- *brightness contrast* between print and its background
- alteration of the *figure/ground* relationship so that the white areas which should be background provide a dominant frame with white rivulets running down the page
- *interference* from neighbouring print in the lines above and below, and the words to right and left
- *jumpy or dazzling print* that moves, perhaps related to the ability to stabilize the image
- an *after-image effect* producing 'shadow' of print which clutters the white spaces and impedes the perception of the real print with clarity.

Serifs, the decorative feet on printed letters maintain a clarity of outline to stem the encroachment of the white and prevent thinning of the letters. Many children's books have sanserif script which may introduce new problems.

There are some interesting comments to be made on Meares' findings. Every psychologist would recognize these variables as operating under certain conditions for all of us. They are not the sign of a cerebral dysfunction. Meares discovered them anew before she read the psychology texts, by sensitive observation of her pupils. And a reduced brightness contrast is very easy for the teacher of new entrants to achieve. Instead of reaching for a black felt-pen and a white sheet of paper she can try some other variations, at least for her slow readers. The changes will not work for all children, and miracles rarely occur with reading. But the daily lesson may be a little easier for all concerned. A tinted sheet of perspex or sunglasses are less suitable alternatives.

Meares provides an experiment for the reader to carry out and she says 'I hope it will not tire you as much as it did me.'

Choose a book at about the 7-year level. You will have no trouble finding one with maximum brightness contrast print.

Read at least two pages at the slow rate of a child with severe reading difficulties. Don't forget to back-track occasionally for self-correction and to employ continued inspection on those words you don't know.

# To Check On What Children See

## Observe eye movements

One study observed children in a controlled way looking at their eye movements while they read to their teachers. High scores of eye-on-print behaviour was related to reading progress and high scores on eyes-wandering were related to slow reading progress. The 'eyes-wandering' children moved their attention to the illustration, to the teacher, to the floor, to other children, perhaps searching away from the book for cues rather than scanning the print for cues (McQueen, 1975).

It is easy to pick up from the turn of the head and the shift of the eyes whether the child is scanning the print before he gives a response to the text.

## Observe how a particular child remembers letters

School entrants can sometimes discriminate between letters quite well before they can name them or write them. I discovered this by accident and recommend it as a technique for checking on the young child's visual analysis. One child was shown a picture of a horse with *h* under it. She said *horse* and then added *A stick and then over.* With nothing to copy she traced the letter in the air. Shown the letter C she said *cat* then *c* and without a copy traced the letter in the air. When shown the letter *m* she said *mouse* and traced the letter in the air. After further exploration of this technique I began to test young children for letter identification in this way, particularly those children who were unable to give a verbal response to letters.

I showed the child a picture, turned the card over to show a single consonant sound and asked 'What is this?' One can accept a response which is a *word*, a *letter name* or a *sound*.

If the child did not respond in one of these ways I would take away the card and ask the child to write the letter in the air, and in this way I could learn whether the child had visually analysed this letter in such a way as to be able to produce the motor pattern for making a copy of it. I soon learned that while some children might find it difficult to remember the word to go with the picture or to be able to name or sound the letter they were often able to write it in the air either with their eyes closed or with the card turned over. They had some kind of model of the letter in their mind and this could produce a response in movement but not a response in language.

Teachers can use this technique to:

● Locate children who cannot analyse letter forms.
● Find out which letters a child does attend to 'in mind's eye'.
● Test whether letters currently being taught have been visually scanned.

The following sample of behaviour was gained from a child who has been at school for two weeks. Shown a display of letters she selected a lower case 'd'. Asked 'What is it?' she made no response. Spontaneously she wrote it in the air. Then she looked at me and said, 'That's Delwyn's little d,' a reference to her sister's name. That was learned at home. She then selected *m*, traced it in the air, and whispered *m-m-mouse*. That was learned at school. Then she selected in turn *i k s c* and gave them their alphabetic names. That was the limit of her skill and she paid no more attention to the letters on the table. Two weeks later this child was tested with a full range of the alphabet sounds and at one point as she was tracing one of the letters in the air *with her eyes closed* she said '*me can see my finger*'.

It is common when children are asked to write the letter in the air for them to close their eyes as if trying to see the letter as they follow out the movement pattern. This is an interesting confirmation of a link between the motor and the visual aspects of early reading skills. And this writing in the air seems to be easier than writing on paper.

## Observe the child's grouping of letters

In the early stages of learning letters the child may deal with the diverse array of letter forms by grouping similar letters together. Researchers have tended to say that children make errors when they do not distinguish between forms such as n and r and each of these from h. Recast in a more positive form this behaviour could mean that as a first stage in learning the child forms a few categories that are distinctly different. For example Rodney was tested on the lower case alphabet, with the following results.

| Alphabet names: | e  o | |
|---|---|---|
| Sounds: | — | |
| From known words: | s (see)  y | (Rodney) |
| Writing form: | h  n  u  w  m | (tunnel) |
| | q  p  b | (ring and stick) |
| | i  l  j | (number one) |

From such gross classifications of sameness new distinctions will emerge.

## Observe early attempts at writing

Another way to observe children's visual scanning of letter forms is to observe their writing, see pages 124 to 127.

## Test letter identification and study the answers

A more systematic check is made when capital and lower-case letters are presented in random order with the instruction 'What do you call this?' The child is credited with a pass if he gives:

● an alphabetic name
● a phonetic equivalent
● a word beginning with the letter.

He is not credited with a pass if he notes correctly a letter in the middle of a word or identifies it as the last letter, for example the 's' in 'is'.

A teacher may wish to check the range of letters that have been taught so far. However, if she presents a wider range of letters she will probably discover that the child knows more than she has taught him.

At 6 years of age the full capital and lower case alphabets should be checked. This checking yields information on the number of letters correctly discriminated, the dominant mode of identification, and the common confusions for any one child. It demonstrated that the average Auckland school entrant knew 3 letters at school entry and that letter identification increased in importance for reading progress throughout the first year of school. At 6 years most children could identify 28 (of the 54 letters tested). By 7 or 8 years one could expect nearly perfect scoring (Clay, 1966).

## A three-piece puzzle

Letters have a constant position. Before a child comes to school things like his toys don't lose their identity even if their position is changed. So a bucket is a bucket whether it's upside down or right way up or on its side. One of the things a child has to learn in writing is that letters change their identity if you turn them around the wrong way. The child must learn this exception to his past 5 to 6 years of experience. That's a very difficult thing for the child to learn. What have been called reversals might be looked upon as behaviours found in a child who believes that shapes have constancy no matter what their orientation. That is true for objects in his environment why should it not be true for letters that he is learning. For me this seems a simpler explanation than the assumption that his brain is turning the letters around.

---

**EXAMPLES OF PROBLEMS WITH LETTER SEQUENCES**
A three-piece jigsaw was made of each child's name and each child was asked to make his own name. Most succeeded after six months at school but these three children were having more difficulty than most with this letter sequence problem.

| | | |
|---|---|---|
| pɹ ᓂo uo | Go | rd | on |
| on Sh ar | Sh | ar | on |
| Cɑ en rm | Ca | rm | en |

---

To test this awareness of the constant position of letters I have used a three piece puzzle. All the vertical sides have identical curves and so they can be fitted together in any order and even inverted with the bottom at the top. I divide the child's name into three groups of letters. It is my guess that three pieces of puzzle is sufficiently difficult at this stage of the child's development. If there are only three letters in the name such as Kay or Jon, then one can go on each piece of the puzzle; if there are nine letters then three can go on each piece. The principle is that the child's name can be constructed with the three piece puzzle that can fit together in many ways. There are many possible arrangements of the puzzle. When the child places the letter groups in correct order and correct orientation he is probably selecting correctly only those ways that are appropriate for printed material. So we have another chance of checking on his conceptions about print.

The task is confined to the use of the child's name for a special reason. It is not a test of reading skill, and the aim is not to find out which words the child can read. The task aims to reveal something about the visual scanning the child is applying to the task and his name is familiar, and likely to be of high interest. By using the child's name we are using a word which he learns relatively early even if it does take him some time to know all its detail.

**A three-piece puzzle**

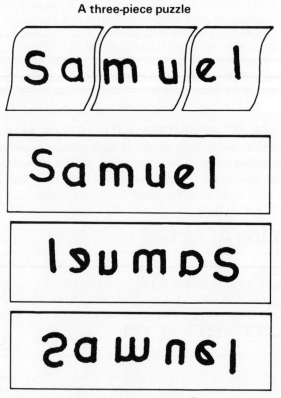

**Which name is yours?**

## Which name is yours?

Write the child's name with a capital letter and small lower case letters, then write it in reversed form (a mirror reflection) and then in inverted form. Scatter these three versions of his name around with about six other names (too many names will make the task too difficult) and ask him to pick out his name. In the earliest stages he will tend to pick out his name in any of these three forms, normal, reversed, or inverted. Perhaps he is judging from its initial letter.

But as time goes on he will reject the 'wrongly printed' words and come to choose only the name in correct orientation. This task would be a poor teaching device for school entrants but it is a useful discovery task. We cannot be quite sure what the child is looking at or what is guiding his choice but we can demonstrate with it when his behaviour is appropriate for the reading task.

## Concepts About Print

In the Concepts About Print Test (Clay, 1979) there are four items that also provide information about visual search and scanning. They are the items that ask the child to find what is wrong with disoriented print.

**1** Can the child detect the displaced lines?  *Item 10*
**2** Can he see that the words have been rearranged?  *Item 12*
**3** Does he notice when the order of first and last letters is changed?  *Item 13*
**4** Does he notice when the arrangement of middle letters is changed?  *Item 14*

Those four items represent a steep gradient of difficulty, a gradient of noticing, a gradient of visual scanning strategies. Many experiences with print are needed before a child will be able to pass a more difficult item. But as an opportunity to observe what a child is noticing those items are very useful.

# The Timing of Letter Learning

When should children be introduced to letter learning? Perhaps they should begin by recognizing words or captions and come to letters later? Most 5-year-olds studied in New Zealand research showed little sign of attending to whole words or the pattern of the word. They were recognizing words by the distinctive features of some letters or by particular associations:

's' in 'is'
'd' Delwyn's little d.

As soon as the child is encouraged to write his name his attention is being directed to letters. Often the first two or three letters that occur in his name become distinctive because of these efforts.

Readers do not have to respond to all the letters in a word to 'read' it correctly. They only have to recognize enough cues to distinguish it from the words that might occur. In this sense they can go straight from a simple recognition of letter, cluster or word to the message. Because words are repeated frequently in controlled vocabulary texts the child has only to distinguish some new feature when his old recognition strategies fail to distinguish between new and old words that are too similar to be separated by his old tricks.

Will the child gather up this knowledge of letters and letter sound relationships as he reads words? The fact that some children do is probably misleading. One child learns that some features of the marks in *Mother* help him to recognize this word. Before long he can approach new words more analytically. He may work by analogy from familiar words and he may read *coat* because he knows *cat* and *boat*.

If a teacher hears the child thinking out a word in this way she will know that the process has been established. She may herself have used analogy as a teaching device. Can the child discover this process for himself and use it by himself? In one experiment English-speaking adults were able to derive their own sound associations from learning words in Arabic (Bishop 1964) but they did not necessarily do so when this was not set as a particular task. Word learning can be as good as letter training if the reader analyses the component relationships for himself.

It is surely false then to assume that children will necessarily be able to learn letters from words. If words or messages are the focus of the teaching programme there must be alternative opportunities to encourage the child to focus on letters. If the child's early attempts at creative writing are handled sensitively this provides for that focus on letters. To get his message conveyed the child must produce letter forms which can be recognized and that means that he must attend to the distinctive features in letters.

# A Gradual Gain in Control

*How long does this learning take?* Research shows that adults report a string of letters flashed on a screen in an order which has been trained by their reading habits. They have an organization of behaviour which leads them to attend to and report the letters in serial order from left to right. How soon after instruction has begun does this behaviour appear in children? The answer is not simple but, by and large, it appears within six months for children who are good at learning to read and has not appeared after eighteen months in children who are failing to learn to read (Clay, 1970). Psychologists may debate whether we read letter by letter or not (Kolers, 1970 ; Gough, 1972) but the young child making good progress probably can, if need be, survey his words letter by letter, left to right.

The New Zealand evidence for this comes from a study in which children were asked to read lists of words printed:

● in the normal way

- reversed
- inverted.

The 89 children were tested each year from entry to school until 8 years of age (Clay, 1970). Beginning readers seemed to be relatively undisturbed over reading word cards upside down. With 6 months, at 5:6, children making good progress were getting better scores on lists of words in normal orientation. These effects became more pronounced as reading improved. When a child who was normally a competent reader was asked to read reversed or inverted words he stumbled, paused for long periods, offered no response, looked puzzled, squinted at the words, backed away from print to take a longer view, or tried some strategy for unravelling the words which would have been easy to read in normal orientation. These signs of disturbance in good readers, imply that the cues and strategies which they commonly use to identify words and discriminate one response from another were seriously disrupted by changed orientation. Curiously enough poor readers were relatively unconcerned about changes in orientation. The more successful experience the children had with reading the greater their expectation for certain letter forms to occur in certain letter sequences.

Good readers were able to overcome the problem of reversed words after two years and to score relatively well on these. They may have learned to mentally flip the word back to its recognizable form. But by this time inverted words had become particularly difficult. Why was this? The answer can only be suggested and it required further testing. If the lower case alphabet is written in reversed orientation only five letters change their identity and can easily be mistaken for another letter (b, d, p, q, g) but if the alphabet is written in inverted presentation 15 letters could readily be identified as other letters (b, d, f, g, h, k, m, n, p, q, r, t, u, v, w) give or take some variations which allow h or k to approximate y when inverted. It seems likely that inverted print becomes more difficult to read because the New Zealand child is paying more attention to letter detail at this stage of his reading progress. The timing would be dependent on the emphases and sequences in the instruction programme. In the New Zealand programme this was after two years of instruction for the top 25 percent and after three years for the next 25 percent.

This research report has been a digression from consideration of the child who has just entered school, but it was necessary to provide evidence that, despite the introduction of the child to letters and to writing close to his entry to school the process of seeing letters is undergoing changes at least for the next three years for the *best readers*, and longer for the poorer readers. What the teacher of new entrants does in introducing children to letters is merely the first contact with letter forms. What the child's brain knows about operating on such forms, continues to change for at least several years.

The graph below describes the progress of a group of children on a Letter Identification Test. The dotted line at the right side of the figure shows the children's attainment at 6 years of age. Most of the children have mastered most of the letters, but a few children are low scorers. In contrast the solid line shows that six months earlier at 5:6 only a few children had mastered all letters whereas many children had a lot more to learn. Sample 1 at 5:6 had an average score of 26 letters known. This group represents the progress of one particular research sample (Robinson, 1973). In another school with different teaching emphases the children might be slower or faster in learning to identify letters and the graphs would take a different shape. It could be useful for a school to know what is happening in its own programme. The change-over time is easy to see if there are at least two sets of results taken from *the same children at* two different times. And the laggards or low scorers need special and individual attention to this problem.

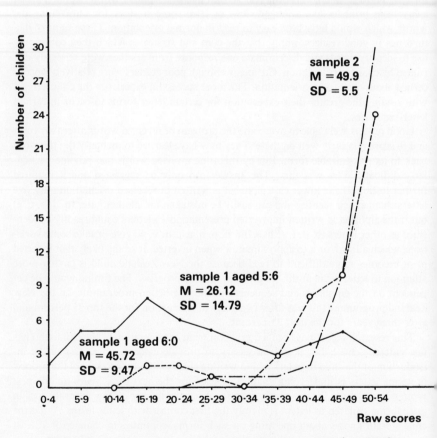

sample 2
M = 49.9
SD = 5.5

sample 1 aged 5:6
M = 26.12
SD = 14.79

sample 1 aged 6:0
M = 45.72
SD = 9.47

**Distribution of scores on Letter Identification Test (total 54)**

Children were asked 'What do you call this?' and were thus invited to give their preferred response. The majority preferred to use alphabetic names for 40 percent of capital letters and 34 percent of lower-case correct answers. Sounds were given for only 2 per cent of capitals and 1 percent of lower-case letters. Perhaps most surprising since the teaching method stressed sounding initial letters, was the limited use made of a word beginning with the test letter, 16 percent for capital and 11 percent for lower-case letters.

## CHILDREN'S RESPONSES TO LETTERS

| Age | Total Correct | | Alphabetic Name | | Sound | | Word Beginning | |
|-----|--------|-------|---------|-------|---------|-------|---------|-------|
| | Capital | Lower Case | Capital | Lower Case | Capital | Lower Case | Capital | Lower Case |
| 5:0 | 8% | 3% | 6% | 3% | 0% | 0% | 1% | 0% |
| 5:6 | 35% | 21% | 18% | 12% | 2% | 2% | 15% | 8% |
| 6:0 | 58% | 46% | 40% | 34% | 2% | 1% | 16% | 11% |

The children's preferred responses were, first, alphabetic; secondly, words beginning with the letter; and last (and by far least), the sound equivalents. This does not indicate poor teaching, nor does it necessarily imply that children did not have more phonic knowledge. It suggests that children found the alphabet an easy and economical way of identifying the visual symbols, one from another. Conversely, to insist that children learn the sound equivalents of the letters first may well increase the difficulty of the visual learning task for slow-learning children.

When instruction did not stress letter or phonetic learning, high progress readers had a mean letter score of 50 symbols after one year of instruction. They were able to give 50 letter names, 50 sounds and 50 words beginning with the letters, on request. They showed not only that they could distinguish almost all the symbols, one from another without confusion, but also that they could categorize each letter in several ways, multiplying their effectiveness for rapid responding or for checking a response. This multiple categorization suggests a flexibility and a competence which makes mere sound associations seem somewhat meagre. The alphabet or the sounds are mere labels which are the tip of the iceberg, used to represent all the stored information about each letter symbol. Even when their letter identification became over-learned and habitual it continued to be enriched by building more extensive associations around these letters.

The letter identification scores of children aged 6:0 (after one full year at school) showed a higher relationship with reading progress at 6:0, 7:0 and 8:0 than any other variable investigated in the Auckland research. (Correlations ranged from 0.80 to 0.86.) The exact nature of this relationship is complex but the child's visual scanning of letter forms and his manner of labelling or categorizing each one to establish its identity as different from all others is important learning. One can say that because the child reads, his letter identification improves and vice versa. High progress readers learn many new letters for every letter identified by the low progress readers so that entrants who do not differ markedly on this variable at 5 years show increasingly wide variability as the first year progresses.

At the end of the first year at school some letters were much more likely to be known than others. The reasons are many and various. Some occur more frequently than others, some have a distinctiveness of form, some capitals and lower-case letters are virtually the same.

Whatever the approach to beginning reading a major learning task for the child in the first year is learning to identify as distinct entities the letter forms commonly used in English orthography. The discrimination of letters one from another is only partially acquired at 6 years and further development must take place during the second year at school. It is a tremendously large set of learning which takes place slowly over a long period of time as new forms are successively distinguished from known ones. Here are some examples of diary entries on letter difficulties:

> *My biggest gripe is the way the home readers vary in the way they print their letters, every book is different and Brent finds great difficulty in sorting out the words because of it. I feel that the books should be of uniform nature starting with the very simple, and not chopping and changing as they are doing now.*

> *Has improved out of sight with his words but finds the different ɑ a and ɡ g very confusing. In the new books they are easier to read. Also gets stuck with capital letters at beginning of sentences.*

There is some evidence to suggest that most children are helped by being introduced to variable print and variable letter forms (such as capital and lower case) early in their programme. Capital letters are very salient and eye-catching in texts. However, for slow learners some reduction of the variety is completely justifiable. Authors of some early reading books have, somewhat arbitrarily, omitted capital letters, quotation marks, and other such symbols. For the average child this is probably unnecessary. In their second year at school, children should not only complete the mastery of the complete set of letter identities but they should also discover both names and sounds for every symbol. Teachers should check for gaps in this knowledge and teach deliberately those names and sounds that are proving to be difficult for individual children. This means specific attention to the particular difficulties of individuals.

A different method of reading instruction could produce higher skill on letter identification in the first year. Undoubtedly this could be done. However, I believe that slower progress in this skill is an appropriate price to pay for fluent responding to interesting stories, and attention to meaning and syntax. The discrimination of letters can be completed during the second year.

# Writing Letters

A series of experiments was conducted with children learning to write Russian letters. The child encounters many difficulties in his attempts to copy words for which he has a model. In the research study (Zaporozhets and Elkonin, 1971) children were taught by three different methods:

| | |
|---|---|
| Just a model: | The experimenter wrote a letter in front of the child and gave him general directions on how to write it. More than 50 presentations were required per letter for mastery by this process. |
| A model plus instructions: | In addition to the above, the experimenter indicated all the basic points of the contour and an explanation of the shifts from point to point. The verbal guidance is what psychologists call orienting; focussing the attention of the child on the significant features and actions. This method reduced the training sessions to 10 per letter on the average. |
| Model and directed search: | The most successful training encouraged the child, independently, to identify supportive points *by analysing the presented model for himself.* The average training sessions per letter was then reduced to 4. |

Under the first type of learning children gained the ability to write correctly each letter on which they were trained. On the second type of programme children were able to write unfamiliar letters but whatever they had learned was unstable and sensitive to changes in the surroundings such as a shift from book to blackboard or to lines of different width. The children trained by the third type of programme shifted to writing unfamiliar letters in varied settings without much difficulty.

. . . . . . . Thus special organization of the orienting-exploratory activity in situations of activity is an important condition in forming motor habits in preschool age' *(under 7 years.)*

(Zaporozhets and Elkonin,1971)

These authors maintain that imitation is the basic method for the mastery of movements that success in imitation gradually increases as a result of the development of observation which refines *the image of the action being copied.* Notice that attention is directed to the sequence of movements in the action to be learnt not to the product of that action — such as a letter written.

The child learns something of great advantage in his future progress when he is allowed to organize the sequential steps in his own learning for himself. But Type 3 learning is different from Type 1. Type 1 might be called permissive — he is left to do it in his own way and those who can, succeed. Type 3 might be called guided learning in that the child is helped to attend to the significant moves in the skill but is allowed to put it all together in his own way.

The danger in applying guided learning approach to skill learning is that we tend to talk too much and often words confuse the young child.

Discussing the organization of early skilled action, Bruner (1974) draws on his research with infants but the general principles that he arrives at, have surprisingly useful explanatory power for children entering school and beginning instruction in reading. How does a child modify an action he is in the process of carrying out? He gets feedback at each stage of the movement. What is feedback? It might be simply called a message of where one is at. But it is not simple.

The child's preliminary level of skill dictates what he can utilize in the modelled behaviour and what he can carry out in imitation.

- A child should be encouraged to venture, rewarded for venturing his own acts and sustained against distraction or premature interferences in carrying them out.
- Opportunities to carry out intentions, initiate and sustain action provide for co-ordinating feedback and knowledge of results.
- Environments must be both supportive and challenging.

# Sequences of Letters

A research test of concepts about print indicated clearly that a child taught to read under the present New Zealand syllabus notices features of lines of print before he notices word order within lines and well before he can detect errors of letter order. The ability to pay close attention to detail deep in the middle of words while continuing to use other cues correctly is apparently a difficult task for a child taught by a natural language sentence approach to reading.

A child finds the beginnings and ends of words easier to 'see' than features embedded within sentences or words. The spaces help him to locate and perceive the letters at the edges of the spaces.

---

**lineorderiseasierthanwordorderwhichiseasierthanletterorder**

---

That example is interesting. Most people are able to locate the familiar word units within it but what is disturbed by the deletion of spaces seems to be the sequential eye movement across the line. It is as if left to right movement is helped by the spacing. In particular, it may be that re-scanning or checking behaviour is most disturbed by the deletion of spaces. I suspect the capital letter at the beginning of a sentence is of similar assistance to the eyes in scanning a text.

The child who is writing stories gives his attention to detail in every part of the word as he learns to construct patterns of letters in left to right sequences. The child at first produces strings of letters. In the accompanying 'illustration and story' it is interesting to imagine why the child wrote what he did. He knew certain letters (d i p A l f e M D c h T ɑ) but he also knew other important things about sequencing letters.

- Letters that follow one another are usually different.

- Letters can recur, together | | or first and last (did).

- Capitals and lower-case letters occur mixed together but lower-case predominate.

- Words are of varying lengths (did, PAll7M, DeliqadM etc.)

- The word concept seems to be indicated by the enclosing of groups of letters —
  (didꝗ)

- There is even a hint that vowel and consonant relationships are sensed.

Before the child can write a sentence he is already becoming aware of factors which are probably important about the sequences of letters which can occur in English.

Lewis Carroll was using similar intuitions about the sequences that can occur when he wrote English-like nonsense words — 'jabberwocky' and 'mome raths'. If adults are given a selection of letters and asked to write down what letter seems to follow they frequently write sequences of letters which have a high probability of occurring in English. Young children develop this awareness of letter sequence as their experience with written language increases.

Although the beginning reader knows that letters follow left to right across a word he makes errors of omission and substitution as he writes, concentrating on forming the letters and forgetting about their sequence. He often loses his place; and his patience, in the complexity of the labour.

> *Copying words from a book John chose only those in capitals from the titles. He concentrated hard while other children danced to a record. He burst into tears when he was interrupted and lost the sequence he was following. He is usually very patient. Shown the place he resumed the job and finished it.*

At this stage an error in letter sequence in the child's writing is caused by the immaturity of the skill and the complexity of the task.

Here is a sample of work from a boy aged 8:6 in his fourth year at school, who had failed to learn to read, despite average intelligence (I.Q. 97-107). He could answer the questions of his mid-year English test correctly when questioned orally, but this is what he wrote:

(a) One who writes poems    *'nanante'*
(b) A man who studies science    *'ntrer'*
(c) A man who sells pills and medicines    *'piken'*
(d) A man who drives an aeroplane    *'piserter'*
(e) Punctuate: john lives near lake taupo    *'Ohn liven ena'*
(f) Give the opposite of
    sad    *'yes'*
    fresh    *'yes'*
    ending    *'no'*
    perfect    *'now'*
    dirty    *'now'*

He uses only a few letters but puts them together in 'probable' sequences. Once or twice he creates an 'unEnglish' sequence like 'ntr' as a word beginning, or 'piken' when English usually uses a 'ck' in medial position. The only words he can produce correctly are 'yes' and 'no'. The same boy's spelling test written in short sentences demonstrates clearly this word production from a few letters.

1   *'lana form vegetabls'*
2   *'her thernenner'*
3   *'Bentern ertert'*
4   *'the threter for'*
5   *'fhteler the Peher'*

When one knows that the boy's name is Peter it becomes obvious that this is the 'theme' of his variations.

What is the basic failure here? Peter has failed to store detailed memories for more than four word forms — yes, no, the, Peter. Peter has the correct visual concept of written language — intricate messages constructed by varying the sequences of a few letter symbols. But he has failed to link these to his rich stores of information about the sounds of his oral language in his sentences, words and symbols, and his problem has gone undetected (Clay, 1975).

A study of how reading behaviours change between 5:5 and 6:5 years for New Zealand children (Robinson, 1973) explored a large number of tests and how they were related to reading progress. She discovered that the number of words in a child's writing vocabulary, that is the number of words he could write with prompting but without help — that list of words which he knew in every detail and which he could produce from within his head — a score in this skill was very highly related to early reading progress. This seems to underline the suspicion that when the reading method calls for analysis of letter and word detail within sentences the complementary process of learning to write words and building words out of letters and sentences out of words is a very important activity.

Eleanor Gibson (1965) reports an experiment to discover how long after beginning reading, children began to anticipate words in terms of clusters of letters which they expected to occur together. She concluded that soon after beginning reading most readers tried to read nonsense words by using clusters of letters. The child learns to differentiate letters one from another. He learns to associate letters with sounds. At one and the same time he learns to use larger building blocks — clusters of letters or sounds. Psychologists describe this as working by 'chunks' rather than 'bits' of information. These terms have technical meanings but they are correctly related to dealing with clusters of signals rather than the items within the cluster.

In early reading, a child typically reads short units and generalizes simple rules on the basis of the regularities he discovers. His skill develops; his span increases and he derives rules for longer units, these require more complex rules. (The child behaves as if he knew the rules but could not state them.)

This skill seems to be the basis of the analogy method of decoding new words. To attempt the new word 'goat' or 'spring' teachers may ask children to read:

| | | | |
|---|---|---|---|
| **boat** | **coat** | **go** | **goat** |
| **rat** | **spat** | **ring** | **spring** |

Without segmenting the sounds of the words many children who are familiar with or who are told the first three have no difficulty with the last. But children should have a store of experiences with letter probabilities in English before this teaching is consciously and systematically introduced in lessons.

Another instance of letter probabilities that good readers 'know' quite early in their schooling is that certain letters probably say one of several sounds — Father, am, said; Mother, oh, on. Advocates of i.t.a. simplify the child's task by writing each sound with a different letter-sign. Some research suggests that if a child must ultimately operate in a flexible way on such confusing patterns as the spelling of English he should learn such flexibility from the start. Other research would emphasize that the child learns best when his first experiences are consistent and from these he can move to flexibility. In a sense both are true. The high progress reader needs only a brief period of consistency before he learns to operate in a flexible way. The slow progress child needs the consistencies of his environment increased.

Knowledge of the sequential probabilities of language is 'hidden learning' which is not readily observable except perhaps in a child's attack upon unknown words. The child who is failing to learn these probabilities is easily overlooked.

# Attention to Details of Orientation

The pictures in children's story books may prepare a child for reading in that they arouse interest in books, add context to an impoverished text, and stimulate recall. But pictures allow freedom to scan in any direction and do not induce any directional habits (unless perhaps when they are in comic strip series).

Some preschoolers are unperturbed when they look at a book upside down, and, in a test situation, 27 percent of a research group at 5:0 did not detect the inversion of a picture when questioned about it. In a laboratory experiment 4-year-old children detected differences in orientation, but they still classified symbols which vary in orientation as the same. They responded without apparent heed to orientation. It is probable that all readers begin with this tendency and that good readers overcome it sooner than poor readers.

The child who overlooks the detail of orientation will make errors on letters which, if reversed or inverted, could become a different letter. A recent study of letters (Dunn-Rankin, 1968) found four groups which tended to produce confusions. These were

1  e, a, s, c, o
2  f, l, t, k, i, h together with y
3  b, d, p, together with o, g, h
4  n, u, m, together with h, r

This does not account for all the confusions that can occur. For some reason Dunn-Rankin excluded j, g, v, x, z from his survey. Other authorities have found y and k confusing (perhaps because of their angular characteristics) and the I, 1, l, L set is a very confusing one, ('I' may be read as 'one').

Children find it easiest to distinguish letters with the maximum of contrast at first. This is a good teaching principle. But they must gradually learn the minimal differences for discrimination within sets of similar letters.

While some symbols change their meaning by reason of changed orientation others change because fragments are removed (h, n; o, c; w, v). Upper and lower-case letters vary, cursive and printed scripts vary, type fonts vary. Overall, the visual constancy permitted and not permitted to each letter in the alphabet is arbitrary, capricious and illogical. All this is independent of any letter-sound irregularity. For the child, the game is really one of categories. Which forms is he permitted to group together as similar? He learns the arbitrary features of our printed code gradually.

Errors of orientation, a problem of space perception, are common in the child's reading and writing during the first year and the child should have the benefit of a year's experience with reading and writing instruction before errors in letter orientation are taken as clinical symptoms of possible problems.

# To Facilitate the Visual Perception of Print

Relatively little research has been done on the legibility of print and layout for children. Conventionally, the type size in beginning reading books is larger (14 to 18 point) and the space between lines is generous. Lines are usually short (20 picas). Reviewing all the literature in this area, Tinker (1966) concludes that all-capital print is extremely difficult for adults to read and that lower-case print is over-whelmingly preferred. It may be presumed that children react similarly.

Teachers of beginning readers have observed that an exaggeration of the spaces between words, and between letters within words assists children's discrimination. It is possible that publishing layout could reduce in some measure the learning problems children have with visual discrimination. Some teachers make large brown paper books with simple texts in 5cm high print. Children span their hands across the large word patterns using gross motor patterns rather than fine coordinations. There may be perceptual advantages in such large print.

Exaggerated spacing of words, letters and lines can be a help. Starting position on a page could be consistent in the early books and could be cued by some standard sign. A reduction in type-face variations for beginning readers is important, and elimination of any features which confuse one letter with another. Increasing the spacing between phrase and clause breaks or before constructions like 'said Mother' would be justified. It would serve the same purpose as limiting lines to full sentences, as is frequently done in beginning books.

# First Direction, Then Individual Letters, Then Categories of Letters

Research findings suggest that when a child first begins to read English texts there is a strong left-to-right, horizontal, directional component to his behaviour, with his attention being focussed on the left ends of lines and of words. The child's attempts to read cannot be matched correctly to the printed text unless he is attending to the correct position when he says a word and is proceeding in the correct direction as he completes the sentence. Any learning about letter-sound relationships must depend on his attending to the correct part of the text. At this time the child is discovering the identity of a few letters, usually locating them at the left end of a word.

Left to right movement across a line of print is usually learned in the first six months.

At a later stage, perhaps after six months to one year, letter identity is an important cue (Clay, 1970). The child is familiar with far more letters and can discriminate between two similar words on the basis of several letters. Mastery of the set of letter symbols is gradual, spreading into the second year of instruction, but the lowest 25 percent of children paid too little attention to word patterns or features through the first year.

Children learn a specific response first in a specific context but reading behaviour must become flexible, and free to be applied to any page of print in different and new contexts. The movement or scanning patterns required in reading must run off in appropriate sequence whenever the child is faced with a page of print. They should not require conscious attention because this detracts from the attempt to extract the message from the text. They must permit pausing to scan word patterns or letter forms without loss of place or message.

The teacher must observe very carefully what her pupils are doing and what they are confusing. She must employ simple discovery techniques to check for learning that cannot be readily observed: the learning of the movement patterns, the spatial concepts, the sequential survey of words and the detailed survey of letter features. The child's writing behaviour provides opportunities to observe his spatial concepts and to train attention to letter and word detail as a complementary activity to reading. Whether the orthography is traditional or i.t.a., whether the method has a decoding or a language experience emphasis (or both), the visual perception of the symbols is a prerequisite to any learned association for phonetic sound or spoken word.

Learning how to scan and produce letters (seeing and writing), appear to be more significant responses than learning to name the symbols of the alphabet. At first glance it seems like a simple task to remember the letters and to produce a response in speech or writing. But there are qualitatively different ways of achieving this.

At the most *abstract* or *flexible* or *generative* level a letter which we intend to produce can be written out in a variety of forms and settings:

and the correct form of a written letter can be produced by a variety of action sequences.

# When Sequential Action is Difficult

A standard reference text among Soviet psychologists and educators on research in early child development deals with the perceptual processes from birth to 7 years (Zaporozhets and Elkonin, 1971). It reports that 3- to 7-year-old children cannot visually isolate elements of a complex form without appropriate training. Children who cannot indicate the elements that make up a complex figure, can do this after a series of practical exercises in which they actually build a figure from the elements using different forms. The children then begin an analysis of the figure by purely visual means, anticipating in the process the paths traced in their practical activity.

These experiments have described a series of changes that occur in the ways a young child explores new objects and forms, by hand, and by eye.

# Hand Exploration of a Hidden Object

● At 3 years hand movements resemble grabbing rather than exploring.
● At 4 to 5 years the child explores gropingly with the palm of his hand.
● At 5 to 6 years he explores with both hands but not systematically.
● At 6 to 7 years he carries out a sequential exploration of the entire outline of the figure with his fingertips.

# Eye Exploration

Changes were also observed in eye movements recorded on film during the perception of an object.

● At 3 years eye movements are few and attention is frequently diverted.
● At 4 to 5 years there are twice as many eye movements directed.
● At 5 to 6 years the eyes appear to pursue the contour of the figure.
● At 6 to 7 years eye movements outline the figure and also dart across it.

During the latter stages of this sequence the exploratory eye movements become successively shorter, the pausing or fixating is for less time, and attention is paid to the more informative characteristics of the object.

There is an interesting in-between stage when the child visually scans the figure but uses some movements of the hand also, movements which model at a distance, the figure's form. It is as if the hand movements organize and adjust the process of visual exploration of this object.

Later still the eye movements observe the entire contour of the figure and perceive its properties in detail.

After more experience, in a quick glance at a figure directed to a particular characteristic aspect of the object, the child can activate the entire 'internal' model leading to an instantaneous judgement of the qualities of the perceived object.

Some distinctive features in the writing of letters have been isolated by Hooton (1975) and built into a training programme. These are —

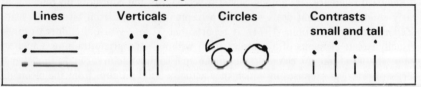

| Lines | Verticals | Circles | Contrasts small and tall |

Patterns or sequences of these different forms can be practised to aid in building the flexibility needed for letter writing, letter identification and letter perception. There is no evidence that these features are the ones used by good readers to perceive letter forms and there is some evidence to the contrary but the tutorial scheme is heuristic which at the present stage of our knowledge has value.

Children who have difficulty with the exploration of new forms can be trained to follow the contour of a figure sequentially. In the formative stages of this behaviour the exploratory movements of the hand performs a key role. The eye registers and pursues the movements of the hand. But in the later stages of training the eye can solve the perceptual task and systematically inspect the form's contour without the support of the hand.

# References and Further Reading

Beadle, Muriel, *A Child's Mind*, Doubleday and Co., New York, 1970.

Bruner, J.S. 'On perpetual readiness', *Psychological Review*, 64, 1957, 123-152.

Bryant, P., *Perception and Understanding Young Children*, Methuen London, 1974.

Clay, Marie M., 'An increasing effect of disorientation on the discrimination of print: a developmental study', *J. Experimental Child Psychology*, 9, 1970, pp. 297-306.

Clay, Marie M., *What Did I Write?*, Heinemann Educational Books, Auckland, 1975.

Clay, Marie M., *The Early Detection of Reading Difficulties: A Diagnostic Survey with Recovery Procedures*, Heinemann Educational Books, Auckland, 1979.

Dunn-Rankin, P., 'The similarity of lower-case letters of the English alphabet', *J. Verbal Learning and Verbal Behaviour*, 7, 1968, pp. 990-995.

Durrell, D., 'First grade reading success study', *Journal of Education*, 140, Feb., 1958.

Elkonin, D. B. USSR, In Downing, J. (ed.), *Comparative Reading*, Macmillan, New York, 1973, 551-580.

Fellows, B. J., *The Discrimination Process and Development*, Pergamon Press, London, 1968.

Gibson, Eleanor J., 'Learning to Read', *Science*, 148, 1965, pp. 1066-1072

Gibson, Eleanor J. & Levin, H., *The Psychology of Reading*, MIT, Cambridge, Massachusetts, 1975.

Gough, P., One second of reading. *Visible Language*, 6, 4, 1972, 291-320.

Hooton, Margaret, *The First Reading and Writing Book*, Heinemann Educational Books, Auckland, 1976.

Juola, J., Development trends in visual search: determining visual units in reading. In Resnick L. and Weaver P., *Theory and Practice of Early Reading*, Lawrence Erlbaum and Associates, Hillsdale, New Jersey, 1979.

Kolers, P.A., Three stages of reading. In Levin, H. and Williams, J. P. *Basic Studies On Reading*. Basic Books, New York, 1970.

McQueen, P.J., Motor Responses Associated with Beginning Reading, Unpubl. M.A. thesis, University of Auckland Library, 1979.

Meares, Olive, Some children talk about print. Takapuna Reading Clinic, Auckland, 1972.

Meares, Olive, Some further notes about print. Takapuna Reading Clinic, Auckland, 1973.

Lynn, R., *Attention, Arousal and The Orientation Reaction*, Pergamon Press, London, 1966.

Moore, O.K., 'Orthographic symbols and the preschool child: a new approach', in E.P. Torrance (ed.), *New Educational Ideas: Third Minnesota Conference On Gifted Children*, Minnesota Center For Continuation Study, University of Minnesota, pp. 91-101.

Pines, Maya, *Revolution in Learning*, Harper & Row, New York, 1967.

Solley, C.M. & Murphy, G., *Development Of The Perceptual World*, Basic Books, New York, 1960.

Tinker, M.A., 'Experimental studies on the legibility of print: an annotated bibliography', *Reading Research Quarterly*, 1, 1966, pp. 67-118.

Zaporozhets, A.V., 'The development of perception in the preschool child', in P.H. Mussen (ed.), 'European Research in Cognitive Development', *Mono Soc. Res. Child Development*, 30, 1965, pp. 82-101.

Zaporozhets, A.V. and Elkonin, D.B. (eds.), *The Psychology of Preschool Children*, MIT Press, Cambridge, Massachusetts, 1971.

Zinchenko, V.P. and Lomov, B.F., 'The functions of hand and eye movements in the process of perception', *Problems of Psychology, 1 & 2, 1960*.

# Exploring Further

**Use a letter identification test with first year children at three different levels of reading skill. Record all their responses and suggest the implications for the teaching programme. Refer to** *The Early Detection of Reading Difficulties: A Diagnostic Survey with Recovery Procedures* **for further help.**

# 14 The Organization of Reading Behaviour

This chapter presents an overview of the reading process in the first two years, to be read last, first, or on its own.

Reading behaviour concerns all the things teachers have always thought it did — word knowledge, meaning, story sense, word study skills. It also includes directional behaviour, letter identities, pronounceable clusters, grammatical sense, fluent processing of cues, and error correction. Reading involves the use of items of knowledge

- to anticipate what can occur in meaning and in language
- to search for cues
- to self-correct
- to form intuitive rules that take the child beyond what he already knows.

The good reader manipulates a network of language, spatial, and visual perception cues, and categorizes these efficiently, searching for dissonant relations and best-fit solutions. Familiar responses which become habitual, require less and less processing and allow attention to reach out towards new information that was not previously noticed.

## The Reading Process

Reading, like thinking, is a very complex process. When you think, all you have to do is produce the responses from within you. When you read you have to produce responses which are precisely the ones the author wrote: you have to match your thinking to his.

Most people are familiar with the old game 'Twenty Questions' or 'Animal, Vegetable or Mineral'. Reading is very much like that. The smartest readers ask, of themselves, the most effective questions for reducing the uncertainty, the poorer readers ask trivial questions and waste their opportunities to reduce uncertainty. They do not search for information in effective ways.

Many remedial programmes direct their students to equally trivial matters. Before they resort to left to right sounding out of letters all readers, from the competent 5-year-old on his first reading book to the efficient adult use —

- the sense
- the sentence structure
- the order of ideas, words, letters
- the size of words or letters
- special features of sound, shape and layout
- and special knowledge from past experience.

As explanations of what we do when we read, the terms 'look and say', 'sight words' and 'phonics' are nonsense. Reading is more complex than that.

By far the most important challenge for the teacher of reading is to make it easier for the child to operate successfully in getting precise messages from books. Because this idea is basic to the research I want to report we must look briefly at the theory of the reading process that was used.

## Language

Reading involves messages expressed in *language*. Usually it is a kind of language which is found in books. Most children bring to the reading situation a fluent oral control of their mother tongue. This consists of an unconscious control of most of the sounds of the language, a large vocabulary of word labels for meanings and relationships that are understood, and cognitive strategies for constructing sentences.

## Concepts about print

Reading also involves something that the skilled reader is not even aware of because he responds automatically to the *concepts about print*, to do with direction, spaces, formats, punctuation cues and so on. In the preschool years children can learn important ideas about print from the print in their environment.

## Visual patterns

Reading involves *visual patterns* — groups of words/syllables/blends/letters — however one wants to break the patterns up. The reading process is so automatic in skilled readers that it is only by drastically altering the reading situation that we can show how adults scan text to pick up cues from patterns and clusters of these components. Children tend to operate on visual patterns in very personal ways.

## Sounds in sequence

Reading involves knowing about the sound sequences in words. The flow of oral language does not always make the breaks between words clear and children have some difficulty breaking messages into words. They have even greater difficulty in breaking up a word into its sequence of sounds and hearing the *sounds in sequence*. This is not strange. Some of us have the same problem with the note sequences in a new melody.

These are four different areas of reading skills, each of which the child can use when reading text.

*Language* was put first because the message embodied in print is of high priority. Language has two powerful bases for prediction, its *structures* and its *meanings*. A third but sometimes confusing and distorting language base exists in letter-sound relationships.

The *concepts about print* were mentioned because although this learning soon becomes subconscious or automatic it cannot be taken for granted in the early stages of learning to read. It is sometimes the source of some fundamental confusions.

The *visual analysis skills* were mentioned because visual cues are basic for correct, fluent functioning but skilled readers tend to use as little visual knowledge as possible, scanning for enough information to check on the meaning. The beginner reader must discover for himself what visual cues are helpful in reading.

The *sound sequences in words* are also used in reading to anticipate a word from a few cues or to check a word one is uncertain about. This requires two kinds of detailed analysis in strict coordination:

- the analysis of the sound sequence in the words we pronounce
- the left to right visual analysis of letters or clusters of letters in a written word.

Reading involves the integration of all four sources of cues. The high progress reader after only one year at school operates on print in an integrated way with high accuracy and high self-correction rates. He uses a central method of word attack; that is, he reads with attention focussed on meaning. What he thinks the text will say is checked by looking for sound-to-letter associations. He also has several ways of functioning according to the difficulty level of the material. Where he cannot grasp the meaning with higher-level strategies he can use other strategies such as letter-to-sound knowledge.

On the other hand, the low progress reader or reader 'at risk' has few resources to fall back on. He tends to operate on a narrow range of strategies all the time. He may rely on what he can invent from his memory for the text but pay no attention at all to visual details. He may disregard obvious discrepancies in his response and the words on the page. He may be looking so hard for words he knows and guessing words from first letters that he forgets what the message is about. These unbalanced ways of operating on print can become habituated and automatic when they are practised day after day. They become very resistant to change as early as 12 to 18 months after entry to school.

That is why a Diagnostic Survey after one year of instruction is important. Intervention at this stage can help children who are stumbling to operate on print in more appropriate ways so they can continue to progress spontaneously in the classroom. Because each child having difficulty will have different things he can or cannot do, different confusions, different gaps in his knowledge of meanings, of letters, and of words, and different ways of operating on print, each child who is failing needs an intervention programme especially tailored to his needs in a one pupil/one teacher situation to supplement his classroom programme. That is, of course, if we are interested in a programme which recovers those readers who are already confused and struggling, accelerates their progress, and replaces them back into the mainstream of class instruction.

Why should we wait until the child has been at school one year? There are several reasons:

● I must assume that children on entry to school will have different levels of ability and will respond to school programmes at different rates.

● I also assume that children will have learned different things from their preschool experiences. Their knowledge will differ in type and quality and they will need to learn many things in the first year at school as a background to later progress in reading.

● I believe that children take time to learn how to learn in the groups they are placed in, and that this social and emotional learning is important as a foundation for success in school.

# Our Preferences for Methods

As teachers we become very committed to the personal theories that we have about our methods, we defend them passionately at times, and we resist their revision. Harper Lee provides a caricature of such commitment in *To Kill a Mockingbird.*

*How do our differences in method arise?*
A language is organized on several levels; sounds, syllables, words or morphemes, phrases, sentences, and larger paragraph or story units. Some adult arbitrarily decides that the child shall learn the smallest units first. This is sometimes referred to as a bottom to top sequence. Alternatively, the child could begin at the level of sentences and, aided by meaning, come to know the word and letter-sound relationships, a top-down approach. Another starting place is with the words, moving both down to sounds and up to phrases or sentences. Written language can be approached via any of these levels.

This is the analytic-synthetic debate. What is usually forgotten in this debate is the developmental fact that the little child does not learn all his sounds before he uses words, nor does he know many words before he knows sentences. He is immature, in his control of language, in his cognition, in his visual perception in his motor activities. Despite this immaturity the child gradually improves in these *and* in his school achievement.

In the early stages of learning to read one way in which we protect children from complexity is by the controls we exercise over the texts. Every device has been tried — control over the letters or the sounds or the words used, the symbol-sound relationships in i.t.a., the sentence structure.

People have advocated and decided the use of capital letters in one case, or lower case letters in another, the inclusion or exclusion of quotation marks and other punctuation, the size and the spacing of print. Controls are also asked for over the topics of interest to children, the sex stereotypes and the middle-class bias. We have even used children's own language as a basis for the text.

In exercising these controls *we are preselecting what the child will have an opportunity to learn,* and therein lies a danger.

• A teacher who uses an approach that is as close to children's literature as she can bring a child will probably not give that child an opportunity to learn a graded sequence of letter-sound correspondences.

• The child in a graded phonics programme may not learn that there are images and expressions to be thought about in reading. A code-cracking set may exclude a sensitivity to literary nuance.

• If we build our reading books with the language that children use we may prevent them from extending their vocabulary by reading.

Consider the cost or risks of any programme emphasis.

• Comprehension might suffer.
• Speed might be slower.
• Reading vocabulary might be less.
• Reading vocabulary might consist of regular words only.
• Accuracy could be less.
• Mean reading age may drop.
• Mean reading age may rise but the slowest children may be left further behind.

There are other costs not so often counted.

• Literal interpreters may look for meaning in single words and miss the meaning in word relationships.
• Speed may be fast and constant rather than varied and flexible.
• Reading vocabulary may be learned in lessons but may not be self-extending.
• Accuracy may be perfect but what strategies can the child use when the text is harder?
• The age at which independent reading is possible may vary.

What happens to particular groups of children in the programme?

# Some Effects of Programmes

*Do these programme differences matter?*
A study of spelling errors by Margaret Peters (1967) reported that learned differences showed themselves clearly in types of spelling errors that children made. In the schools she studied in Britain three groups of children were compared with 'look-and-say', 'phonic', and 'i.t.a.' programmes. All three groups had been rigorously taught by teachers and head teachers who were totally committed to the method used and were heavily prejudiced against other methods. To bring out the differences clearly one would have to describe the error categories that Peters used. However, in brief, the differences in method or medium seemed to produce differences in attention to words. These showed themselves in the quite different types of spelling errors commonly made in each programme.

Different training schedules may produce at least three kinds of differences in children.

- They may attend to different cues in the text.
- They may use different strategies for working on the text.
- They may store this information in different ways.

I am particularly interested in another finding of Peters'. When she divided her groups by intelligence into a broad average group, I.Q. 85 to 115, and a bright group above I.Q. 115, Peters found these differences held only for that broad average group. *They entirely disappeared for the brighter children.* For the group with higher intelligence differences due to teaching method or medium vanished almost completely.

If programmes do focus on some components of the reading process rather than others then it follows from Peters' finding that:

- the broad band of average children seem to be good learners of what their teachers want them to master.
- the children of higher ability acquire more than the programme offers.

I carried out a pilot study to explore this question during a visit to Scotland. With the help of local reading advisers I was able to work in four schools, each of which appeared to be committed to a particular type of reading programme: phonics, sentence makers, language and story experience, and a word emphasis. I studied the children's skills after three months at school, and after a year and three months and the different programmes did produce different patterns of subskills.

- After three months at school children making good progress scored well on the subskills emphasized in a particular programme.
- In the second year at school subskills that were not emphasized or were neglected in the programme showed the highest relationships with reading progress.

For example, in the second year in School A with a *phonics* programme it was the measure of *Concepts About Print* that showed a high relationship to reading progress. In the *language experience* programme it was the *Letter Identification test.* Results like these suggest that when a teaching programme pays minimal attention to a particular skill *those children who make good progress are those who gain that skill in spite of, or in addition to what they are taught.* This neglect hypothesis is worthy of further research. I offer it only as a hypothesis as this study was only a pilot exercise.

Theodore Harris (1976) warns that variability in reading tasks and purposes must be kept in mind if we are to train flexible readers. He warns that *careful, systematic and detailed reading for total recall can become counterproductive if continued to the point of habituation.* It may then be too difficult for the reader to become flexible and adaptable. He has overlearned the programme emphasis. This is the risk in any programme *and it may be a greater risk in some well-taught, well-organized programme.* Our enthusiasms act like blinkers; they give us tunnel vision. We select our course, measure what is important on that course, practise and habituate those skills we value. The worst thing that can happen then is for us to have children who learn too well and teachers who teach effectively. Any programme can become counterproductive if children are helped to habituate only a narrow range of strategies.

Guthrie (1973) reported his study which seemed to show that a good reader can build the subskills of reading into a single process so that the components of the process become mutually facilitating. The poor reader had a number of independent subskills. Perhaps in Guthrie's study the better readers (50 percent) transcended any limitation in the programme and discovered for themselves other useful things about written language. If this were the explanation then, in evaluating any scheme it would be important to look at what is happening to the lower 50 percent of readers.

A recent research by Board at the Ontario Institute for the Study of Education showed that the role of the teacher may be complex. Board studied what instruction does to children in the DISTAR scheme, basal reader, Sullivan linguistic approach and a language experience method. He found that instruction does not seem to interfere with the best readers, that the average readers also learn to read well enough, *but that the poorest readers tend to be doing exactly and only what they are told*. The more structured the programme the more effect this had. Board identifies these struggling readers as *instruction dependent*. The results from Peters, from Guthrie and from Board may all imply differences occurring in some general information-processing strategies of putting it all together rather than merely learning the particular skills. For the poor readers it is as if the items are entered in the computer without a programme for getting from one store to another. In the good readers the strategies for access are also available.

I don't believe we know how this occurs, and every time a programme emphasizes some things to the neglect of others, to the extent that it reaches its goals with good teaching, it will constrain children's functioning. Why then do not more children fail in our chosen emphases? Fortunately the child's contribution to the act is paramount. He out-reaches our limitations and learns more than we imagine. He goes beyond the information given. The bright child and the high progress reader can transcend the limitations of our teaching. The poor readers may be the captives of our methods.

# The Child's Contribution

Our thinking about individual differences in reading has been dominated by our attention to differences in abilities like intelligence and language knowledge. We have not thought very much about *the child's contribution to his learning*.

'The child enters the classroom equipped to learn language and able to do so by methods of his own.'

(C. Chomsky, 1972)

● Before the child comes to school he has already learned how to learn by making a response and getting feedback about its appropriateness.
● He has developed a complex differentiated internal representation of his world.
● He has strategies for remembering, grouping, problem-solving.
● He has constructed a complex system of language rules which enable him to understand and produce the sentences of his language. He builds these rules by a process that is as yet little understood, but his language learning is innovative and rule-governed.

There are some important aspects of learning to read which the child must teach himself *because we do not understand them* (Smith, 1971). For example:

- The child has to discover for himself the distinctive features of print that distinguish letters and words. Nobody knows enough about these to help him.
- The child has to discover for himself the sources of redundancy in written language. This knowledge is not accessible to our awareness. We acquire and use it unconsciously.

I am not implying that reading instruction programmes are unnecessary but there are critical aspects of learning to read which we do not yet fully understand.

The best of the British infant schools have long been admired for the teacher's ability to act as a facilitator or consultant and not as a didactic expert.

'Where the teacher's expertise really counts . . . is in knowing what the child is going to want . . . the more they can allow themselves to hold back and allow the student to do his own learning the more effective and better judged will be their interventions when they are really needed. There are two ways in which we can help the child to learn. One of them is by attempting to teach him; the other is by facilitating his attempts to teach himself. We need to give the child freedom to explore and to learn on his own. . . . The child is self-stimulating and self-starting provided conditions are right for him.'

(Cashdan, 1976 )

We can be instructors in those areas where we know what the task involves. But in other areas we can only act as someone whom the child can consult.

## Independence in reading

It is the aim of most reading programmes to bring children through the beginning reading scheme to a stage called independence in reading. At this point the teacher has to do less teaching. She provides the structure, the time and acts as a resource but the child pursues a large amount of the activity by himself, pushing the boundaries of his own skills as he tries more and more material of increasing difficulty.

The child reading to himself knows when he is more or less correct because 'one of the beautiful advantages of reading sense is that it provides its own feedback' (Smith, 1971). One way to describe this independence is that the child has learned how to work out new words for himself. He finds this activity rewarding. Once the child learns to search for cues to a word the reinforcement lies within the reading process, in the agreement he can achieve between all those signals and messages in the code. He no longer needs as much outside help to confirm whether his response is right or wrong. The activity of making all the cues fit, of eliminating any misfit is rewarding to the child who succeeds.

*But is word decoding the essence of independent reading?*

Jessie Reid (1973) thinking about the young readers in four studies where error behaviour was analysed said they were using prediction in many cases as a substitute for word-decoding or word recognition, in situations where their knowledge was inadequate. These intermediate skills enabled a reader to use prediction to narrow the field of possibilities, and to reduce the decoding load.

'It may well be that a great deal of the hold-up with poorer readers resides in their inability to perform such cognitive acts as suspending judgement until more information is processed; modifying a first guess (or hypothesis) in the light of further information; transferring information from the short-term to medium term memory, or fusing information from different cognitive systems.'

Independence in reading is not being able to decode words. It is a much larger cognitive enterprise relating to thinking and understanding.

# Is The Child Aware Of What He Does?

Developmental psychologists have been studying how children remember. What do they do when they are told to remember something? One interesting discovery is labelled by Flavell as the 'production deficiency'. A young child may be able to rehearse a list of numbers of words if he is required to by the instructions that he is given but *left to himself he does not think to do so*. He does not seem aware that he, himself, can relate one area of knowledge or one cognitive strategy to another. John Flavell and Ann Brown have written extensively of the importance of how the child orchestrates these strategies he has. Does he bring them into play, can he use them when they are appropriate? Does he know what the task is about? Does he look? search? try to remember? Does he predict? generate? hypothesize? plan? select? check? monitor? test? change? recycle? recheck? Although the child has these subskills can he bring them into the complex orchestrated activity of obtaining full meaning from a text? These authors would claim that many of the strategies needed in reading *are not taught by the reading teacher they are already available from other cognitive activity*. Self-correction strategies for example are a response to confusion that operates whenever messages from the environment are not clear. Not only do teaching methods with demands for meaning draw upon strategies that were there before the child began to read, they also help the child to practise prediction, self-correction, weighting the evidence and decision-making processes that will have application to other situations and to other subject areas. Too focussed an approach to reading may limit the repertoire the orchestra may play. Why should we encourage children to specialize in limited behaviours just for reading? The competent children resourcefully cast around all their experience to find clues, strategies and solutions.

The independent reader reads; and because he reads he improves his reading ability. Why is this? A quick unthinking answer might be that he is repeating the words so often that they are becoming part of his automatic responses. That can be only part of the story. For his responses do not just get speedier, and more often correct. *He becomes able to read more difficult text*. What accounts for the rise in level of performance? How does he improve his own skill and pull himself up by his bootstraps?

At the moment of making an error, a child reading for meaning will notice the error; it will become self-evident. This is a *monitoring* activity. The reader takes some action. At this moment he is observing his own behaviour closely because he will have to decide which response is the best fit, which to retain and which to discard. As he searches and selects he must carry out two further types of self-regulatory action. He *observes* his own behaviour and he assesses his own behaviour. Has he solved it? Has he got it right? Do all the sides of the jigsaw piece fit that particular slot?

In the processes of self-observation, self-assessment and self-reinforcement the young reader discovers new features of written language, new instances of things he learnt earlier, new relationships, and best of all for fluent reading, new short-cuts to storing and retrieving information.

The child's contribution is quite considerable.

# Learning Tasks on Natural Language Texts

A sequence of skills to be gained in the early book reading stages when the method is based on natural language texts can be proposed.

A 'natural language' text purports to use the language of the child. The English to be read is not simplified according to logic, or linguistics, or by drastic reduction of sentences to noun-verb or verb-noun dyads. Authors have used their knowledge of children's language to guide the construction of texts. A language experience approach which is somewhat similar uses the language produced by children to form wall-charts and class-made books. In both approaches language learning is based on an acquisition sequence — that is, the order in which children gain command over the structures of English, rather than a simplified adult version of English. If oral language is to be a driving force for gaining control over written language this is appropriate.

Natural language texts will differ from texts controlled for letter-sound associations or for vocabulary, in that words and sounds will tend to occur in the frequencies in which they are found in adult language. This helps the reader or listener who knows the language to predict what is likely to occur. According to Kenneth Goodman (1970):

> We have understood the importance of using the learner's own experiences in making charts for early reading for many years but we have not sufficiently understood the importance of using the child's own grammar; phrasing, and vocabulary.

There is research evidence to show that although learning that takes place on a constant task may be faster and easier, it is more readily transferred to a new and variable task if it is practised on a variable task. The child who learns a set for diversity is a more efficient performer when faced with diversity than the child who learns a set for constant relationships. Natural language texts probably require and train a set for diversity.

The teaching method practised with these natural language texts is thrown into perspective by contrasting it with a scheme described by McKee, Brzeinski and Harrison (1966). These authors evaluated the long-term effects of a large-scale project for 'teaching reading in the kindergarten' which means, in Denver, U.S.A., to 5-year-old children. They concluded that the experimental programme, followed by an accelerating programme in Grades 1 to 5, gave a continuing advantage to the children. A strictly controlled sequence of skills was taught prior to the introduction of printed words or books. The instruction trained children to think of a word that could come next or make sense in a spoken sequence; to listen for consonant sounds used at the beginning of words; to distinguish letter forms from one another, and name them; to think of a word which began with a given sound and could come next to make sense; to give letter-sound associations for the specific list of consonants; to use together spoken context, a shown consonant letter, the sound of that letter and sense to think what could come next. At this stage the children were shown a word and used these skills to 'read' it.

The remaining consonants were introduced and practised; then 14 printed 'function' words were practised for instant recognition. Finally the pupils read the pre-primers of the basal reading series. Each new word was introduced in spoken context, and the pupils were expected to use that context and the beginning sound, to decide what the word was.

In this programme reading is by word recognition checked by first consonant. The method minimizes the opportunity for the young child to use syntactic information.

The *Ready to Read* series was introduced in New Zealand to replace a similar approach in which prior teaching of sight vocabulary and word recognition had been emphasized. In contrast, the new method:

● introduced children to caption books they could not read
● used discussion to encourage children to think of sentences about the pictures
● taught directional habits on print, not on pictorial material
● encouraged any discoveries about sentences, words and letters including cues from longer stretches of language
● derived teaching points about words and letter-sounds from discussions with a group of children about a page of the book (using also a small blackboard for demonstration)
● encouraged children to express ideas in print, writing letters and words with any help needed and without any requirement to memorize the forms.

In this method, context allows the child to predict not only the word but a whole phrase or group of words likely to occur. He has far more cues than are available from the word in isolation. This approach gives the able child an opportunity to order his experience at a faster rate than the teacher can teach it, bit by bit and in more flexible ways than a planned teaching sequence will allow. Scrapping the controlled introduction of letter or word items opens up possibilities for very fast progress. It also introduces many hazards and confusions unless the teacher uses an evaluation programme to check that progress is being made.

The natural language text is not being upheld as the ideal approach. An either/or argument about method is inappropriate since both analytic and synthetic skills are required by a good reader. But there does seem to be some economy of teaching and learning time when larger units than phonetics are the main focus of the programme. The child who begins on this text

**Timothy is five today**

with letter-sound relationships has to group these into syllables, regroup into words and regroup these into phrases, and link the phrases into sentences. If the child begins with the sentence he can take in the sentence, phrase structure, word elements at one time. He reads the sentence practising its structure, meaning, words, sounds, intonation, punctuation. He can take time to pause and study any feature on any level of linguistic analysis and relationships between levels, but if he is skilled he practises all levels of analysis on the run with one anticipation of what the sentence is. Natural language texts focus on sentences and large segments of meaningful English. This brings the child to mature reading by quite a different route from the letter-sound or word approach with reduced and controlled types of English. A probable sequence of appropriate learning is described in the following pages.

## First concepts

The child who is to begin to read on sentences must quickly become aware of several features in written language.

● He must appreciate the directional pattern of movement needed to read English. There are three stages to this learning:
  (i) left to right sweep across lines
  (ii) word — space — word matching within the left to right sweep
  (iii) letter analysis left to right across a word, within the word-by-word analysis, within the left to right sweep across a line.
● He must realize that the language he speaks is related to the written English he is trying to read, and is a valuable source of cues.
● He must become aware that there are visual cues which he can use.
● He must actively search for cues from different sources, check his own responses, and correct his own errors.

With these concepts the child can 'read' in the sense of the following definition of reading.

*(1) Within the directional constraints of the printer's code (2) verbal and (3) perceptual behaviour are (4) purposefully directed (5) in some integrated way (6) to the problem of extracting a sequence of cues from a text (7) to yield a meaningful and specific communication.*

Emphasis is on the on-going, sequential, message-grasping process.

Development in the first three areas can be observed at the Early Reading and First Book stages and one can predict that children whose records show these behaviours are likely to make good progress. Conversely, readers may gain word recognition reading ages of over 6:0 and yet be omitting several aspects of the behaviour defined above.

What is the sequence of behaviour acquired in good reading progress?

## A willingness to decide between alternatives

The beginning reader may, and often does, 'read' his first book by a low level strategy of memory for sentence, page, and story. His memory for oral language is driving the process. There is nothing wrong with such a starting point if it leads on to the development of new skills. However, some intelligent children with good oral language continue for their first year to produce approximate responses to the text, apparently unaware that a precise message is conveyed and has to be decoded. When a child realizes that there is only one response equivalent to the text, he develops a need or willingness to decide between alternative possibilities. The child then has a vague awareness that he must discover the best-fitting response, which is an excellent beginning.

## When is a child likely to succeed on books?

At the point of transfer from the Early Reading period to formal reading instruction a child likely to succeed

● moves with some consistency across print within the broad directional constraints of written English (left to right, return down left)
● produces a nearly perfect rendering of a simple caption book
● matches speech and text word by word and space by space with some accuracy using hand or voice to synchronize the matching
● locates a few familiar words on the basis of cues although he is vague about what these are
● expects what he reads to sound meaningful and sensible.

Children's performance is varied and fluctuating, with adequate responses appearing and disappearing. Gradually the responses become more controlled and accurate, although it is not always the most appropriate consistency that is arrived at.

When these behaviours become purposefully directed in some integrated way to the problem of extracting a sequence of cues from a text the child is usually placed in a reading group.

## 'In some integrated way'

Synchronization of the visual, directional, and speech aspects of reading is evident in word-by-word reading, and in self-correction strategies. The teacher has reason to take notice when the child begins to use cues from two different sources, as cross-checking different kinds of cues during the fluent decoding of a message in print is important.

What factors can interfere with this smooth blending of skills? In a complex activity such as reading, strong responses may mask a weak aspect of behaviour. The record of a boy aged 5:6 with fast fluent oral language and poor motor and directional learning states:

> *Depends on picture interpretation and story invention. Does not use auditory memory for the text. Points rarely and then only with a sweeping movement along the line. The speed of his oral response prevents any linking of speech to visual forms.*

Later the early, inconsistent stage of a better integration of skills seems to be indicated by this record for the same child when aged 5:10:

> *Has slowed his response and does some visual matching with a few known words. Slips readily into old habits of fast inventing.*

There are problems in observing this 'integration' of skills. Newly learned responses are unstable and do not occur consistently so that the new behaviour appears and disappears. Thus, directional control which guides visual survey from left to right may lapse into invention. Or, reading controlled by a small recognition vocabulary may lapse into auditory memory of the text. A fast reader, capable of word-by-word decoding, may speed up to a rate where motor matching is impossible. Or the fluency possible with auditory memory may be dropped as the child begins to search for cues in the text, and to read word by word. As a child tires, his integration of cues tends to break down. It seems unlikely that a prescribed sequence of learning could be devised to bring about this delicate meshing of several activities because it must be dependent on the strengths and weaknesses of individual children who differ markedly. It is obvious, however, that only by sensitive, close observation can the teacher create learning conditions for the individual child that will facilitate the development.

This observation by a teacher describes some behaviour which points to an emerging integration of skills.

> *She is improving on reading some words, not confusing so much and adding less. As word-by-word correspondence has improved, self-correction is beginning to appear.*

# Reading to Discover the Code

Learning to identify the letters of the alphabet, and concepts about print are highly related to success in reading. While full awareness of these two sets of learning would not, in itself, ensure reading, a gain in one leads to gains in the other. Although the everyday speech of the child is important for successful reading, language skill does not ensure reading success either, as there are other things to be learnt. Oral language creates appropriate expectations which narrow the field of possible responses and make the final selection quicker and more accurate. Goodman (1970) wrote:

'The ability to anticipate that which has not been seen . . . is vital in reading, just as the ability to anticipate what has not yet been heard is vital in listening.'

It is in this respect that grammatical structure facilitates fluency in reading because it helps the child to anticipate what comes next.

Habitual responses to the directional requirements of printed texts are a prerequisite for reading progress. Directional behaviour can be observed in these early stages if the child is asked to, 'Read it with your finger'. It seems to take a developmental course from a sensory-postural awareness supported by finger pointer, to 'voice pointing' in word by word reading, and then to visual survey only. The sensory-postural habits must be learnt before the child can perform successfully in reading but the conditioning of visual perception continues over a long period, as the child learns more and more about orientation and patterns of print. Even in older children errors may result from the difficulty of scanning a single line at a time. For the text

**from a nest long . . .**
**had been reared . . .**

the child reads 'from a near. . . .' gathering and integrating cues from two lines.

There appear to be two different trends here. Some behaviour related to direction and visual perception is learned in a conscious way, overtly, but should retreat to a level of habitual response which facilitates fluent responding. (It should be allowed to retreat in its own time and not be forced too early.) Oral language skills have to be used in new ways in the new activity, and the manipulation of language has to become more and more explicit, conscious and considered as the child reads more difficult texts.

## A search for difference

Awareness of a few letter or word characteristics permits the child to search actively for differences, similarities or identities between what he says and the text. Differences are by far the easiest to detect because they need only occur in one detail or dimension. Identity must establish a correspondence in every respect. Children can detect errors on occasions when they cannot supply the correct response. One can hear the doubt or uncertainty in their voices. They should be praised for such awareness even if they need to be helped to the solution.

How does a reader check for identity or difference? How does he select from his stock of responses the significant ones to match the input signals?

*Comparison of visual form.* If a word resembles another in visual form they may be judged to be identical, e.g.

| 100 | It was round |
| too | I saw round |

*Comparison of parts.* Parts of a word may come to be identified with that word, e.g. 'is' recognized by 's' may lead to error with 'as'.

*Abstract comparison.* An arbitrary group may be learned as when the forms '*Q*', '𝕴, and 'q' each represent an arbitrary, abstract whole which is made up of the sounds /kw/ or when 'dog, DOG, Dog', are known to be 'the same'. Once the groupings have been learned there is no essential difference between this and other perceptual reactions.

Children search for identity and differences by each of these methods.

## Increased attentiveness to cues

The learning tasks for the remainder of the first year relate to developing new ways of discovering cues in the text, and increasing accurate responding. A small amount of error or an occasional prompt in a predominently correct text leads the child to notice new differences. A large quantity of material read fluently will allow many opportunities for new discoveries to be made.

When the child reads a Little Book an appropriate question is 'What new feature(s) about the print did he notice for himself today?' Rarely can a teacher introduce the child by lessons to the thousands of possible cues in print. The teacher's lessons orient the children to features they can use and good readers go on to many self-discoveries.

The child who knows very few letters or words but who is actively searching for cues and confirmation will make more and more perceptual comparisons. He increases his own attentiveness to finer differences in print and in language. Here is an example of this behaviour near the beginning of book reading.

| *Child:* | *You* (SC) | *up to the top* |
| Text: | Go | up to the top |

| *Child:* | *Janet went up* | *to* (SC) | *slide* |
| Text: | Janet went up | the | slide |

● This child is visually checking for words she knows.
('Go' and 'the' are self-corrections)
● She is using meaning.
('to the top' predicted the idea needed in the second line)
● She is anticipating language structures.
('You' is appropriate for a sentence beginning. 'Up to the top' could be used more frequently than 'up the slide'.)

She has achieved fluency and accuracy, uses self-correction and has a good balance of visual skill and language prediction.

Such increased attentiveness is by no means inevitable. A child who has been repeating the text of Red Book 1 for 6 months may know the text by heart and not yet realize that there are visual cues in print to help him. His long contact has served to make him inattentive to the print!

There are various ways in which printed language can provide cues. If the reader decodes the following sentence he could then analyse how he solved it. What were the cues used?

**Lxttxxx xxx xxx xxx xxly clxxx xxed xxx rxxxxxg xxrds.**

The adult reader is helped by knowing

- the letter symbols
- the sounds of English
- the frequently used function words of English and their patterns of occurrence
- the pronounceable sequences of English words
- the sentence patterns of English.

He not only knows that language varies in the distribution of letters, words and structures but he is familiar with the full range of variation along each dimension.

The beginning reader knows only a few letters, and a few words. He controls easily only some of the structures of English sentences. He has hardly begun to think about probabilities of occurrence and he has not needed to analyse the language he speaks beyond the word level to the sound level. Should he be taught to deal with letters before he attempts words?

There is a critical distinction here between claims that the most easily learned signals differ in many respects, or differ in only one attribute. Natural language texts and a language experience approach use signals which differ in many respects. If the child is presented with words in sentence structures which mirror the distribution of words and structures in the language he speaks, this will help the child match his response to the text and will increase his opportunities to develop self-correcting strategies. This is how the child's control over the grammatical aspects of language, word order, and word agreement, contributes to his reading success. What he is liable to overlook are the dimensions of letters and sounds.

There is another advantage of texts rich in cues. In the initial stage of learning to read a teacher cannot easily find a baseline of common experiences or strengths among children who have idiosyncratic experiences. Experience is individual and private particularly for the young child. Meanings common to a group are gained only with extensive experience. A text, rich in information sources, is likely to provide cues that suit a wide range of beginning readers.

The immaturity of the 5-year-old learner and the instability of early learning lead to the firm conviction that material rich in information is more appropriate for communication than material that has been controlled and regularized down to the just-noticeable-difference level.

## Discovering new words and new features of words

The child who has learned how to use cues to work out new words for himself shows considerable enthusiasm when he decodes a new word successfully. He finds this activity rewarding and reinforcing.

When the book is interesting this encourages responding, that is, continued participation in the reading situation. Such automatic reinforcement of an interesting activity will increase the likelihood of responding without any assurance of accurate response. A close check on the learner with praise for accurate responses is very necessary in the early stages of learning to read. Once the child learns to search for cues the reinforcment lies in the agreement between all the signals in the code and the child no longer requires so much outside help to confirm whether his response is right or wrong. The activity of making all the cues fit, of eliminating any misfit, is rewarding to the child if he succeeds. MacKinnon (1959) who observed groups of children working together reported that the children evinced great enthusiasm when they apprehended a new word. They said the word with stress, often repeated it aloud, and sometimes clapped their hands.

Children differ in the devices they use to extract cues from print placing varying dependence on

- letter-sound analysis,
- syllabification and clusters,
- little words in bigger words,
- visual analysis by analogy,
- syntactic and semantic context.

Pupils must acquire a variety of approaches and develop flexibility in dealing with new words and although they may learn to use several of these devices to some degree in the first few months of beginning reading, development in word discovery techniques goes on for many years.

The mature reader may read a phrase as a single unit or he may read a word, sound by sound. He can use cues from large chunks of language or parts-within-wholes. Good readers after one year of instruction show a similar flexibility and awareness of parts within wholes. Poor progress readers are more specific in what they know and more rigid in what they can do with it.

## Substitution strategies: not mere guessing

When a child omits, inserts, or changes words he seems to be using strategies that keep the activity going. Sometimes these are looked upon as 'indiscriminate guessing', or 'not seeing words'. For the child they serve useful purposes. They lower the risk of 'senseless reading' or the effort of 'prolonged searching' or the embarrassment of 'failure to respond'. The substitutions tend to be prompted by the child's oral language habits and are useful predictions of what might occur (which is related to later fluent reading). The teacher must listen closely to the substitutions being made, preferably recording these for analysis. Questions she might ask are

- Does it make a good sentence? (grammatical expectation)
- Does it make sense? (semantic expectation)
- Is he merely juggling sight words?
- Is he afraid to search? Has he been urged to hurry or has he been criticized for self-correction? Is he so lacking in confidence that he dare not try to search for cues?
- Is he confident enough to say 'I don't know' and can he expect acceptance and help? Or will he feel less conspicuous if he flings in any word?

To reduce the use of inappropriate substitutions for words in the text the child must be taught some additional means of gaining cues and checking his responses. What these should be can only be decided by analysing the substitutions that particular child is currently making. In addition the child must feel that he will not be hurried, harrassed or criticized because he searches at length or because his efforts are eventually unsuccessful. The willingness to search and to choose between alternatives must be preserved. The child who gives up searching becomes the problem reader.

## Re-reading

To confirm a response the young child tends to re-read a word, or a word group. Repetitions may be a check upon correct responses. Most frequently young children return to the beginning of a line or a sentence. This clears away the memory of any previous error. It helps the child to recall cues which he had forgotten because of a long delay at a difficulty. It allows the child to use relationships between words as cues. It may arouse memories which were not activated on the first run. If re-reading succeeds it places the correct response in its correct matrix of association (so that sound patterns, grammar, intonation and meaning are all correct). This should make for better responding on subsequent occasions.

Teachers believe that children can and do read ahead to complete the semantic context. There was little evidence in research that beginning readers do this, and many reasons why the strategy of repetition of sentences is better at the stage of early reading.

## Re-hearing: oral reading

Oral responding may facilitate the mental processing of new or difficult information. The mature reader increases self-stimulation by reading aloud when the text is difficult. Oral language plays a supportive role in reading behaviour. Saying words and sentences aloud resulted in greater ability to recognize and understand written words and sentences among beginning readers in a research comparing oral and non-oral approaches. Oral reading is then, an aid to learning at this level and not something to be minimized lest it create slow readers.

Data available on self-correction behaviour suggests that young children respond, hear their errors, and correct them. As reading skill increases, this thinking aloud, after the error has been made, disappears and with it observable self-correction. The trying out, rejecting and new attempts are probably being carried on in the brain. If this hypothesis can be further supported in research then oral reading may be a necessity to get the feed-back system working. Because at an early stage errors are heard by the child and fed back into the processing activity of his brain he may become able to mentally correct his errors. Oral reading remains important as the only situation the teacher can use to observe, check and reinforce appropriate reading behaviour in the first few years.

## Perceptual or reasoned operations

Downing (1967) describes the child as a code-breaker who consciously breaks up his words into sound units, who finds simple, rational relationships between spoken language and letters, who appreciates the logic of the connections, and who is possibly encouraged to reason by the reading task. He believes that children have ability to appreciate and benefit from the logic of i.t.a. which '. . . may have an important role in that early training in empiricism and reasoning'. According to Downing, the child needs to be taught problem-solving techniques to consciously break the code of written English.

Spache (1963) does not agree. He supports the view that reading responses are not made at the level of conscious awareness even by older readers:

> In all probability, the reader is seldom aware of the particular type of context clue which aids him in deducting word meaning. He hardly recognizes whether the word meaning was clarified by some structural aspect of the sentence, by his own inferential thinking, or by some other type of clue.

MacKinnon (1959) studied children learning in a group teaching situation which seemed to make the working out of cues more explicit. The group of children rarely allowed a reader to make an undetected error, forced him to make choices from among the group's suggestions, and increased the pressure to be right, therefore to preview rather than review material. By actively engaging in search and check the child seemed to become more aware of what he was doing. The reader 'pulls himself up by his bootstraps' as it were, and, as a result, gradually becomes aware of how he is behaving.

# Two Years After School Entry

By 6 years the high progress reader had completed the Little Books and one or two of the readers. He had fast, efficient techniques for reading continuous texts. Directional behaviour was established very early, and so was an expectancy for meaningful, grammatically-probable sentences. Letter-sound awareness was paid much less attention than syntax, and sound associations were not used overtly. This early behaviour for good reading of continuous material had changed by the third year in school.

After two years of instruction children sampled from six Auckland schools were good to excellent oral readers. They read with accuracy, solved unknown words, corrected errors, and read at a comparatively fast rate. The most powerful cues in their reading came from oral language. The errors made by good readers seemed to occur as a result of pressures from context, grammatical and semantic. They predicted from the previous text what the following text would say. Poor readers made more errors, misusing visual cues. Their errors were more often cued by letters and were less contextually and grammatically adequate (Williams, 1967).

Another study of children at the same level showed good readers pausing at punctuation points, after whole phrases and sentences, but poor readers stopping and stressing a word at a time, and often a syllable at a time. Their reading behaviour was organized at the letter, syllable and word level, not at the phrase and sentence level (Clay and Imlach, 1971).

By 7:6 years the good readers were well beyond the *Ready to Read* books. They had increased their speed because they paused less often. Oral language expectations for grammar were used but the children also predicted from semantic cues. Synonyms for the actual words in the text were selected which also match the first and last letter sequences. Reversals and phonic attack rarely occurred. Rapid re-reading was a good strategy and self-correction remained a good indicator of a problem-solving approach and an attentiveness to the vagaries of print. The good reader was able to operate on large stretches of language, at the phrase and sentence level and even on cues that held across sentences.

# Checking the Effects of a Programme

If one were to try to study the effects of programmes on the type of readers we are producing how would we go about this? Let me explore this at two levels.

Firstly, for the teacher in a particular school, what would this mean? Teachers commonly keep some record of the levels of test scores or reading ages that their children are reaching, often from a word-recognition test.

If a teacher is really interested to know whether she is getting what she plans for in reading she will have to test more widely, *testing for what she plans for*, and she should test the other component skills which she thinks can be de-emphasized to see whether her judgement is correct. Will time permit this testing? The teacher could decide to follow a small number of advantaged new entrants and an equal number of disadvantaged new entrants through the first 3 years of their schooling, say a minimum of ten of each. Her problem will be to find tests for the subskill components; a letter identification test, a word test, an early writing test, an oral language test, a test of phonic knowledge, concepts about print and an analysis of the child's reading behaviour as he reads his book. This is to tap the orchestration of strategies. She will find it very difficult to think of tests for the aspects of her programme which she does not consider as important as others, but in reading about new ideas that other people are trying she will encounter measures of those things which she rejects. These are to be included in the testing I suggest.

Within the first six months the results will produce material of interest — she will find results that need to be talked over with others. After a longer period of time she should begin to notice which components of her programme her school's population do particularly well on. She should notice what the good readers do well, and where the poor readers have difficulty with the programme. She may notice that the good readers do things she has never really paid much attention to, and that the poor readers do not. This would be an example of my 'neglect hypothesis'. The observant teacher might then devise ways to add something to her programme without changing its nature. This happened in New Zealand recently where an interest in improving letter recognition has led to alphabet corners where children can choose to use letters in a variety of ways during developmental periods.

In a larger and more formal study of the emphases in a curriculum for a school district, very careful consideration must be given to the selection of tests because some tests favour progress under some programmes. We are not looking merely for those which will confirm our biases but for a range of tests that will reveal the biases of our programmes. Also, like child development, reading behaviours change as the child moves through a programme. In some components the children move from no score through to perfect scoring after about two years. This happens in letter identification which is a set of learning which one can master completely. There is a rather complex patterning of these components of the reading process in the first two or three years of instruction and any evaluation of it must be designed with an understanding of the shifts that might occur.

There is some justification for such *a study of curriculum* to look at a scheme's operation in schools with fewest handicaps, schools from high socio-economic districts with advantaged children.

# Reading Failure

I have read two definitions of a dyslexic child which appealed to me for their simplicity:

One who is bad with written words.
One who cannot read, for causes unknown.

Magdelene Vernon (1968), who is an acknowledged authority on the psychology of reading, wrote this summary of reading difficulties.

Dyslexics would appear to fall into four main groups: (1) those characterized principally by impairment of the language functions, which may be classified as cases of developmental dysphasia; (2) those probably suffering from brain damage, who are deficient in the ability to perceive and remember complex visual forms and ordered sequences, and show directional confusion; (3) cases in which there may be an inherited disposition, who may exhibit any of the above symptons, together with difficulty in matching visually and auditorily perceived sequences, and weak lateralization; (4) cases in which there are deficiencies in concept formation rather than perceptual deficits. Although group (3) has been attributed to 'maturational lag' which children may grow out of, it is suggested that both in (3) and (4) there is a basic disability in dealing with complex integrated structures which may show itself at either the perceptual or the conceptual level.

Vernon's analysis of reading failure refers to the same areas of reading development discussed throughout this book — (1) language, (2) visual perception of print, and (3) complex integration of behaviour. Children who fail early may be children

- who have not applied their oral language skill to reading because they became overdependent on visual memory for words
- who have not developed visual control over printed symbols
- who have not learned the directional constraints on behaviour required for the visual analysis of print
- who have not added a baseline of letter-sound relationships and pronounceable clusters of earlier language skills
- who have not shown evidence of integrating complex sources of information by developing error correcting or problem solving strategies.

Any one of these may be the hurdle at which the younger reader has fallen. When children suffer from several low levels of functioning they have little useful prior learning on which the school can build.

The child will have lost faith in his ability to penetrate the complexities of the task, which leads to lowered effort and an accumulated limitation of reading experience. He can read so little that he seldom reads. The emotional reactions that arise from knowing that he is doing a poor job, compound the problem from the first time he becomes aware of it, which is as early as six months after instruction begins.

Better understanding of the reading process should make it easier for teachers to monitor closely the gradual accumulation of reading skill to ensure continuing progress. Diagnostic teaching can reduce the number of readers who become disorganized because their experiences have been inadequate for their needs, and then we can discover the nature of the residual group of children who may perhaps be organically impaired.

# In Summary

At this point we should summarize how the beginning reader processes coded information on natural language texts.

Beginning reading is a communication system in a formative stage. At first the child is producing a message from his oral language experience and a context of past associations. He verifies it as probable or improbable in terms of these past experiences and changes the response if the check produces uncertainty.

At some time during the first year at school visual perception begins to provide cues but for a long period these are piecemeal, unreliable and unstable. This is largely because the child must learn where and how to attend to print. Slowly the first sources of cues from experience and from spoken language are supplemented by learning along new dimensions, such as letter knowledge, word knowledge, letter-sound associations and pronounceable clusters of letters. As differences within each of these dimensions gradually become differentiated the changes of detection and correction of error are increased.

The oral language habits of the linguistically average child provide a source of relatively stable responses which can give some success in predicting what a text will say and when an error has occurred. However, it is not inevitable that under the support of oral language habits visual perception will proceed to more refined knowledge of letters within words. Some children maximize the importance of oral language and fail to attend to the visual cues. Seen in perspective the child's oral language skills make an excellent starting point since they provide a set of well-established stable responses. Adequate learning must proceed in the direction of more and more receptiveness to visual cues which must eventually be a critical component of the reading process. They do not do so in the first year of reading when the average 6-year-old can only discriminate half the letter symbols in his reading, and yet in the third year they are a very important source of information.

# References and Further Reading

Cashdan A., Who teaches the child to read. In J. Merritt, *New Horizons in Reading*, IRA, Newark, Delaware,1976.

Chomsky, C., Stages in language development and reading exposure. *Harvard Educational Review*, 22, k, 1972, 1-33.

Clay, Marie M. and Imlach, R. H., 'Juncture, pitch and stress as reading behaviour variables', *J. Verbal Behaviour and Verbal Learning*, 10, 1971, pp. 133-139.

Downing, J., *The i.t.a. Symposium*, National Foundation For Educational Research For England and Wales, 1967.

Goodacre, Elizabeth, *Children and Learning to Read*, Routledge, London, 1971.

Goodman, K. S., 'Reading: a psycholinguistic guessing game', in H. Singer and R. B. Ruddell (eds.), *Theoretical Models and Processes Of Reading*, International Reading Association, Newark, Delaware, 1970.

Guthrie, J. T., Reading comprehension and syntactic responses in good and poor readers, *Journal of Educational Psychology*,1973, 65, 294-299.

Harris, T. L., Reading flexibility: a neglected aspect of reading instruction. In Merritt, J. (ed.), *New Horizons in Reading*, IRA, Newark, Delaware, 1976.

Luria, A. R., 'The functional organisation of the brain', *Scientific American*, March, 1970.

McKee, P., Brzeinski, J.E. and Harrison, M.L., 'The effectiveness of teaching reading in kindergarten', Report of the Co-operative Research Project, Denver Public Schools, Colorado, 1966.

MacKinnon, A. R., *How Do Children Learn To Read?*, Copp Clarke, Toronto, 1959.

Peters, M. J., The influence of reading methods on spelling. *British Journal of Educational Psychology*, 37, 1. 1967, 47-53.

Reid, J. F., Towards a Theory of Literacy in Reading and Related Skills, Ward Locke, London,1973.

Smith, F., *Understanding Reading*. Holt, Rinehart and Winston, New York, 1978.

Spache, G. E., *Toward Better Reading*, Garrard Publishing Co., Champaign, Illinois, 1963.

Strang, Ruth, *The Diagnostic Teaching of Reading*, McGraw-Hill, New York, 1969.

Vernon, Magdelene, 'The dyslexic syndrome and its basis', in R. C. Staiger and O. Andresen (eds.), *Reading: A Human Right And A Human Problem*, International Reading Association, Newark, Delaware, 1968.

Williams, B. 'The oral reading behaviour of Standard One children', Unpubl. M.A. thesis, University of Auckland Library, 1968.

# Exploring Further

'Strengthening one's control by roaming around the known'. How does this quotation relate to the ideas discussed in this chapter?

# In Conclusion

In the first two years of instruction the child learns how to teach himself to read. He learns the

- aspects of print to which he must attend
- aspects of oral language that can be related to print
- kinds of strategies that maintain fluency
- kinds of strategies that explore detail
- kinds of strategies that increase understanding
- kinds of strategies that detect and correct errors.

He also learns how to relate new information to what he has already learned.

In the process of learning how to learn he masters a reading vocabulary of familiar words, the set of letters used to record language, and the sound equivalents of common spelling patterns and of single letters.

At school entry old learning must be transformed into useful ways of dealing with a new medium, print, with its own special rules. Group instruction calls for an independence and initiative that is different from the learning of preschool years. And perceptual and cognitive functioning change markedly between 5 and 7 years.

It is my belief that, at this important time, we begin the production of our reading failures by allowing some children to build inefficient systems of functioning, which keep them crippled in this process throughout their school careers. As older readers they are difficult to help because they are habituated in their inefficiency. In the terms of the computer age, they have been poorly programmed.

Children who fail at reading do not all have damaged brains. At least half if not more, have developed inefficient behaviour responses for finding, using, checking and correcting information as they read. If we are to reduce the incidence of functionally disorganized readers these principles must be accepted.

- The first two years of instruction are critical for learning to read, because this is the formation stage of an efficient or inefficient behavioural system.
- The best approach is to teach and then to observe behaviour rather than to apply tests which can only predict failure, or merely describe a level of performance.
- Remedial efforts will be most economical when applied close to the point where the faulty learning begins, after one year of instruction.
- Visual exploration, visual scanning and visual perception of the symbol system used in print are first-year learning tasks of major importance which have been neglected because they are difficult to observe and record.
- Language skills are very important for reading progress but cannot be applied to the task unless and until the child has learned where to direct his attention, and how to explore the text with his eyes.

There is research evidence to suggest that reading behaviour becomes organized into a complex system of functioning during the first two years of instruction, in a way that sets the pattern for subsequent gains in skill. If the system functions efficiently the child reads fluently without much error and adds to his skill with every exposure to this task. If the system functions inefficiently the child establishes habits of inefficient processing of cues with every extra reading lesson he has.

The significant question at any stage of progess is not 'How much does he know?' but rather 'What operations does he carry out and what kinds of operations has he neglected to use?'

The child who cannot read is often considered to be deficient in certain skills with letters, sounds and words, and remediation is directed towards teaching the missing items of knowledge. A different remedial approach proceeds on the assumption that children who have failed to learn to read have stopped producing many appropriate responses. They have specialized rather rigidly in particular kinds of responses. Research has demonstrated that some retarded readers are better on visual perception tasks than good readers — an example of over-specialization or imbalance in the system. Other research has shown an exaggerated attention to words, overstressed and separated by pausing, to the detriment of phrasing and meaning. It is also noticed that good readers have both reading and writing vocabularies but the very poor readers have no writing vocabulary. They have approached the 'knowing' of words in some narrow way. Good reading depends upon rich sources of information.

If the problem reader is young, any 'lost' behaviour which he no longer tries to apply to his reading will not be buried too far below the surface and with encouragement (that is, positive reinforcement) it can be recovered. The longer the narrow, specialized responding has been practised the harder it will be to build new learning into the old system. This is a good reason why reading failure should be detected early (Clay, 1979).

There may be many ways of learning successfully to read. We need not over-instruct. In fact, if we believe that all reading stems from our instruction, our programmes may lack the flexibility needed for individual children to succeed. Children may fail because we believe we know all.

Any programme will have its own risk areas. This seems to me to be inevitable for at least three major reasons.

1   Decisions will have to be made *about the order* in which the components of reading behaviour are fostered in a programme.
2   Teachers with limited access to the theoretical discussions will make decisions in selecting programmes that fit with their personal understanding of the reading process and they will reinforce children for those behaviours which led them to choose the programme.
3   There are many aspects of reading behaviour for which we have little understanding, like the feature analysis that children do, how they learn to select the critical information for rapid recovery of responses, how they learn to use the redundancies of language.

If every method has risk areas what can be done about this?

The problem for education is how to retain the advantages and minimize the risks. This means that the building of checks, insurance and recovery processes is an implication of choosing any programme.

(Singer, Samuels and Spiroff, 1974)

How one manages to time the steps of pedagogy to match unfolding capacities, how one manages to instruct without making the learner dependent and how one manages to do both of these while keeping alive zest for further learning — these are very complicated questions that do not yield answers.

(Bruner, 1974)

# References and Further Reading

Bruner J., *The Relevance of Education*, Penguin Education, Middlesex, 1974.
Singer H., Samuels S. J., Spiroff J., The effect of pictures and contextual conditions on learning responses to printed words. *Theoretical Models and Processes of Reading 2nd Edn.*, Newark, Delaware 1976.
Clay, Marie M., *The Early Detection of Reading Difficulties: A Diagnostic Survey with Recovery Procedures*, Heinemann Educational Books, Auckland, 1979.

# Index